THE
ULTIMATE
MARILYN

THE ULTIMATE MARILYN

Ernest W. Cunningham

BOOKS

RENAISSANCE BOOKS
Los Angeles

For permission, write: Renaissance Books,
5858 Wilshire Boulevard, Suite 200,
Los Angeles, CA 90036.

Library of Congress Cataloging-in-Publication Data
Cunningham, Ernest W.
The ultimate Marilyn / by Ernest W. Cunningham.
p. cm.
Filmography: p.
Includes bibliographical references and index.
ISBN 1-58063-003-0 (paperback : alk. paper)
1. Monore, Marilyn, 1926–1962—Miscellanea.   I. Title.
PN2287.M69C86 1998
791.43'028'092—dc21   97-53167
[B]   CIP

Norman Rosten, "For Marilyn Monroe: Sunday Morning," from *Thrive Upon the Rock*,
Trident Press, New York, 1965. With permission of Patricia Rosten.

10 9 8 7 6 5 4 3 2 1

Printed in the United States of America
Distributed by St. Martin's Press
First Edition

Design by Tanya Maiboroda

ACKNOWLEDGMENTS

The Academy of Motion Picture Arts & Sciences: Margaret Herrick Library; Archive Photos (Michael Shulman), Steve Campbell, Freddy Collado, Lloyd Curry, Diane and George Fain, Ernie Garcia, Bebe Goddard, Maretta Hambrick, J. C. Archives (John Cocchi), Carlos Lamboy, Carlton Maddox, Patrick V. Miller, Sara and Keith Musgrove, Photofest (Howard Mandelbaum), Robert Simons, Jim Tamulis, Allan Taylor, Mark Vieira, David Wills.

Special thanks to Greg Schreiner and the Marilyn Remembered Fan Club for their inspiration and support.

This book is for

my sister Mildred,

and my friends

Ed Gori,

Carla Rich,

and

James Robert Parish

FOREWORD

Somewhere along the way, the image of Marilyn Monroe as Superstar, as Sex Goddess, as Legend, has been tarnished by the image of Marilyn as Tragic Victim.

She has become Marilyn the Conspiracy, with each new claim more outlandish than the one before. Flying saucers are now part of the scenario.

Marilyn is too much of a good thing to disappear into this black cloud—she still has much to offer and inspire us.

This book would like to rescue Marilyn from the conspiracy industry by lining up the different, conflicting stories, hoping, at least, to make readers pause for a moment and wonder, and question.

Above all, I would hope that the material collected here will help restore Marilyn's humanity, by reminding the reader of her great wit and beauty and talent, and her luminous spirit.

CONTENTS

Part 3—Marilyn's World

Part 4—The Annotated (and Opinionated) Guide to Marilyn in Print

Marilyn

THE WOMAN

Chapter 1

The Anatomy of a Sex Symbol

◆

As a legend of Hollywood sensuality, Mae West (1892–1980) was memorable for her ample bosom and sashaying walk. Betty Grable (1916–1973) had beautiful, shapely legs. Helen Kane (1903–1966) had a lovable *boo-poo-pe-doop* voice. And Jean Harlow (1911–1937) had startling platinum blonde hair. But Marilyn Monroe had them all—and more—in one amazing package. Anatomical part by part, there's probably been more said about Marilyn's body than anyone else's—and not even her toes escaped scrutiny!

That Hair!

Marilyn was born (in 1926) with brown hair that was naturally curly, very fine, and hard to manage. (See Susan Doll, *Marilyn: Her Life and Legend*, page 9, for a photo of eighteen-year-old Norma Jeane with cascading curls.) When she sought work with the Blue Book Model Agency, owner Emmeline Snively advised that blondes not only had more fun but found more work.

Emmeline sent Marilyn to Frank and Joseph's Beauty Salon on Wilshire Boulevard, where beautician Sylvia Barnhart supervised the straightening and bleaching of her hair to a golden blonde. This was in the winter of 1945.

In March 1948 Marilyn was signed to a six-month contract at Columbia Pictures. Her hairline was permanently heightened by electrolysis, and the basic brown of her dyed blonde hair entirely stripped away. In *Ladies of the Chorus*, Marilyn's glistening blonde hair is styled like Rita Hayworth's, then the screen queen at Columbia.

From *The Asphalt Jungle* in 1950 through *O. Henry's Full House* in 1952, Marilyn's hair went from ash blonde, to golden blonde, to smoky blonde, to dark blonde, to honey blonde, and beyond.

In March 1954, when she showed up for the *Photoplay* awards, her hair was now the brilliant platinum of her idol Jean Harlow.

In 1962, hairstylist George Masters toned down the Harlow platinum to what he called "the Lana Turner white-on-white look." Marilyn called it "pillowcase" white.

Actress friend Simone Signoret spoke of Marilyn's widow's peak:

> "She hated it because, curiously, the roots of that hair, fluffy as the hair of a small child, didn't take the platinum dye well. The lock that fell over her eye so casually and so accidentally was produced by a hairdresser's vigorous teasing, and it was a shield protecting those darker roots, which might be seen when the camera came in for close-ups."

Those Ears!

When superfan James Haspiel first saw Marilyn, he was surprised by how large her ears were.

Others found her ears ugly, so they were usually hidden by hair—on- and offscreen.

Those Eyes!

"Her cornflower-blue eyes were the right distance apart."

—*cinematographer Jack Cardiff*

That Nose!

In 1949, a Beverly Hills surgeon removed a slight bump of cartilage from the tip of Marilyn's nose. Agent and lover Johnny Hyde paid the bill.

Cinematographer Jack Cardiff said:

"I had to be careful about her nose, so delightfully retroussé [turned-up], for, if the key light was too low, a blob would show up on the tip. She actually mentions this in the film [*The Prince and the Showgirl*], saying to Larry's [Olivier] paean: 'You skipped my nose, because you noticed the bump on the end.'"

Those Lips! That Mouth!

"Marilyn Monroe had the most beautiful mouth ever. No one has ever been able to convey so much sex appeal with just one feature."

—*hairstylist George Masters*

"The definition of glamour shifts from period to period. In the twenties, the erotic emphasis was legs. Clara Bow. In the thirties, it went from the legs to the eyes. Garbo, Dietrich, Crawford—all eyes.

"Next came Marilyn Monroe, and the focus shifted to the mouth. Marilyn never closed her mouth. A lot of girls had great laughs, but she took it to the furthest point, so that it became iconic—the gasping mouth, the laughing mouth, the open mouth, which represented the possibility of pleasure."

—*photographer Richard Avedon*

"There isn't enough upper lip between the end of your nose and your mouth," modeling agent Emmeline Snively told Marilyn. She instructed Marilyn to pull her upper lip down when she smiled. Marilyn mastered the smile, but her lip usually quivered as she did—and this quiver became one of her famous traits.

Those Teeth!

In the early photos of Marilyn, she appears to have near-perfect teeth. But Laszlo Willinger, an early photographer of Marilyn, remembers, "She had one bad front tooth which I had fixed at my expense. Her hair was kinky, which someone else fixed."

In 1948, an orthodontist fitted Marilyn with a retainer to correct her slightly protruding front teeth. Vocal coach and lover Fred Karger paid the bill.

> "[Marilyn] took exceptionally good care of herself, washing her face constantly to prevent clogged pores, taking long baths, and spending what little money she had on monthly trips to the dentist to ensure she had no cavities. 'Natasha [Lytess, acting coach], these are my teeth!' she cried when asked if these appointments were not excessive."
>
> —*Donald Spoto,* **Marilyn Monroe: The Biography**

That Chin!

Remember the Beverly Hills surgeon who removed the bump from Marilyn's nose? He also inserted a crescent-shaped silicone prosthesis into her jaw, beneath the lower gum, to give her face a softer line. Johnny Hyde paid the bill.

> "You very seldom saw her with her mouth closed, because when it was closed she had a very determined chin, almost a different face."
>
> —*film director George Cukor (1899–1983)*

That Face! That Skin!

Film director Billy Wilder (1906–   ) explains Marilyn's "flesh impact":

"It's very rare. Three I recall [who had it] are Clara Bow, Jean Harlow, and Rita Hayworth. Such girls have flesh which photographs like flesh. You feel you can reach out and touch it."

Actress Susan Strasberg wrote in *Marilyn and Me: Sisters, Rivals, Friends*: "Marilyn's skin had something like a translucent glow. A fine mist of down on her face captured a kind of halo, a nimbus of light around her: photographs seemed to canonize her, to offer a creature almost ethereal as well as sensual."

"Her skin was translucent, white, luminous. Up close, around the periphery of her face there was a dusting of faint down. This light fuzz trapped light and caused an aureole to form, giving her a faint glow on film, a double plus."

—*photographer Eve Arnold*

A photo showing the "fuzz" or down on Marilyn's face, which caught the light from flashbulbs or studio lights and made her face glow. [Photo courtesy of Photofest.]

Marilyn's facial hair is visible in many photos and very much so in Bert Stern's "Last Sitting" photos.

Foster sister Bebe Goddard remembers that the mole on Marilyn's left cheek was flesh-colored, hardly noticeable.

Makeup artist Whitey Snyder says, "She had a very slight imperfection [i.e., a tiny mole on her face]. We wouldn't always put it in the same spot. Sometimes we had it on the other side. If we hadn't darkened it, nobody would know it was there. But she thought she could see it."

> "About her beauty mark—a mole on the left cheek near her mouth—she [Marilyn] shrugged, 'Sometimes I darken it, sometimes I don't.' "
> —*photographer Jock Carroll*

In summer of 1997, the German car manufacturer Mercedes-Benz launched a major advertising campaign using a large head shot of Marilyn—but a closer look reveals the Mercedes-Benz insignia (an upside-down Y in a circle) in place of Marilyn's beauty mark. The message of the advertisement: Two top-of-the-line images—Marilyn Monroe and Mercedes-Benz—two names you can count on.

That Bosom!

While Marilyn was living on Catalina Island in 1943, she started exercising on gym equipment previously used only by men, and worked out with light weights and barbells—"I'm fighting gravity!" was her explanation.

Marilyn's bust-waist-hip measurements fluctuated, apparently depending on who was asking. The accepted dimensions are those she once suggested for her epitaph: "Here lies Marilyn Monroe, 37–22–35."

While making *The Seven Year Itch* in 1955, Billy Wilder recalled:

> For the scene in which Marilyn snuck down a back staircase to visit Tom Ewell, she was wearing a nightdress, "and I could see she was wearing a bra. 'People don't wear bras under nightclothes,' I told her, 'and they will notice your breasts simply because you are wearing one.' Marilyn replied, 'What bra?' and put my hand on her breast. She was not wearing a bra. Her bosom was a miracle of shape, density, and an apparent lack of gravity."

"Her exuberant breasts defied Newton's law of gravity."

—*cinematographer Jack Cardiff*

"She had one long blonde hair on her chest that she wouldn't let me cut off. She liked to play and fondle it. It was her security blanket."

—*hairstylist George Masters*

That Body!

"Her whole body had a touch of overripeness—how Renoir would have adored her! She was indeed a little overweight and was worried very much about her tummy protruding in her tight white dress."

—*cinematographer Jack Cardiff*

Marilyn had her gallbladder removed on June 29, 1962, which helped create the new slim figure that's so striking in the footage from *Something's Got to Give*.

The gallbladder operation also left a prominent scar that's revealed in a number of Bert Stern's "Last Sitting" photos.

Those Hands!

"I wish I could wear rings, but I hate people to notice my hands. They're too fat," said Marilyn.

That Butt!

Journalist Brad Darrach interviewed Marilyn for *Time* magazine in the May 14, 1956, issue:

> "...there were those extraordinary jutting breasts and jutting behind. I've never seen a behind like hers; it was really remarkable, it was a very subtly composed ass."

"Jut butt" is said to have been an early nickname for Marilyn.

> "Her derriere looked like two puppies fighting under a silk sheet."
>
> —*columnist James Bacon*

Her derriere was prominent in publicity photos taken in New York during filming of *The Seven Year Itch*, with Marilyn,

Marilyn between takes on *Some Like It Hot* (1959)... which brings to mind Constance Bennett's comment about Marilyn being "a broad with her future behind her." [Photo courtesy of Photofest.]

photographed from behind, leaning out the window waving to the crowd below. (For example, see *Magnum Cinema*, page 123.)

Marilyn's dress for the yacht scene in *Some Like It Hot* (1958) also put emphasis on her rear.

In early 1949, Marilyn auditioned for *Love Happy*: "There were three girls there and Groucho [Marx] had us each walk away from him. I was the only one he asked to do it twice. Then he whispered in my ear, 'You have the prettiest ass in the business.' I'm sure he meant it in the nicest way."

Those Legs!

"She had also said, 'I have knobby knees and my legs are too short.'"
—*Simone Signoret, Nostalgia Isn't What It Used to Be*

The Artists Institute of America rejected Marilyn as the standout pinup of 1952, saying that her legs were too short and her derriere too sloped.

That Walk!

"It has often been remarked . . . that Marilyn's walk in *Niagara* [1953] is what made her a star—that she turned her back on the camera and walked her way toward immortality. Marilyn's 116-foot walk in *Niagara* was, up until that time, the longest, most luxuriated walk in cinema history. Clad in a tightly sewn black skirt and blazing red top, Marilyn simply walked—in her distinctly exaggerated style—while Henry Hathaway's camera remained transfixed on Marilyn's bottom."
—*Randall Riese and Neal Hitchens, The Unabridged Marilyn*

"The picture [*Niagara*] features three walking sequences; the one that received the most attention is often referred to as 'the longest walk in cinema history'—116 feet of film of Marilyn in a black skirt and red sweater walking away from the camera into the distance. In a daring shot for the era, the camera eye remains firmly focused on Marilyn's swaying posterior."

—*Susan Doll,* **Marilyn: Her Life and Legend**

"She walks a long distance away from the camera, but the uneven cobblestone street throws her high heels off, resulting in the seductive swivel she used forever after."

—*Donald Spoto,* **Marilyn Monroe: The Biography**

"Ralph Roberts, her masseur, traces the walk to the time she was studying with Michael Chekhov. Either he or Lotte Goslar gave her a book called *The Thinking Body* by Mabel Ellsworth Todd. Marilyn was a slow but thorough reader. She reported back to Chekhov that she hadn't understood one word. Chekhov told her to read it again, and again, and again. She did reread the book frequently and found in it an exercise to move from one buttock to the other while sitting. Roberts says the walk stems from this."

—*photographer Eve Arnold*

According to *Unsung Genius,* a biography of choreographer Jack Cole, Cole worked behind the scenes with Marilyn, "helping her develop her sensuous walk and breathlessly sexy mode of speaking."

Photographer Philippe Halsman takes credit for being the first to photograph Marilyn's distinctive walk, trying to capture what he described as its "turbinoid undulations" (*American Photo* magazine, May/June 1997).

Halsman also has said, "With every step her derriere seemed to wink at the onlooker. It is incredible that Twentieth Century–Fox had had her under contract for many years and had never thought of photographing her from behind."

Arthur Miller, playwright and Marilyn's future third husband, visited the set of *As Young As You Feel* in 1951:

"Marilyn, in a black openwork lace dress, was directed to walk across the floor, attracting the worn gaze of the bearded Monty Woolley. She was being shot from the rear to set off the swiveling of her hips, a motion fluid enough to seem comic. It was, in fact, her natural walk: her footprints on a beach would be in a straight line, the heel descending exactly before the last toe print, throwing her pelvis into motion."

"The girl with the horizontal walk."

—Hollywood reporter Pete Martin, in the mid-1950s

"... a long white dress that suited her perfectly. It made her walk with an amazing wiggle, but a wiggle which is somehow naive not brazen." *—Colin Clark, **The Prince, the Showgirl and Me***

"She walks as if the whole earth were a tightrope on which she has to balance." *—novelist-biographer Gavin Lambert*

OTHERS JOINING THE WALK:

- Drama coach Natasha Lytess claimed she invented it for Marilyn.
- Modeling agency owner Emmeline Snively insisted it was the result of weak ankles or double-jointed knees.
- Columnist Jimmy Starr believed Marilyn simply shaved a bit off one high heel to undulate in that manner.
- Marilyn said she had always walked that way.

Those Feet! Those Toes!

Arthur Miller mentions that a podiatrist group named Marilyn as having the most perfect feet.

Photographer Joseph Jasgur photographed Marilyn in 1946. In the late 1980s, he started telling people that Marilyn had six toes on her left foot. In 1991, he published the book to prove it

(*The Birth of Marilyn: The Lost Photographs of Norma Jean* by Joseph Jasgur, text by Jeannie Sakol).

There is a two-page color photo in the book that *seems* to show just such a physical abnormality... but you turn the pages to find black-and-white photos that clearly show only five toes.

To Put Them All Together...

"Marilyn Monroe had manufactured hair; a baby face with a round forehead, sad eyes, a button nose, a shapeless mouth, and an imperfect smile; an overripe bosom; a Betty Boop alto; knock-knees; and an ocean motion rather than a walk. But even through the distortion of film it is clear how these irregularities almost always corrected each other."

*—Whitney Balliett, **The New Yorker**, July 27, 1963*
*reviewing the **Marilyn** compilation film*

"My eye roved her face, searching. I couldn't find the secret of her beauty in any one feature. She didn't have a great nose like Liz Taylor, or perfect lips like Brigitte Bardot. She didn't have gorgeous almond-shaped eyes like Sophia Loren. And yet she was more to me than all of them put together."

*—photographer Bert Stern, **The Last Sitting***

"If what she wore influenced fashion, her makeup and hair redefined beauty. Red lips, dark eyes, the painted mole. Hookers may have owned the look before, but Marilyn refreshed its appeal."

*—Patty Fox, **Star Style***

Chapter 2

Best Things She Said

◆

Wearing Only Chanel No. 5 to Bed

(and other witty remarks made by Marilyn ... or maybe not)

Think of the wonderful movie musical *Singin' in the Rain* (MGM, 1952), with the silent-screen star who's going to be destroyed by the talkies because she *can't* talk—her voice is like fingernails on a blackboard. But hey, no problem, they'll get someone to sing *for* her: Debbie Reynolds gets the chore, conveniently hiding behind the curtain. Good thinking.

During Hollywood's Golden Age, the studio publicity departments played a major role in creating movie stars. They told the talent what to wear, where to live, what to say, what *not* to say. Silent-screen hero Francis X. Bushman was a romantic leading man to die for, because the studio didn't let his swooning fans know that not only was he married, but also that he had a houseful of kids.

In Greta Garbo's early days in Hollywood, she spoke openly of her live-in arrangement with lover/director Mauritz Stiller. A shocked Louis B. Mayer, the head of MGM, gave orders to keep his Swedish import away from the press. Pete Smith, MGM publicity chief, came up with the line that would become Garbo's trademark—"I vant to be alone!"—and the legend of Garbo was born. Suddenly, she became a fascinating world-famous recluse.

A gag shot between takes for *Don't Bother to Knock* (1952), Marilyn's first starring role for Twentieth Century–Fox. Note that she's wearing a bra. [Photo courtesy of Archive Photos.]

Marilyn made many witty and clever and insightful comments. Or did she? Think of it: What kind of a reporter looks at a photo of a naked woman and asks the subject, "You had *nothing* on?!"

Answer: A reporter who's been fed the question so Marilyn can respond on public record, "Oh, yes—the radio." Or, "Oh, yes. I had on Chanel No. 5."

On the other hand, Marilyn was invited to a dinner in honor of the actor Peter Lawford and his wife Patricia, at the home of Attorney General Robert Kennedy in Virginia. But a week before the party, Marilyn was fired from her current movie *Something's Got to Give*. So, in a telegram of June 13, 1962, she sent her regrets:

"Dear Attorney General and Mrs. Kennedy:
"I would have been delighted to have accepted your invitation honoring Pat and Peter Lawford. Unfortunately, I am

involved in a freedom ride protesting the loss of the minority rights belonging to the few remaining earthbound stars. After all, all we demanded was our right to twinkle.

—Marilyn Monroe"

At best, this "right to twinkle" is naive and romantic; at worst it's silly, cornball, childish. But it's not the work of a professional publicist. It's Marilyn's own words.

On the other hand, Marilyn's response to the question whether she wore falsies—"People who know me better know better"—is too clever by far. Marilyn *might* have thought of it, sure, but probably not. It has the ring of a professional.

Marilyn was intelligent and had a sense of humor, but intelligence and cleverness don't necessarily go together. Most often, cleverness is an acquired skill.

In Ezra Goodman's *The Fifty Year Decline and Fall of Hollywood*, Twentieth Century–Fox publicist Roy Craft denies he ghosted Marilyn's wisecracks for her, but Goodman thinks "there was good reason to believe he had a hand in the witticisms."

One of Marilyn's most quoted lines is:

"Hollywood's a place where they'll pay you a thousand dollars for a kiss and fifty cents for your soul. I know, because I turned down the first offer enough and held out for the fifty cents."

Wow!

But then you track down the quote and you find she said it to Ben Hecht.

Oh.

If you've ever seen one of writer Ben Hecht's many films or read one of his screenplays, you'll recognize his fingerprints—footprints?—all over that quote. One of Hecht's biographers describes his writing as having a "filigreed irony"—that it "ranged from ornate observations to sharp urban observations."

Example. In the Ben Hecht–scripted *Specter of the Rose* (Republic, 1946), a guy picks up Lionel Stander's large brief-case: "Say, that's quite an object to lug around—what's in it?" Stander: "Very little—my soul. And an extra can of tobacco."

♦

Best Things Marilyn Said

(most likely by her)

"Our marriage [to baseball great Joe DiMaggio] was a sort of crazy, difficult friendship with sexual privileges. Later I learned that's what marriages often are."

Susan Strasberg, daughter of acting coach Lee Strasberg and a longtime Marilyn friend, once said she was in conflict about something, that she felt she had another voice clamoring inside her head. Marilyn remarked:

"You have only one voice? I have a whole committee!"

George Cukor directed Marilyn in *Let's Make Love* and *Something's Got to Give*. He tells her not to be nervous. She answers:

"I was born nervous!"

Explaining her avoidance of the sun:

"I like to feel blonde all over."

From *Conversations with Marilyn* by W. J. Weatherby:

"I sometimes felt I was hooked on sex, the way an alcoholic is on liquor or a junkie on dope. My body turned all these people on, like turning on an electric light, and there was so rarely anything human in it."

"So I take extra time with my hair; a little extra eye shadow around the eye, a little more glitter...just my way of saying, 'Hah!'"

On Sir Laurence Olivier, costar of Marilyn's *The Prince and the Showgirl*:

"He gave me the dirtiest looks, even when he was smiling."

The unit manager on *Niagara* criticized the actress on her tardiness. Her reply:

"Am I making a picture or punching a time clock?"

Reporter: "What inspired you to study acting?"
Marilyn: "Seeing my own pictures."

From *Gentlemen Prefer Blondes*, a dialogue line added at Marilyn's suggestion:

"I can be smart when it's important, but most men don't like it."

Asked if she knew that, as a Gemini, she was born under the same astrological sign as star performers Rosalind Russell, Judy Garland, and Rosemary Clooney, Marilyn replied:

"I know nothing of these people. I was born under the same sign as Ralph Waldo Emerson, Queen Victoria, and Walt Whitman."

"I want to be an artist and an actress with integrity. As I said once before, I don't care about the money, I just want to be wonderful."

A scene from *Gentlemen Prefer Blondes* (1953): Lorelei had assumed Henry Spofford III to be a man of means. He turns out to be very young but he's not indifferent: "You're full of animal magnetism," George Winslow tells her. [Photo courtesy of Photofest.]

Journalist Richard Meryman interviewed Marilyn on July 4, 5, 7, and 9 of 1962. The interview appeared in the August 3, 1962 issue of *Life* magazine.

Meryman said in 1986: "She did something that no one had ever done before or since with me—she asked for the questions in advance. She was really prepared, yet spontaneous. Either she was a good actress or very well rehearsed. Let me say that she handled the interview in a very businesslike manner. Very businesslike."

The Meryman interview has become Monroe's "Gettysburg Address," with many of her statements widely quoted and reprinted:

"I remember when I got the part in *Gentlemen Prefer Blondes*. Jane Russell ... got $200,000 [this figure is usually reported as $150,000] for it and I got my $500 a week. But that, to me, was considerable. The only thing was I couldn't get a dressing room. I said, finally, 'Look, after all, I am the blonde and it is *Gentlemen Prefer Blondes*.' Because still they always kept saying, 'Remember, you're not a star.' I said, 'Well, whatever I am, I am the blonde.'"

"And I want to say that the people—if I am a star—the people made me a star—no studio, no person, but the people did."

"I guess people think that why I'm late is some kind of arrogance and I think it is the opposite of arrogance.... The main thing is, I do want to be prepared when I get there to give a good performance or whatever to the best of my ability... [Clark] Gable said about me, 'When she's there, she's there. All of her is there! She's there to work.'"

"I never quite understood it—this sex-symbol thing—I always thought symbols were those things you clash together! That's the trouble, a sex symbol becomes a thing. I just hate to be a thing. But if I'm going to be a symbol of something I'd rather have it sex than some other things they've got symbols of!"

"Fame to me certainly is only a temporary and a partial happiness—even for a waif and I was brought up a waif. But fame is not really for a daily diet, that's not what fulfills you. It warms you a bit but the warming is temporary."

"I like people. The 'public' scares me but people I trust."

"It might be kind of a relief to be finished [as a celebrity]. It's sort of like I don't know what kind of yard dash you're running, but then you're at the finish line and you sort of sigh—you've

Marilyn with her Henrietta Award, given by the Foreign Press Association for "The Best Young Box Office Personality of 1951." The gown she's wearing—or not wearing—is red. [Photo courtesy of Archive Photos.]

made it! But you never have—you have to start all over again. But I believe you're always as good as your potential."

"Fame will go by and, so long, I've had you, fame. If it goes by, I've always known it was fickle. So at least it's something I experienced, but that's not where I live."

The single best thing Marilyn said (also from the Meryman interview):

"It was the creative part that kept me going—trying to be an actress . ... And I guess I've always had too much fantasy to be only a housewife."

which opens up a fascinating new area....

◆

The Fantasy World of Marilyn Monroe

The childhood dream that recurred throughout Marilyn's life:

"I dreamed that I was standing up in church without any clothes on, and all the people there were lying at my feet on the floor of the church, and I walked naked, with a sense of freedom, over their prostrate forms, being careful not to step on anyone."

Also from Richard Meryman's 1962 *Life* interview:

"It's nice to be included in people's fantasies, but you also like to be accepted for your own sake."

"I always felt I was a nobody, and the only way for me to be somebody was to be—well, somebody else."

A preproduction dinner for *The Misfits* (1961). John Huston and Clark Gable study the menu, while Marilyn studies Gable. A look that speaks volumes. [Photo courtesy of Photofest.]

On actor Tony Curtis's famous "it was like kissing Hitler" remark, about his *Some Like It Hot* costar:

> "You've read there was some actor that once said about me that kissing me was like kissing Hitler. Well, I think that's *his* problem. If I have to do intimate love scenes with somebody who really has these kinds of feelings toward me, then my fantasy can come into play. In other words, out with him, in with my fantasy. He was never there."

In 1959, as her marriage to playwright Arthur Miller was in swift decline:

> "I guess I am a fantasy."

In 1960, to film director Henry Hathaway:

> "When I married [Arthur Miller], one of the fantasies in my mind was that I could get away from Marilyn Monroe through him."

To photographer Jock Carroll, quoted in *Falling for Marilyn; The Lost Niagara Collection*:

> "I remember in mathematics I used to write down figures, just any figures, instead of trying to do the questions. I used to think it was a waste of my brain, using it up with mathematics, when I could be imagining all sorts of wonderful things."

To W. J. Weatherby in *Conversations with Marilyn*:

> "Being a movie actress was never as much fun as dreaming of being one."

Chapter 3

Best Things Others Said

◆

"She Threw Herself at Us with the Off-color Innocence of a Baby Whore"

(and other great quotes about Marilyn)

Leon Shamroy, Oscar-winning cinematographer (*The Black Swan, Wilson, Leave Her to Heaven*), who photographed Marilyn's screen test on July 19, 1946:

> "When I first watched her, I thought, 'This girl will be another Harlow!' Her natural beauty plus her inferiority complex gave her a look of mystery.... I got a cold chill. This girl had something I hadn't seen since silent pictures... and she got sex on a piece of film like Jean Harlow. Every frame of the test radiated sex."

Comedian Groucho Marx, after Marilyn's appearance in his screen vehicle *Love Happy*:

> "She's Mae West, Theda Bara and Bo Peep all rolled into one!"

Actor George Sanders on working with Marilyn in *All About Eve*:

> "She showed an interest in intellectual subjects which was, to say the least, disconcerting. In her presence it was hard to concentrate."

Sidney Skolsky, columnist:

"She appeared kind and soft and helpless. Almost everybody wanted to help her. Marilyn's supposed helplessness was her greatest strength."

Pauline Kael, film critic, reviewing Norman Mailer's *Marilyn*, in the *New York Times Book Review*, July 22, 1973:

"She would bat her Bambi eyelashes, lick her messy suggestive open mouth, wiggle that pert and tempting bottom and use her hushed voice to caress us with dizzying innuendoes. Her extravagantly ripe body bulging and spilling out of her clothes, she threw herself at us with the off-color innocence of a baby whore."

Donald Spoto, in *Marilyn Monroe: The Biography*:

"Like many busy and distracted performers, Marilyn was sloppy to the point of genius."

Norman Mailer, author of the biography *Marilyn*:

"She was our angel, the sweet angel of sex."

Philippe Halsman, photographer:

"While the movie studios had yet refused to make this girl their star, the still photographers had made her theirs. Through them she had become better known than many actresses who had been on the screen for ten years or more. Here was a girl nobody could remember having seen in a movie, but men from one end of the country to the other whistled when you mentioned her name."

London *Daily Mirror*, October 30, 1956, after Marilyn was presented to Queen Elizabeth II:

"Marilyn Monroe, the sleek, the pink and the beautiful, captured Britain."

Truman Capote, writer:

"She labors like a field hand to please everybody."

Dame Sybil Thorndike, quoted in Colin Clark's *The Prince, the Showgirl and Me*, in defending Marilyn's on-set behavior to her movie costar Sir Laurence Olivier:

"[She is] the only one of us who knows how to act in front of a camera."

Sir Laurence Olivier, quoted in Colin Clark's *The Prince, the Showgirl and Me*:

"You know, I actually fancied her when I first met her. She's a freak of nature, not a genius. A beautiful freak."

I. A. L. Diamond, screenwriter, on working with Marilyn:

"Our relationship was not unlike that of Chaplin and his drunken friend in *City Lights* [United Artists, 1931]. Sometimes I would run into her and get a big greeting; other times, she would look at me blankly, as if she'd never seen me before in her life. It was like trying to communicate with someone through a plate-glass window."

Sam Shaw, photographer, introduced Marilyn to poet Norman Rosten and his wife Hedda as "a friend of my camera":

"I wanted them to meet her as a young woman, not a movie star."

Eve Arnold, photographer:

"The truth is that she was not only a natural to the camera but that she had a sure knowledge of how to use that affinity. It was to her what water is to a fish—it was her element and she exulted in it."

Catherine David, writer, in her biography, *Simone Signoret*:

"Since the cinema was invented and stars appeared, there was never such a discrepancy between an actress and her image. Marilyn's sensual perfection was all her own invention, a work of art created by herself. But behind the look, beneath the legend, there was nothing but a frightened, abandoned child. She knew that she was only an impostor, and the knowledge hurt her deeply."

Jean Negulesco, director of *How to Marry a Millionaire*:

"She represents to man something we all want in our unfulfilled dreams."

Time magazine:

"Marilyn Monroe's unique charisma was the force that caused distant men to think that if only a well-intentioned, understanding person like me could have known her, she would have been all right."

Fred Lawrence Guiles, biographer:

"[She was] an actress able to instill more excitement into a role than it deserved."

The Russian propaganda machine, on Marilyn's trip to Korea in 1954 to entertain the soldiers:

"The Monroe intoxication is supposed to make people forget why [American soldiers] had to die in Korea."

Otis Guernsey, reviewing *Gentlemen Prefer Blondes* in the July 16, 1953, issue of the *New York Herald Tribune*:

"Marilyn looks as though she would glow in the dark."

Arthur Schlesinger, Special Assistant at the White House, observed Marilyn at the party after the Kennedy birthday salute at Madison Square Garden, the night of May 19, 1962:

He was "enchanted by her manner and her wit, at once so masked, so ingenuous and so penetrating. But one felt a terrible unreality about her—as if talking to someone under water."

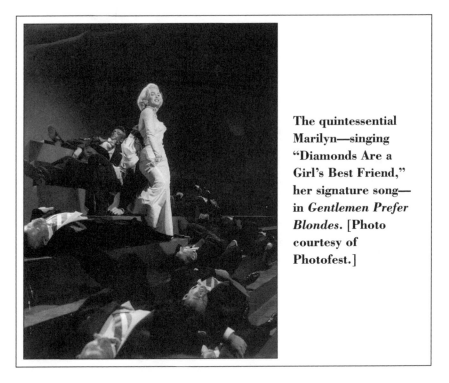

The quintessential Marilyn—singing "Diamonds Are a Girl's Best Friend," her signature song—in *Gentlemen Prefer Blondes*. [Photo courtesy of Photofest.]

Constance Collier, veteran actress, acting coach to Marilyn, in 1955:

"I hope, I really pray, that she survives long enough to free the strange lovely talent that's wandering through her like a jailed spirit."

Sammy Davis, Jr., entertainer:

"She hangs like a bat in the heads of the men that knew her."

Johnny Hyde, talent agent, to Marilyn:

"It's hard for a star to get an eating job. A star is only good as a star. You don't fit into anything less."

Arthur Miller, husband, to *Time* magazine, November 11, 1960:

"She's got more guts than a slaughterhouse. Being with her, people want not to die. She's all woman, the most womanly woman in the world."

Philippe Halsman, photographer:

"When she faced a man she didn't know, she felt safe and secure only when she knew the man desired her; so everything in her life was geared to provoke this feeling.

"Her talent in this respect was very great. I remember my experience in her tiny apartment with my assistant and the *Life* researcher. Each of us felt that if the other two would leave, something incredible would happen."

Jerry Wald, co–executive producer of *Clash by Night*:

"She walks like a young antelope, and when she stands up it's like a snake uncoiling."

Bill Kobrin, photographer:

"I don't think a photographer ever walked away from Marilyn empty-handed."

Collier's magazine reporter, September 5, 1951, on Marilyn's late entrance at the 1951 studio party for Twentieth Century–Fox exhibitors:

"Amid a slowly gathering hush, she stood there, a blonde apparition in a strapless cocktail gown, a little breathless as if she were Cinderella, just stepped from the pumpkin coach."

Joe DiMaggio, husband number two:

"It's no fun being married to an electric light."

"If it hadn't been for her friends she might still be alive."

Edward Wagenknecht, historian, biographer:

"Marilyn played the best game with the worst hand of anybody I know."

Harry Brand, head of Twentieth Century–Fox publicity:

"She's the biggest thing we've had at the studio since Shirley Temple and Betty Grable. With Temple, we had twenty rumors a year that she was kidnapped. With Grable, we had twenty rumors a year that she was raped. With Monroe, we have twenty rumors a year that she has been raped and kidnapped."

George Masters, hairstylist to the stars:

"As a general rule Marilyn would begin turning on about eight hours after I had started with her, while I was applying her lipstick or adjusting her dress. Until then she was a girl you wouldn't look at twice. When she became secure enough to turn into this other person named Marilyn Monroe, then all of a sudden something happened. That's when it was goose bump-time.

"You could really see it with your own eyes, you could feel it in the room—the complete transformation, like Dr. Jekyll and Mr. Hyde. Her mannerisms, her gestures, everything was changed, not only her dress and makeup. She was a totally different person, an exploding image, a projection of sexuality and magnetism beyond belief. Even remembering it now I get goose bumps. She was phenomenal to watch."

Cecil Beaton, photographer:

"She romps, she squeals with delight, she leaps onto the sofa. She puts a flower stem in her mouth, puffing on a daisy as thought it was a cigarette. It is an artless, impromptu, high-spirited, infectiously gay performance. It will probably end in tears."

Billy Wilder worked twice with Marilyn: *The Seven Year Itch* and *Some Like It Hot*—two of her best films. Give him medals for that. As one of the wittiest minds in the business, witty but often stinging or even vicious, Wilder made a number of outrageous comments about Marilyn. But he always calmed down, and came back to say that he would work with her again:

"Anyone can remember lines, but it takes a real artist to come on the set and not know her lines and yet give the performance she did!"

On filming *Some Like It Hot*:

"We were in mid-flight, and there was a nut on the plane."

"I don't think Marilyn is late on purpose. Her idea of time is different, that's all. I think maybe there's a little watchmaker in Zurich, Switzerland, he makes a living producing special watches only for Marilyn Monroe."

"The question is whether Marilyn is a person at all or one of the greatest DuPont products ever invented. She has breasts like granite and a brain like Swiss cheese, full of holes. She defies gravity. She hasn't the vaguest conception of the time of the day. She arrives late and tells you she couldn't find the studio and she's been working there for years.

"There are certain wonderful rascals in this world, like Monroe, and one day they lie down on an analyst's couch and out comes a clenched, dreary thing. It is better for Monroe not to be straightened out. The charm of her is her two left feet."

Shelley Winters, actress:

"She wasn't what she sold.

"You don't realize when you make these deals early in life—and she certainly did with publicity—that you have to live with them forever. And I don't think she was able to do it."

Ben Hecht, novelist, screenwriter, ghostwriter:

"The truth about Marilyn Monroe is that she was *saved* by Hollywood. Fame saved her. The spotlight beating on her twenty-four hours a day made the world seem livable to her. . . . It was the only world in which she could thrive. The real world held only hobgoblins for her, terrors that harried her nights."

Diana Trilling, critic, essayist:

"Hollywood, Broadway, the nightclubs all produce their quota of sex queens, but the public takes them or leaves them; the world is not as enslaved by them as it was by Marilyn Monroe, because none but she could suggest such a purity of sexual delight."

"She was alive in a way not granted the rest of us. She communicated such a charge of vitality as altered our imagination of life, which is the job and wonder of art."

Constance Bennett, screen star:

"There's a broad with her future behind her."

Ayn Rand, novelist, philosopher:

"Anyone who has ever felt resentment against the good for being the good, and has given voice to it, is the murderer of Marilyn Monroe."

Chapter 4

The Men Who Made Merry

◆

A Quiz on Men Who Not Only Liked Her, But Claimed They Went to Bed with Her

Marilyn was wife, lover, or friend to a number of men...and many more claimed to have been there. Can you match the lover to his description? (Some names may be used more than once.)

a. Milton Berle

b. Jose Bolanos

c. Marlon Brando

d. Charlie Chaplin, Jr.

e. David Conover

f. Andre de Dienes

g. Joe DiMaggio

h. James Dougherty

i. Milton Greene

j. Johnny Hyde

k. Fred Karger

l. Elia Kazan

m. John F. Kennedy

n. Douglas Kirkland

o. Arthur Miller

p. Yves Montand

q. Hal Schaefer

r. Joseph Schenck

s. Frank Sinatra

t. President Sukarno

u. Robert Slatzer

1. This man denies that Norma Jeane was raped as a child, claiming that he was Marilyn's first lover and that she was a virgin.

2. "Do you think I'm made of stone?" Marilyn asked this photographer. "Don't you find me desirable? We've slept in separate beds for a week!"

3. Dracula and this guy were sons of Transylvania.

4. This older lover spent time in prison for income tax evasion.

5. This guy was married to the most beautiful of three famous sisters—no, not the Gabors. And not the Andrews Sisters. Keep thinking.

6. In 1948, Marilyn moved in with this lover... and his mother, and his daughter, and his sister and her children.

7. He photographed her wearing a white bathing suit and twirling a dotted parasol.

8. (A) Paid dental bills to correct her overbite, and (B) paid to have a lump of cartilage removed from the tip of her nose.

9. This guy's family sold spaghetti for a living.

10. He almost succeeded in killing himself during a secret affair with Marilyn.

11. Marilyn's code name for this lover was "Carlo."

Johnny Hyde, the man Marilyn always credited with her success. Vice president of the William Morris Agency, and one of the most powerful men in Hollywood, Hyde left his family to devote his time to Marilyn. He died calling her name. [Photo courtesy of Photofest.]

12. (A) This lover was accused of being a Communist, who (B) had to leave town because of his father's Communist militancy.

13. A popular entertainer, Marilyn named her dog in his honor.

14. Marilyn invited this man to come down out of the loft, but he kept taking pictures.

15. He introduced Marilyn to Arthur Miller...but is an unsympathetic character in one of Miller's plays.

16. "Just a boy." "Just a girl."

17. He was married to a blonde showgirl before he met *the* blonde.

18. He thought it was true love until he caught Marilyn with his brother.

19. He was the master of ceremonies when Marilyn rode a pink elephant at Madison Square Garden.

20. He spoke the language of love.

21. When he and Marilyn were guests of Bing Crosby in Palm Springs, Bing said it was okay for them to use the bedroom.

22. Marilyn was quoted as saying of this lover that "nobody in her life was as good in bed...but at some point you have to get out of bed and start talking." And they couldn't do it.

23. According to the usual sources, the CIA had a plan to get Marilyn into bed with this individual, and then take blackmail photos.

24. Marilyn was a "house guest" of this man who had been married to the actress after whom Norma Jeane Mortensen was named.

25. This guy insists he married Marilyn, but he never talks about what happened...later.

ANSWERS ON PAGE 355

Chapter 5

The Women in Her Life

◆

Four Fantasies

In one of their conversations in New York City, in an Eighth Avenue bar, Marilyn said to journalist W. J. Weatherby:

> "I was remembering Monty Clift. People who aren't fit to open the door for him sneer at his homosexuality. What do they know about it? Labels—people love putting labels on each other. Then they feel safe. People tried to make me into a lesbian. I laughed. No sex is wrong if there's love in it."

There have been at least four stories of Marilyn's relationships with women. It is probably necessary to point out that the sources here are not famous for their reliability.

1. Natasha Lytess

Natasha Lytess was an emigrant from Germany who had become head of the drama department at Columbia Pictures. In March, 1948, she was assigned to coach starlet Marilyn Monroe, who had just been signed to costar in the low-budget musical *Ladies of the Chorus*. For the next six years, Natasha dedicated herself to Marilyn.

In its November 19, 1991, issue the *Star* tabloid shouted from the cover, "I Was Marilyn Monroe's Lesbian Lover."

Marilyn lived here in 1950–1951, off and on, with acting coach Natasha Lytess and her young daughter. This is Harper Avenue, just off Sunset Boulevard, in West Hollywood. In 1948, Marilyn lived across the street with vocal director Fred Karger and his family. [Photo courtesy of Patrick V. Miller.]

Inside was the story of "a secret lesbian fling," "a shocking affair revealed in newly released notes from an interview with acting teacher Natasha Lytess."

"She was *mio amore*—my love," says Natasha. "It started when I taught her to kiss. Her sweetness rushed into me. We lived together as man and wife. I was the man . . . and she was the wife. It was the first affair . . . of that nature . . . for me. The only. But there were a lot of women [chasing] after Marilyn, and after a while, I lost her."

2. Lili St. Cyr

In his book *Norma Jean: My Secret Life with Marilyn Monroe*, Ted Jordan writes of Marilyn's secret lesbian loves, beginning when she was six years old and was seduced by a foster mother—a relationship that continued over the next eight years. During her starlet years, she was involved with an aspiring actress who later became quite famous.

Later, still an unknown, Marilyn asked her lover Ted Jordan to take her to see Lili St. Cyr (born in 1918), the reigning striptease queen, a very beautiful blonde. Norma Jeane was totally enraptured by St. Cyr as she went through her routine: "To have that kind of presence, to have that kind of sex appeal—that's the way I have to look."

She and Lili became close friends, and Norma Jeane soon was patterning herself after Lili—who gave her tips on looking and acting sexier. "I think Lili's in love with me," giggled Norma Jeane. "At least she acts that way in bed. She really knows how to please a woman, let me tell you."

3. A Mystery Woman in "The Wrong Door Raid"

In October of 1954, Marilyn was granted a provisional divorce from Joe DiMaggio—after nine months of marriage.

DiMaggio, however, apparently wasn't ready to give up. He was said to suspect Marilyn of a continuing affair with Twentieth Century–Fox musical director Hal Schaefer. He hired a private detective to follow Marilyn to their love nest—which was identified as being in an apartment building at 8122 Waring Avenue in Hollywood.

On November 5, DiMaggio, Frank Sinatra, and a crew of men furnished by Sinatra, stormed the building and broke down a door to catch Marilyn in the act—but the bozos broke down the wrong door. Whatever Marilyn was up to, she wasn't caught in the act.

In Kitty Kelley's unauthorized biography of Frank Sinatra, *His Way*, she says the raid was geared to catch Marilyn in a lesbian relationship.

4. Brigitte Bardot

Another tabloid story originated in the *Globe* of October 15, 1996.

The headline: "Brigitte Bardot Bares All: How Marilyn Monroe Seduced Me!"

"Beautiful Brigitte Bardot has had more than a hundred lovers—but no man seduced the fifties sex kitten as completely as her voluptuous American counterpart, legendary screen siren, Marilyn Monroe."

Said to be recounted in Brigitte's autobiography, *Initials B. B.*, the French star of *And God Created Woman* (French, 1956), told of seeing Marilyn "at a party for Queen Elizabeth of England in 1956."

The two blonde bombshells wind up in the ladies' room together. Bardot adjusts her gown, Marilyn looks at herself in the mirror, smelling of Chanel No. 5. Bardot stands there staring at her...."She seduced me in thirty seconds."

The *Globe* quotes a Bardot watcher, a veteran journalist, on the "intimate friendship" that developed.

Chapter 6

The Great Marilyn Trivia Challenge

◆

Part One

1. In August 1945, Marilyn made her first trip to the swanky Ambassador Hotel, on Wilshire Boulevard near downtown Los Angeles, to register with Emmeline Snively at the Blue Book Model Agency. Years later, she returned to the Ambassador to film scenes for which of her movies?

2. Marilyn's body measurements varied from year to year, publication to publication. By which measurements did Marilyn wish to be known?

3. What did Marilyn do for Darryl F. Zanuck, Twentieth Century–Fox mogul, in the privacy of his office?

4. Sir Laurence Olivier and his then wife Vivien Leigh starred in the original London production of *The Sleeping Prince* (later *The Prince and the Showgirl*).
   a. Who played the lead roles on Broadway?
   b. Who played the key parts in the Los Angeles production?

5. Who was "Mister Sir"?

6. Tony Curtis says he made the movie *Sextette* (Crown International, 1978) with Mae West, because then he could

say that only two actors had worked with both Marilyn Monroe and Mae West. Who was the other actor?

7. Marilyn didn't like to show her _____, because she thought they were too fat.

8. Of the top entertainment columnists of the 1940s—Hedda Hopper, Louella Parsons, Walter Winchell, Sidney Skolsky—who was the first to mention Marilyn's name?

9. What is the Marilyn film you might not have had an opportunity to see?

10. "He's the only person I know who's in worse shape than I am," said Marilyn—referring to whom?

11. (1) Monroe's birth certificate lists her name as Norma Jeane Mortensen. (Also found spelled "Mortenson.") "Mortensen"

Marilyn with Jeffrey Lynn in *Hometown Story* (1951). The sweater-dress she wears (which is her own) is probably more familiar than the movie—she also wore it in *The Fireball* (1950), *All About Eve* (1950), and for her 1950 screen test with Richard Conte. [Photo courtesy of Photofest.]

is from Martin Edward Mortensen, to whom her mother was briefly married, but who was not Marilyn's father.

(2) "Norma" was after Norma Talmadge, a glamorous silent film star.

(3) "Jeane" was after Jean Harlow, the platinum blonde superstar to whom Marilyn was often compared.

Which statement here is not correct?

12. Who was "the woman with the red hair"?

13. Which literary great *narrated* a film in which Marilyn starred?

14. Because of her associations with better-read friends, and pals from Europe, Marilyn developed an interest in the literature of which country?

15. Marilyn first appeared in *Life* magazine for the October 10, 1949, issue, in a photo essay titled "Eight Girls Try Out Mixed Emotions." Philippe Halsman photographed seven starlets and an ex-model.

    Of the group, Marilyn had the most notable screen career, but another of the starlets had the *longest* career. Who was she?

16. A photographer who lensed some of Marilyn's sexiest photos won an Emmy Award for directing a TV show—a 1974 CBS *Afterschool Special*. Who was he?

17. Name another blonde superstar who stuttered.

18. True or False:
    Marilyn was *Playboy* magazine's first Playmate of the Month.

19. Some of the sexiest all-American pinups of Marilyn were taken by a man whose father had been the court photographer to Emperor Franz Josef of Vienna! Name him.

20. In *The Asphalt Jungle*, watch closely and see Marilyn, at the end of her first scene, glance offscreen as she walks off-camera. Who is she looking at?

ANSWERS ON PAGE 356

Marilyn

AT WORK

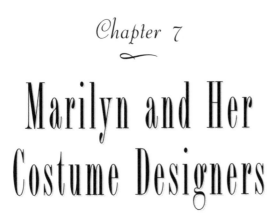

Chapter 7

Marilyn and Her Costume Designers

◆

A Woman Who Had to Be Sewn into Her Clothing

Just as Marilyn posed for so many of the top photographers, she also sought out or attracted the outstanding costume designers.

Beatrice Dawson

A British designer (1908–1976), she created Marilyn's long white dress for *The Prince and the Showgirl.*

> "[It] suited her perfectly. It made her walk with an amazing wiggle, but a wiggle which is somehow naive not brazen. It also showed just enough of the famous Monroe bosom."
>
> —*Colin Clark, The Prince, the Showgirl and Me*

Rene Hubert

Hubert was responsible for the first costume to be designed for Marilyn at Twentieth Century–Fox: the rather ornate dress for a nineteenth-century chorus girl, in *A Ticket to Tomahawk.*

Hubert (1899–1966) was born in Switzerland, studied art in Paris, and was designing costumes for the Folies-Bergere while still in art school.

He came to America in 1928. The Famous Players–Lasky Studio hired him to design clothes for film star Gloria Swanson—for Swanson and no one else. Hubert and Swanson together created many style trends.

Twentieth Century–Fox put him under contract in 1942. His unusual flair for color made him ideal for the studio's vibrant Technicolor movies with such beauties as Betty Grable (*Sweet Rosie O'Grady*, 1943), Linda Darnell (*Forever Amber*, 1947), and June Haver (*Irish Eyes Are Smiling*, 1944).

Dorothy Jeakins

She designed the magenta dress that Marilyn wore in *Niagara*, her wardrobe for *Let's Make Love*, and had started work on *The Misfits*.

Dorothy Jeakins (1914–1995) won the first Academy Award for Costume Design, outfitting Ingrid Bergman for *Joan of Arc* (RKO, 1948). She shared a second Oscar with Edith Head for *Samson and Delilah* (Paramount, 1949), and won again for *Night of the Iguana* (MGM, 1964).

She studied art at the Otis Art Institute in downtown Los Angeles, and entered the movie industry painting cels for the Walt Disney Studio.

Charles LeMaire

Edith Head designed all of Bette Davis's costumes for *All About Eve*, while Charles LeMaire was responsible for the wardrobe of everyone else, including the gown Marilyn wore in the party sequence.

LeMaire (1897–1985) was a vaudeville actor who became a Broadway costume designer. He worked on many Broadway shows in the early 1920s, including the showgirl spectaculars produced by Ziegfeld, George White, and Earl Carroll.

He became Executive Designer and Director of Wardrobe for Twentieth Century–Fox in 1943, and held the title until 1960, when he left to open his own salon.

It was LeMaire who persuaded the Academy of Motion Picture Arts and Sciences to establish an Oscar category for film costume design. He was nominated seventeen times, winning for *All About Eve* (Twentieth Century–Fox, 1950), *The Robe* (Twentieth Century–Fox, 1953), and *Love Is a Many-Splendored Thing* (Twentieth Century–Fox, 1955).

Jean Louis

Jean Louis (1907–1997) was born in Paris, where he became a sketch artist at a couture house. He was head designer for Columbia Pictures from 1944 to 1958, then went over to Universal. He created many striking and memorable costumes:

- The near-nude beaded gown Marilyn Monroe wore when she sang "Happy Birthday, Mr. President" at Madison Square Garden on May 19, 1962. It was made of a transparent flesh-colored material designed to make Marilyn appear nude. Its six thousand beads reflected different colors in different lighting. (Where are the *color* photos from that night?) This gown now hangs in the Smithsonian Institute.

- Jean Louis also designed Marilyn's outfits for *Ladies of the Chorus*, the white dress with red cherries for *The Misfits*, and was working with her on *Something's Got to Give*.

- The strapless black satin gown worn by Rita Hayworth for her "Put the Blame on Mame" number in *Gilda* (Columbia Pictures, 1946).

- Fifty-two different gowns for friend (later wife) Loretta Young for her long-running television show.
- The famous "see-through" gowns for Marlene Dietrich's Las Vegas acts—ingeniously designed to make her appear nude but for strategically placed rhinestones and fur.

Jack Orry-Kelly

He won Academy Awards for Costume Design for *An American in Paris* (MGM, 1951), *Les Girls* (MGM, 1957), and *Some Like It Hot* (1959)—which featured Marilyn in a very provocative, bosom-revealing dress.

Jack Orry-Kelly (1897–1964) was born in Australia, of Irish immigrants. In New York he illustrated title cards for silent films, and designed stage costumes for Ethel Barrymore, Katharine Hepburn, and *George White's Scandals*.

In Hollywood, friend Cary Grant introduced him to Warner Bros., where he worked in wardrobe for eleven years. He then moved to Twentieth Century–Fox, Universal, RKO, and MGM, returning to Warners only to work on Bette Davis movies.

His friends called him Jack; his drinking buddies, including Errol Flynn, nicknamed him Killer. He died while working on Billy Wilder's *Kiss Me, Stupid* (Lopert, 1964). *Tony Curtis: The Autobiography* has a photo of Tony being fitted by Orry-Kelly (page 167).

Helen Rose

She is credited with the costumes for the movies Marilyn made for MGM: *The Asphalt Jungle* (1950), *Right Cross* (1950), and *Hometown Story* (1951).

Helen Rose (1904–1985) was under contract to MGM from 1943 to 1966, designing for more than two hundred movies. She was nominated for Oscars eight times, and won for *The Bad and the Beautiful* (1952) and *I'll Cry Tomorrow* (1955). She designed two wedding gowns for Grace Kelly: one for the religious ceremony, one for the public service.

William Travilla

Travilla (1921–1990) was born on Santa Catalina Island, California. At twenty-four, he was the youngest designer under contract at a major studio (Warner Bros.). He won an Oscar for his costumes in the Errol Flynn satirical classic *The Adventures of Don Juan* (1948).

Once Marilyn became a film star, most of her screen costumes were designed by William Travilla, including the billowing white dress for *The Seven Year Itch*.

He also created the gold lamé gown for *Gentlemen Prefer Blondes* that was considered too daring, and is only glimpsed in the final cut of the film. That's it on the cover of this book.

There is a photo of Travilla with screen sexpot Sheree North in Elizabeth Leese's *Costume Design in the Movies*.

Michael Woulfe

He designed Marilyn's working-girl wardrobe for *Clash by Night*.

Born in New York City in 1918, Woulfe began as a sketch artist in the garment industry. He went to Hollywood to design costumes for Sylvia Sidney in *Blood on the Sun* (United Artists, 1945). He became head designer for RKO in 1949.

Marilyn wore her own dress—a tightly woven sweater-dress from her own wardrobe—in *All About Eve*, for the sequence in the theater lobby; for *The Fireball*; for her second screen test at

Twentieth Century–Fox, in 1950, with Richard Conte; and for *Hometown Story*.

Marilyn rejected the showgirl costume designed for *Bus Stop*, thinking it too glamorous and out-of-character for a "chantoosie" like Cherie. So she went poking around the wardrobe department until she found a seen-better-days costume she thought ideal. Fishnet stockings with holes poked in them completed the outfit.

Chapter 8

The Films of Marilyn Monroe

◆

**The Movies We Remember Her by...and the
Treasures that *Might* Have Been**

Marilyn's films (listed in chronological order)

Marilyn may have been an extra in *The Shocking Miss Pilgrim*
(1946), *Mother Wore Tights* (1947), *You Were Meant for Me* (1948),
and *Green Grass of Wyoming* (1948). No one yet has been able con-
clusively to pick her out of the crowd scenes in these Twentieth
Century–Fox movies.

1. *Scudda Hoo! Scudda Hay!* (Twentieth Century–Fox, 1948),
Color, 98 minutes.
    Producer, Walter Morosco; director, F. Hugh Herbert; (from a
story by George Agnew Chamberlain) screenplay, F. Hugh Herbert.
    June Haver (Rad McGill); Lon McCallister (Snug Dominy);
Walter Brennan (Tony Maule); Anne Revere (Judith Dominy);
Natalie Wood (Bean McGill); Henry Hull (Milt Dominy); Tom
Tully (Roarer McGill); Colleen Townsend, Marilyn Monroe (girls
in canoe, not billed).

2. *Dangerous Years* (Twentieth Century–Fox, 1948), Black-
and-White, 77 minutes.
    Producer, Sol M. Wurtzel; director, Arthur Pierson; story
and screenplay, Arnold Belgard.

William Halop (Danny Jones); Ann E. Todd (Doris Martin); Jerome Cowan (Weston); Anabel Shaw (Connie Burns); Richard Gaines (Edgar Burns); Scotty Beckett (Willy Miller); Darryl Hickman (Leo Emerson); Dickie Moore (Gene Spooner); Marilyn Monroe (Evie).

3. *Ladies of the Chorus* (Columbia, 1948), Black-and-White, 61 minutes.

Producer, Harry A. Romm; director, Phil Karlson; (from a story by Harry Sauber) screenplay, Joseph Carol and Harry Sauber.

Adele Jergens (May Martin); Marilyn Monroe (Peggy Martin); Rand Brooks (Randy Carroll); Nana Bryant (Mrs. Carroll).

MM songs: "Every Baby Needs a Da-Da-Daddy," "Anyone Can Tell I Love You."

4. *Love Happy* (United Artists, 1949), Black-and-White, 85 minutes.

Producer, Lester Cowan; director, David Miller; (from a story by Harpo Marx) screenplay, Frank Tashlin and Mac Benoff.

Harpo Marx (Harpo); Chico Marx (Faustino the Great); Groucho Marx (Sam Grunion); Vera-Ellen (Maggie Phillips); Ilona Massey (Madame Egilichi); Marion Hutton (Bunny Dolan); Paul Valentine (Mike Johnson); Marilyn Monroe (Grunion's client).

5. *A Ticket to Tomahawk* (Twentieth Century–Fox, 1950), Color, 90 minutes.

Producer, Robert Bassler; director, Richard Sale; screenplay, Mary Loos and Richard Sale.

Dan Dailey (Johnny); Anne Baxter (Kit Dodge, Jr.); Rory Calhoun (Dakota); Walter Brennan (Terrance Sweeney); Connie Gilchrist (Madame Adelaide); Marilyn Monroe (Clara).

MM song: "Oh, What a Forward Young Man You Are!" (with cast).

Two scenes from *Ladies of the Chorus*, a romantic musical made in eleven days in 1948. Marilyn played Peggy, a burlesque chorus girl who falls in love with wealthy Rand Brooks. [Photo courtesy of Photofest.]

Peggy and her mother, played by popular Adele Jergens, dance in the same chorus line. Marilyn is twenty-two at the time, Jergens is thirty. [Photo courtesy of Photofest.]

6. *The Asphalt Jungle* (MGM, 1950), Black-and-White, 112 minutes.

Producer, Arthur Hornblow, Jr.; director, John Huston; (from the novel by W. R. Burnett) screenplay, Ben Maddow and John Huston.

Sterling Hayden (Dix Handley); Louis Calhern (Alonzo D. Emmerich); Jean Hagen (Doll Conovan); James Whitmore (Gus Minissi); Sam Jaffe (Doc Erwin Riedenschneider); Marilyn Monroe (Angela Phinlay).

7. *All About Eve* (Twentieth Century–Fox, 1950), Black-and-White, 138 minutes.

Producer, Darryl F. Zanuck; director, Joseph L. Mankiewicz; (based on a story by Mary Orr) screenplay, Joseph L. Mankiewicz.

Bette Davis (Margo Channing); Anne Baxter (Eve Harrington); George Sanders (Addison DeWitt); Gary Merrill (Bill Sampson); Celeste Holm (Karen Richards); Hugh Marlowe (Lloyd Richards); Thelma Ritter (Birdie); Marilyn Monroe (Miss Caswell); Gregory Ratoff (Max Fabian); Barbara Bates (Phoebe).

8. *The Fireball* (Twentieth Century–Fox, 1950), Black-and-White, 84 minutes.

Producer, Bert Friedlob; director, Tay Garnett; screenplay, Tay Garnett and Horace McCoy.

Mickey Rooney (Johnny Casar); Pat O'Brien (Father O'Hare); Beverly Tyler (Mary Reeves); James Brown (Allen); Marilyn Monroe (Polly).

9. *Right Cross* (MGM, 1950), Black-and-White, 90 minutes.

Producer, Armand Deutsch; director, John Sturges; screenplay, Charles Schnee.

June Allyson (Pat O'Malley); Dick Powell (Rick Gavery); Ricardo Montalban (Johnny Monterez); Lionel Barrymore (Sean O'Malley); Marilyn Monroe (Dusky Ledoux) [unbilled].

10. *Hometown Story* (MGM, 1951), Black-and-White, 61 minutes.
Producer/director/screenwriter, Arthur Pierson.

Jeffrey Lynn (Mike Washburn); Donald Crisp (John MacFarland); Alan Hale, Jr. (Haskins); Marilyn Monroe (Miss Martin).

11. *As Young As You Feel* (Twentieth Century–Fox, 1951), Black-and-White, 77 minutes.

Producer, Lamar Trotti; director, Harmon Jones; (based on a story by Paddy Chayefsky) screenplay, Lamar Trotti.

Monty Woolley (John Hodges); Thelma Ritter (Della Hodges); David Wayne (Joe); Jean Peters (Alice Hodges); Constance Bennett (Lucille McKinley); Marilyn Monroe (Harriet); Albert Dekker (Louis McKinley).

12. *Love Nest* (Twentieth Century–Fox, 1951), Black-and-White, 84 minutes.

Producer, Jules Buck; director, Joseph Newman; (from a novel by Scott Corbett) screenplay by I. A. L. Diamond.

June Haver (Connie Scott); William Lundigan (Jim Scott); Frank Fay (Charley Patterson); Marilyn Monroe (Roberta Stevens); Jack Paar (Ed Forbes); Leatrice Joy (Eadie Gaynor).

13. *Let's Make It Legal* (Twentieth Century–Fox, 1951), Black-and-White, 77 minutes.

Producer, Robert Bassler; director, Richard Sale; (based on a story by Mortimer Braus) screenplay, I. A. L. Diamond and F. Hugh Herbert.

Claudette Colbert (Miriam); Macdonald Carey (Hugh); Zachary Scott (Victor); Barbara Bates (Barbara Denham); Robert Wagner (Jerry Denham); Marilyn Monroe (Joyce).

14. *Clash by Night* (RKO, 1952), Black-and-White, 105 minutes.
Producer, Harriet Parsons; director, Fritz Lang; (from the play by Clifford Odets) screenplay, Alfred Hayes.

Barbara Stanwyck (Mae); Paul Douglas (Jerry); Robert Ryan (Earl); Marilyn Monroe (Peggy); Keith Andes (Joe Doyle).

15. *We're Not Married* (Twentieth Century–Fox, 1952), Black-and-White, 85 minutes.

Producer, Nunnally Johnson; director, Edmund Goulding; (from a story by Jay Dratler and Gina Kaus) adaptation, Dwight Taylor; screenplay, Nunnally Johnson.

Ginger Rogers (Ramona); Fred Allen (Steve Gladwyn); Victor Moore (Justice of the Peace); Marilyn Monroe (Annabel Norris); David Wayne (Jeff Norris); Eve Arden (Katie Woodruff); Paul Douglas (Hector Woodruff); Eddie Bracken (Willie Fisher); Mitzi Gaynor (Patsy Fisher); Louis Calhern (Freddie Melrose); Zsa Zsa Gabor (Eve Melrose).

A setup not in the final cut of *We're Not Married* (1952), which featured Marilyn as the Mrs. Mississippi beauty-contest winner. The man with his back to the camera could be Twentieth Century–Fox studio president Spyros Skouras. [Photo courtesy of J. C. Archives.]

16. *Don't Bother to Knock* (Twentieth Century–Fox, 1952), Black-and-White, 76 minutes.

Producer, Julian Blaustein; director, Roy Baker; (based on the novel by Charlotte Armstrong) screenplay, Daniel Taradash.

Richard Widmark (Jed Towers); Marilyn Monroe (Nell Forbes); Anne Bancroft (Lyn Leslie); Donna Corcoran (Bunny); Jeanne Cagney (Rochelle); Lurene Tuttle (Mrs. Ruth Jones); Elisha Cook, Jr. (Eddie); Jim Backus (Peter Jones).

17. *Monkey Business* (Twentieth Century–Fox, 1952), Black-and-White, 97 minutes.

Producer, Sol C. Siegel; director, Howard Hawks; (from a story by Harry Segall) screenplay, I. A. L. Diamond, Ben Hecht, and Charles Lederer.

Cary Grant (Barnaby Fulton); Ginger Rogers (Edwina); Charles Coburn (Mr. Oxley); Marilyn Monroe (Lois Laurel).

18. *O. Henry's Full House* (Twentieth Century–Fox, 1952), Black-and-White, 117 minutes.

Episode number four: producer, Andre Hakim; director, Henry Koster; (based on a story by O. Henry) screenplay, Lamar Trotti.

Charles Laughton (Soapy); Marilyn Monroe (Streetwalker); David Wayne (Horace).

19. *Niagara* (Twentieth Century–Fox, 1953), Color, 89 minutes.

Producer, Charles Brackett; director, Henry Hathaway; screenplay, Charles Brackett, Richard Breen, and Walter Reisch.

Marilyn Monroe (Rose Loomis); Joseph Cotten (George Loomis); Jean Peters (Polly Cutler); Casey Adams (Ray Cutler); Richard Allan (Patrick).

MM song: "Kiss."

20. *Gentlemen Prefer Blondes* (Twentieth Century–Fox, 1953), Color, 91 minutes.

Producer, Sol. C. Siegel; director, Howard Hawks; (based on the musical comedy by Joseph Fields and Anita Loos) screenplay, Charles Lederer.

Jane Russell (Dorothy); Marilyn Monroe (Lorelei Lee); Charles Coburn (Sir Francis Beekman); Elliott Reid (Malone); Tommy Noonan (Gus Esmond); George "Foghorn" Winslow (Henry Spofford III).

MM songs: "Two Little Girls from Little Rock" (with Jane Russell), "When Love Goes Wrong" (with Jane Russell), "Bye Bye Baby," and "Diamonds Are a Girl's Best Friend."

21. *How to Marry a Millionaire* (Twentieth Century–Fox, 1953), Color, 96 minutes.

Producer, Nunnally Johnson; director, Jean Negulesco; (from plays by Katherine Albert, Zoe Atkins, and Dale Eunson) screenplay, Nunnally Johnson.

Marilyn Monroe (Pola); Betty Grable (Loco); Lauren Bacall (Schatze); David Wayne (Freddie Denmark); Rory Calhoun (Eben); Cameron Mitchell (Tom Brookman); Alex D'Arcy (J. Stewart Merrill); William Powell (J.D. Hanley).

22. *River of No Return* (Twentieth Century–Fox, 1954), Color, 91 minutes.

Producer, Stanley Rubin; director, Otto Preminger; (from a story by Louis Lantz) screenplay, Frank Fenton.

Robert Mitchum (Matt Calder); Marilyn Monroe (Kay); Rory Calhoun (Harry Weston); Tommy Rettig (Mark Calder); Murvyn Vye (Colby); Barbara Nichols (Dancer).

MM songs: "The River of No Return," "I'm Gonna File My Claim," "One Silver Dollar," and "Down in the Meadow."

23. *There's No Business Like Show Business* (Twentieth Century-Fox, 1954), Color, 117 minutes.

Producer, Sol C. Siegel; director, Walter Lang; (based on a story by Lamar Trotti) screenplay, Henry and Phoebe Ephron.

Ethel Merman (Molly Donahue); Donald O'Connor (Tim Donahue); Marilyn Monroe (Vicky); Dan Dailey (Terrance Donahue); Johnnie Ray (Steve Donahue); Mitzi Gaynor (Katy Donahue).

MM songs: "After You Get What You Want You Don't Want It," "Heat Wave," "Lazy" (with Mitzi Gaynor and Donald O'Connor), "There's No Business Like Show Business" (with cast).

24. *The Seven Year Itch* (Twentieth Century–Fox, 1955), Color, 105 minutes.

Producers, Charles K. Feldman and Billy Wilder; director, Billy Wilder; (from the play by George Axelrod) screenplay by George Axelrod and Billy Wilder.

Marilyn Monroe (The Girl); Tom Ewell (Richard Sherman); Evelyn Keyes (Helen Sherman); Sonny Tufts (Tom MacKenzie).

25. *Bus Stop* (Twentieth Century–Fox, 1956), Color, 96 minutes.

Producer: Buddy Adler; director, Joshua Logan; (from the play by William Inge) screenplay, George Axelrod.

Marilyn Monroe (Cherie); Don Murray (Bo); Arthur O'Connell (Virgil); Betty Field (Grace); Eileen Heckart (Vera); Robert Bray (Carl); Hope Lange (Elma).

MM song: "That Old Black Magic."

26. *The Prince and the Showgirl* (Warner Bros., 1957), Color, 117 minutes.

Producer/director, Laurence Olivier; (based on the play *The Sleeping Prince* by Terence Rattigan) screenplay, Terence Rattigan.

Marilyn Monroe (Elsie); Laurence Olivier (Grand Duke Charles); Sybil Thorndike (The Queen Dowager); Richard Wattis (Northbrook); Jeremy Spencer (King Nicholas).

27. *Some Like It Hot* (United Artists, 1959), Black-and-White, 122 minutes.

Producer/director, Billy Wilder; (based on a story by M. Logan and R. Thoeren) screenplay, I. A. L. Diamond and Billy Wilder.

Marilyn Monroe (Sugar Kane); Tony Curtis (Joe/Josephine); Jack Lemmon (Jerry/Daphne); George Raft (Spats Colombo); Pat O'Brien (Mulligan); Joe E. Brown (Osgood Fielding); Joan Shawlee (Sweet Sue).

28. *Let's Make Love* (Twentieth Century–Fox, 1960), Color, 118 minutes.

Producer, Jerry Wald; director, George Cukor; screenplay, Norman Krasna; additional material: Hal Kanter, Arthur Miller (uncredited).

Marilyn Monroe (Amanda); Yves Montand (Jean-Marc Clemens); Tony Randall (Howard Coffman); Frankie Vaughan, Milton Berle, Bing Crosby, and Gene Kelly as themselves.

MM songs: "My Heart Belongs to Daddy," "Let's Make Love," "Incurably Romantic," and "Specialization."

29. *The Misfits* (United Artists, 1961), Black-and-White, 124 minutes.

Producer, Frank Taylor; director, John Huston; screenplay, Arthur Miller, from his own short story.

Clark Gable (Gay Langland); Marilyn Monroe (Roslyn Taber); Montgomery Clift (Perce Howland); Thelma Ritter (Isabelle Steers); Eli Wallach (Guido); Kevin McCarthy (Raymond Taber).

30. *Something's Got to Give* (Twentieth Century–Fox, 1962, unfinished), Color.

Producer, Henry T. Weinstein; director, George Cukor; (based on the screenplay *My Favorite Wife* by Bella and Samuel Spewack) screenplay, Nunnally Johnson and Walter Bernstein.

Marilyn Monroe (Ellen Arden); Dean Martin (Nick Arden); Cyd Charisse (Bianca); Tom Tryon (Steven Burkette); Wally Cox (Shoe Clerk); Phil Silvers (Insurance Man); Steve Allen (Dr. Herman Schlick).

(Also see Part 4, Chapter 25, for a list of books on Marilyn's films.)

◆

The Marilyn Filmss You Didn't See

It's always fascinating to speculate about what might have been: if Claudette Colbert had played Margo Channing in *All About Eve*; if Paulette Goddard had played Scarlett O'Hara in *Gone with the Wind*; if Marilyn Monroe had played Sadie Thompson in *Rain*, or Holly Golightly in *Breakfast at Tiffany's*.

In her relatively brief screen career, Marilyn had more than her share of bad movies. One looks at the remnants of *Something's Got to Give* and wonders if anyone could have saved it. You look at *Let's Make Love* and realize that almost any of the projects listed below *must* have been better suited to the star's talents. There are a couple of these projects that make something inside of you go *thwang!* when you realize what might have been, what we've lost.

Born Yesterday (Columbia, 1950)

Garson Kanin, then at Columbia (at the time of *Ladies of the Chorus*, 1949), wrote that Marilyn had done a screen test for the Billie Dawn role in *Born Yesterday*, but that studio head Harry Cohn refused to look at it.

Judy Holliday, who created the role in the original Broadway production, won an Oscar for her performance as the not-so-dumb blonde in the 1950 film. Melanie Griffith starred in a 1993 remake.

(In 1960, after Marilyn had completed filming *The Misfits*, Frank Sinatra wanted her to star with him in a musical remake of Garson Kanin's classic comedy *Born Yesterday*, for his own company.)

The Last Man on Wagon Mound (Twentieth Century–Fox, early 1950s)

Marilyn as a frontier widow? *The Unabridged Marilyn* lists this title as an early-1950s Twentieth Century–Fox project, to costar Mitzi Gaynor, Debra Paget, and Jean Peters.

Pink Tights (Twentieth Century–Fox, 1953)

Marilyn was to report to work at Twentieth Century–Fox on December 15, 1953, for *Pink Tights*, a remake of Betty Grable's 1943 musical *Coney Island*, to costar Frank Sinatra. (The project had already been remade in 1950 with Grable herself, as *Wabash Avenue*.) Marilyn chose to go on suspension rather than make the film. The project was permanently shelved.

The Egyptian (Twentieth Century–Fox, 1954)

After the success of *How to Marry a Millionaire*, Marilyn asked to star in the upcoming biblical epic *The Egyptian*. Studio head Darryl F. Zanuck ignored her request, giving the role of the exotic courtesan to his current protégée Bella Darvi.

Other cast members of this 1954 costume spectacle were Edmund Purdom, Victor Mature, Gene Tierney, Jean Simmons, and Michael Wilding.

Of Human Bondage (Twentieth Century–Fox, 1954)

In 1954, Henry Hathaway (who had directed *Niagara* in 1953) proposed a new version of W. Somerset Maugham's classic *Of Human Bondage* to costar Marilyn Monroe and James Dean. Indifferent to Marilyn's career, Darryl F. Zanuck refused to discuss it.

In the 1934 version, Bette Davis put her mark on the role of the sluttish waitress who torments sensitive medical student Leslie Howard.

Eleanor Parker starred in a 1946 version with Paul Henreid; Kim Novak tried it in 1964 opposite Laurence Harvey.

The Girl in the Red Velvet Swing (Twentieth Century–Fox, 1955)

Many fans think Marilyn would have been good in this project, playing showgirl Evelyn Nesbitt, the center of the sensational 1906 society scandal when millionaire Harry K. Thaw killed architect Stanford White over his love of Evelyn.

Marilyn was forming her own company at the time, and refused this project. Joan Collins later did the 1955 film. The Nesbitt-Thaw-White scandal was featured in the movie *Ragtime* (Paramount, 1981), with Elizabeth McGovern as Evelyn, and in the 1997 Broadway musical version of *Ragtime*.

Guys and Dolls (MGM, 1955)

Producer Samuel Goldwyn paid over a million dollars for movie rights to this popular Broadway musical. He sought to cover his expensive bet by signing the biggest stars of the day... hence the casting of Marlon Brando and Frank Sinatra as the Damon Runyon–style, lovable underworld characters. Director Joseph L. Mankiewicz capitulated to Goldwyn on those two, but insisted that Vivian Blaine re-create her Broadway role. So Mankiewicz didn't tell Goldwyn that Marilyn Monroe was eager to be in the film.

How to Be Very, Very Popular
(Twentieth Century–Fox, 1955)

After *The Seven Year Itch*, Twentieth Century–Fox had scheduled *How to Be Very, Very Popular* to be Marilyn's next screen assignment. She had no intention of doing it, as she and photographer-partner Milton Greene were busy forming Marilyn Monroe Productions.

Sheree North was cast in *How to Be Very, Very Popular* (Twentieth Century–Fox, 1955), with Betty Grable (her last film), Robert Cummings, and Charles Coburn.

The two blondes play strippers on the run, hiding out in a college fraternity house.

The million-dollar blondes of Twentieth Century–Fox. Marilyn and Betty Grable arrive at a party for Walter Winchell (before he turned against Marilyn). [Photo courtesy of Photofest.]

The Lieutenant Wore Skirts
(Twentieth Century–Fox, 1956)

Sheree North also starred in the comedy *The Lieutenant Wore Skirts* (1956), another Twentieth Century–Fox project meant for Marilyn. Sheree enlists in the Air Force to be near husband Tom Ewell—but he's been rejected by the service, and so becomes the only civilian husband on the base.

The Revolt of Mamie Stover
(Twentieth Century–Fox, 1956)

After *The Seven Year Itch*, producer Buddy Adler and Twentieth Century–Fox wanted Marilyn to star in *The Revolt of Mamie Stover*, a Sadie Thompson–inspired story of a San Francisco "dance-hall hostess" who is thrown out of San Francisco and takes her business to Hawaii.

Jane Russell starred in the 1956 film with Richard Egan and Agnes Moorehead.

The Jean Harlow Story
(Carroll Baker version, Paramount, 1965;
Carol Lynley version, Magna, 1965)

In 1955, Marilyn said that the first film of Marilyn Monroe Productions might be the story of screen legend Jean Harlow (1911–1937).

This was a project she and columnist Sidney Skolsky had talked about for years. Reportedly, they were to discuss it again on August 5, 1962, the day Marilyn died.

The closest Marilyn got to playing Harlow was posing as her for Richard Avedon's "Fabled Enchantresses" photo series in *Life* magazine.

Baby Doll (Warner Bros., 1956)

In her book *Baby Doll: An Autobiography* (1983), Carroll Baker writes of doubting she would get to play the southern child bride in the movie version of the Tennessee Williams black comedy, as Marilyn was campaigning hard for it. Marilyn was Williams' first choice, as he wanted a fleshier, sexier actress. Elia Kazan, who produced and directed the 1956 film, insisted on Baker.

Charles Chaplin project (circa 1957)

As the partnership with Milton Greene was being dissolved, "they had discussed plans for the future—among them a film with Charles Chaplin, who was indeed interested."

—*Donald Spoto, **Marilyn Monroe: The Biography***

The Brothers Karamazov (MGM, 1958)

In the summer of 1955, Marilyn was saddened to hear of the death of acting teacher Michael Chekhov—he had encouraged her to undertake the role of Grushenka. Arthur Miller promised to write a screenplay of the novel for Marilyn, but it never happened.

The eventual 1958 MGM film starred ever-smiling Maria Schell as Grushenka, with Yul Brynner, Claire Bloom, Lee J. Cobb, Richard Basehart, and William Shatner.

Middle of the Night (Columbia, 1959)

Marilyn read an advance copy of Paddy Chayefsky's play *Middle of the Night*, the drama of a middle-aged man in love with a much younger woman, and made him promise he would sell the screen rights to Marilyn Monroe Productions. Chayefsky waited and waited, until Milton Greene told him Marilyn was no longer interested—apparently husband Arthur Miller had badmouthed the script.

Edward G. Robinson and Gena Rowlands had costarred in the original 1957 Broadway production. The 1959 Columbia black-and-white feature film starred Fredric March and Kim Novak.

The Goddess (Columbia, 1958)

Marilyn had made playwright Paddy Chayefsky promise he'd sell her the screen rights to his acclaimed play *Middle of the Night*...then kept him waiting...and then dumped him. An angry Chayefsky sat down and wrote the original screenplay *The Goddess*, a harsh retelling of the Norma Jeane Baker–Marilyn Monroe story. He sent the first copy of the screenplay to Marilyn, who responded that she wanted to play the part. However, husband Arthur Miller said no.

The 1958 black-and-white film starred Kim Stanley, and the depiction of Marilyn had been softened.

(See Part 3, Chapter 14, "Paddy Chayefsky," for full details on *Middle of the Night* and *The Goddess*.)

Some Came Running (MGM, 1958)

In May 1958, Marilyn was eager to go back to work—not having made a film in America in two years, because of her determination to appear in quality movies of her own choosing.

Twentieth Century–Fox discussed a movie of *Some Came Running*, from the James Jones novel (1957) about postwar disillusionment, to costar Frank Sinatra. It was filmed at MGM in 1958 with Sinatra and Shirley MacLaine as the boisterous honky-tonk girl Ginny.

Director Vincente Minnelli wrote, in *I Remember It Well*, "[Shirley's] part represented the failure of sex rather than the triumph that would be implied if a sex bomb had been cast in the role."

Pillow Talk (Universal, 1959)

Marilyn wanted it but couldn't get it. No more details.

Pillow Talk is a bright comedy of two people who dislike each other, but fall in love via a telephone party line they don't realize they share. This 1959 smash hit with Doris Day and Rock Hudson was the most successful film either star had made, and launched a series of similar comedies.

The Sound and the Fury (Twentieth Century–Fox, 1959)

Twentieth Century–Fox suggested to Marilyn a project based on William Faulkner's novel *The Sound and the Fury*. The movie appeared in 1959, with Joanne Woodward as a defiant southern girl seeking independence from her strict family, and bore little resemblance to the book.

Can-Can (Twentieth Century–Fox, 1960)

In 1958, Twentieth Century–Fox offered to produce a film of the Broadway musical *Can-Can* to star Marilyn and Maurice Chevalier. It was finally made in 1960 with Frank Sinatra, Shirley MacLaine, and Chevalier.

The Story on Page One (Twentieth Century–Fox, 1959)

Jerry Wald, who had produced *Clash by Night*, told Marilyn of Clifford Odets' new script. *The Story on Page One* was about a lonely, neurotic woman who seeks refuge in men—a story that sounded to Marilyn too much like her own life.

This stark drama was filmed in black-and-white in 1959 with Rita Hayworth and Anthony Franciosa. Hayworth won very high praise for her acting.

They Shoot Horses, Don't They? (Cinerama, 1969)

"I told [Marilyn] the story of *They Shoot Horses, Don't They?*, a book I knew backward because I had done it on the radio in 1946...and I advised her to buy the rights as fast as possible."

—*Simone Signoret, Nostalgia Isn't What It Used to Be*

Jane Fonda starred in the 1969 film, a story of the grueling dance marathons popular during the Depression years. She won an Oscar nomination for Best Actress.

Breakfast at Tiffany's (Paramount, 1961)

"I was on a plane with Marilyn Monroe from New York to California, and we spoke about *Breakfast at Tiffany's*; before our trip was over, Marilyn insisted she was the only one to play Holly. We agreed that we would speak to her adviser and see whether we could mutually find the time to do the film. Within forty-eight hours, we were advised by the adviser, Paula Strasberg, that Monroe would not be available; she would not have her play a lady of the evening."

—*producer Martin Jurow, in a letter to the editor of the New York Times, March 14, 1993*

Author Truman Capote himself said he pleaded for Marilyn to play Holly Golightly—the insouciant call girl with an amazing collection of secrets, friends, and fantasies. However, Paramount Pictures was adamant that Audrey Hepburn star in the 1961 film, which was written by George Axelrod and directed by Blake Edwards.

Paris Blues (United Artists, 1961)

"Brando thought he might star in *Paris Blues*, a story of American jazz musicians in Paris, hopefully with Marilyn Monroe as his costar. Miss Monroe...liked the idea of working with Marlon. She agreed to do *Paris Blues* if Brando costarred, but he stalled on committing himself. When the film was produced in 1961, it starred Paul Newman and Joanne Woodward."

—*Gary Carey, Marlon Brando: The Only Contender*

Freud (Universal, 1962)

In his autobiography, *An Open Book*, director John Huston says that Marilyn had been his first choice for *Freud*, for the role eventually played by Susannah York in the 1962 film—but that her own analyst advised against it.

Huston writes that Marilyn "was appreciated as an artist in Europe long before her acceptance as anything but a sex symbol in the United States. Jean-Paul Sartre considered Marilyn Monroe the finest actress alive. He wanted her to play the leading female role in *Freud*." (Sartre wrote the first, unfilmed, screenplay for *Freud*.)

In Lawrence Grobel's book, *The Hustons*, Marilyn is quoted as saying, "I can't do it because Anna Freud doesn't want a picture made. My analyst told me this."

Rain (NBC, 1961)

In 1961, Marilyn and drama coach–mentor Lee Strasberg proposed a TV dramatization of *Rain*, W. Somerset Maugham's story of floozy Sadie Thompson.

Fredric March and his wife Florence Eldridge were to play the repressed Reverend Davidson and his wife, Rod Serling was to write the script, George Roy Hill was to direct, and Lee Strasberg was to be "production supervisor."

After a year of negotiations, Marilyn had still not signed a contract. The Marches pulled out of the project. Serling became disenchanted. Strasberg insisted on directing, and Marilyn stood by him. When the network said no, Strasberg canceled the project.

Obviously, the loss is ours. After all these years, Marilyn as Sadie Thompson still sounds like a very good idea.

Gloria Swanson starred in the 1928 United Artists movie *Sadie Thompson*; Joan Crawford was Sadie in *Rain* (United Artists, 1932), and Rita Hayworth was *Miss Sadie Thompson* (Columbia, 1953). The stage careers of Jeanne Eagels (1894–1929) and Tallulah Bankhead (1902–1968) will always be associated with the role. June Havoc starred in the 1944 Broadway musical *Sadie Thompson*, written by Vernon Duke and Howard Dietz.

Irma La Douce (United Artists, 1963)

Billy Wilder reportedly offered Marilyn the title role in the movie version of *Irma La Douce*. This had been a musical on Broadway, but Wilder took out the music and played it strictly for laughs. It is the story of a Paris gendarme who falls in love with a prostitute and tries to keep her all to himself.

It was filmed in 1963 with Shirley MacLaine, who received a Best Actress nomination, and Jack Lemmon.

The Stripper (Twentieth Century–Fox, 1963)

Marilyn was offered the role of Lila—a girl from a foster home who fails in Hollywood and resorts to stripping—and rejected it. At this point in her career why would she do a project like this?

The script is from the Broadway failure *A Loss of Roses* (1959) by William Inge (who also wrote *Bus Stop*, which became one of Marilyn's biggest critical and personal successes). Joanne Woodward starred in the 1963 film, with Richard Beymer and Claire Trevor.

I Love Louisa (aka What a Way to Go!) (Twentieth Century–Fox, 1964)

When Twentieth Century–Fox decided to resume production on *Something's Got to Give*, Marilyn had also decided to appear in a new screen comedy with Dean Martin called *I Love Louisa*, and scheduled a meeting on that project with director J. Lee Thompson for Monday, August 6, 1962.

I Love Louisa became *What a Way to Go!*, released in 1964, with Shirley MacLaine in the role Marilyn had wanted. The film's other stars were Dean Martin, Robert Mitchum, Paul Newman, and Gene Kelly.

What a Way to Go! is maybe even dumber than *Let's Make Love*. The story is of a jinxed woman who marries a series of wealthy men who promptly die, making her richer and richer. It's hard to imagine what Marilyn saw in it, what she saw in Thompson's ability as a director of comedy (he was an action director known mainly for *The Guns of Navarone*, Columbia, 1961) and what she thought she could bring to it.

Goodbye Charlie (Twentieth Century–Fox, 1964)

George Cukor, who'd had his problems with Marilyn on *Let's Make Love* and *Something's Got to Give*, was planning to risk his luck again, with a film of George Axelrod's stage comedy *Goodbye Charlie*. Lauren Bacall originated the part on Broadway, that of a crude gangster who is murdered and comes back to Earth as a blonde female.

Eventually, Vincente Minnelli directed the 1964 Twentieth Century–Fox feature film, which starred Debbie Reynolds, Tony Curtis, Pat Boone, and Walter Matthau.

The Clara Bow Story (never made)

Marilyn reportedly once tried to obtain the rights to the life story of screen star Clara Bow (1905–1965), the very popular "It" girl of the Roaring Twenties. Clara's career was cut short by physical and emotional problems, and by rumors of scandalous offscreen behavior. Bow was said to have declined Marilyn's offer because she didn't want the movie made while she was still alive.

Marilyn posed as Clara Bow for Richard Avedon's "Fabled Enchantresses" photo essay in *Life* magazine, December 22, 1958.

A Tree Grows in Brooklyn (musical version, never made)

Jule Styne, who had agreed to compose songs for *I Love Louisa* in 1962, proposed another project to Marilyn—a musical version of Betty Smith's novel *A Tree Grows in Brooklyn*, which had been a big Twentieth Century–Fox success in 1945. Frank Sinatra would be her costar. Marilyn made an appointment to meet Styne in New York City on August 9, 1962.

"Rat Pack" project

At the time of Marilyn's death, in 1962, producer William Asher was in negotiations for a new film. It was a comedy about a train heist to star Marilyn, Peter Lawford, Frank Sinatra, Dean Martin, and Sammy Davis, Jr. Screenwriter Harry Brown, who had written *Ocean's Eleven* (1960) for the Rat Pack, had completed a treatment for the new project, and Milton Rudin was already negotiating contracts.

Pauline Kael on the roles Marilyn didn't get

"The pity is that she didn't get more of the entertaining roles that were in her range; she hardly had the stability to play a mother or even a secretary and she was a shade too whorey for *Daisy Miller* or her descendants, but she was the heroine of every porny-spoof like *Candy* come to life, and she might have been right for *Sweet Charity* or for *Lord Love a Duck* or *Born Yesterday* or a remake of the Harlow comedy *Bombshell* or another *Red Dust*. She might have had a triumph in *Breakfast at Tiffany's* and she probably could have toned down for Tennessee Williams's *Period of Adjustment* and maybe even *Bonnie and Clyde*. Plain awful when she suffered, she was best at demi-whores who enjoyed the tease, and she was too obviously a product of the movie age to appear in a period picture."

—*from her* **New York Times** *book review of Norman Mailer's* **Marilyn**

Chapter 9

The Documentary Films

♦

In Search of the Real Marilyn

A documentary film about Marilyn will usually begin with black-and-white footage, in slow motion, of Marilyn's blanket-covered body being wheeled out of her home and into an ambulance. Or it may begin with color footage of an ambulance screaming down Hollywood Boulevard—miles away from where Marilyn lived and died—and going in the wrong direction anyway.

The early documentaries will feature rare footage of important players in Marilyn's life: her first foster parents, the Bolenders; Emmeline Snively of the Blue Book Model Agency; photographers Tom Kelley and Laszlo Willinger. The regulars will include first husband Jim Dougherty, costars Robert Mitchum and Jane Russell, friend Susan Strasberg, and actress Sheree North who always impresses you with her sincerity.

Added to the mix later will be publisher Hugh Hefner, feminist Gloria Steinem, columnist Liz Smith, early fan James Haspiel, and biographer Donald Spoto. Then the Marilyn documentaries basically become exposés or attempts to prove conspiracies, and the guests will speak of ominous government agencies, mafiosi, wiretapping, and take-your-choice versions of single incidents. "Best friend" Jeanne Carmen will tell of driving Marilyn and Bobby Kennedy to a nude beach, and "confidant" Robert Slatzer will growl, "She was a little girl that knew too much."

Marilyn's documentaries (listed in order of release)

Marilyn Monroe, Why? (CBS-TV, 1962), Black-and-White, 30 minutes.

Executive producer, Les Midgeley; host, Charles Collingwood.

On August 10, 1962, less than a week after Marilyn's death, CBS aired this documentary—initially titled "Who Killed Marilyn Monroe?"— on its *Eyewitness* program.

Marilyn (Twentieth Century–Fox, 1963), Color, 83 minutes.

Narrator, Rock Hudson; writer, Harold Medford; editor, Pepe Torres. A tribute produced for theatrical distribution. Released on April 18, 1963, eight months after Marilyn's death.

Basically it is a collection of scenes from the films she made at Twentieth Century–Fox, omitting important films made elsewhere. The costume and makeup test shots from *Something's Got to Give*, brief as they are, always thrill viewers.

The Marilyn Monroe Story (ABC-TV, 1963), Black-and-White, 30 minutes.

Producer, Art Lieberman; writer, Malvin Wald; narrator, Mike Wallace; original music, Elmer Bernstein.

The Legend of Marilyn Monroe (ABC-TV, 1966), Black-and-White, 60 minutes.

Aka *Portrait: Marilyn Monroe* (Ciné Productions) and *The Marilyn Monroe Story* (Madacy Music Group, Canada).

Producer, David L. Wolper; director/editor, Terry Sanders; writers Terry Sanders, Theodore Strauss; narrator, John Huston.

Marilyn Remembered (ABC-TV, 1974), Black-and-White, 60 minutes.

A 1974 television pastiche that takes *The Legend of Marilyn Monroe* (above) and adds thirty minutes of actor Peter Lawford interviewing Marilyn's housekeeper Eunice Murray and others.

Marvelous Marilyn (Syndicated, 1979), Color and Black-and-White, 30 minutes.
 Producer/writer, Phillip Savenick; narrator, Tom Bosley.
 A segment of *That's Hollywood!*, the syndicated television program.

In Search of: "The Death of Marilyn Monroe" (Syndicated, 1980), Black-and-White, 30 minutes.
 Producer, Alan Landsburg; writers, John D. Ackelson, Annette Marie Bettin, and Abraham Lewenstein.

Marilyn, In Search of a Dream (ABC-TV, 1983), Color and Black-and-White, 30 minutes.
 Producer, Jonathan Kaplan; executive producers, David Kellogg, Frank Kelly; narrator, Kevin McCarthy.
 Special documentary on Marilyn featured on the *Hollywood Close-Up* television series.

The Last Days of Marilyn Monroe (BBC-TV, 1985), Color and Black-and-White, 60 minutes. Aka *Say Goodbye to the President* (American television version) and *Marilyn, Say Goodbye to the President* (home video release).
 Executive producer, Ted Landreth; director/writer, Christopher Olgiati; narrator, Christopher Olgiati; consultant, Anthony Summers.

Marilyn Monroe: Beyond the Legend (Cinemax Cable, 1986), Color and Black-and-White, 60 minutes.

Producers-writers, Gene Feldman and Suzette Winter; director, Gene Feldman; narrator, Richard Widmark; consultant, James Haspiel.

This documentary focuses on Marilyn as an actress, with a generous amount of footage, even including the non–Twentieth Century–Fox films (*The Asphalt Jungle, Some Like It Hot, The Misfits*).

Remembering Marilyn (ABC-TV, 1988), Color and Black-and-White, 60 minutes.

Producer, Andrew Solt; in association with Scott/Vinnedge Television; director, Andrew Solt; writer, Theodore Strauss; host, Lee Remick.

The Hollywood Studio Club on Lodi Place, a safe place for aspiring actresses. Marilyn lived here for a time in 1946–1947 and in 1948–1949.

Other notable tenants: Sharon Tate, Kim Novak, Linda Darnell, Sally Struthers. It opened in 1926, closed in 1975. [Photo courtesy of Patrick V. Miller.]

Marilyn: Something's Got to Give (Twentieth Century–Fox, 1990), Color and Black-and-White, 60 minutes.

Producer/writer, Henry Schipper; coproducer/editor, Ken Turner; executive producer, William K. Knoedelseder, Jr.

Marilyn Monroe, The Early Years (Ashley Entertainment Productions, 1991), Color, 50 minutes. Aka *The Discovery of Marilyn Monroe* (United American Video, 1991).

Producers, Thomas J. Ashley and Clay Cole; writer/director/narrator, Clay Cole. Distributed by Maier Communications.

Virtually a commercial for the photos of army photographer David Conover (who took the first professional photos of Marilyn in 1944).

Marilyn: The Last Interview (HBO, 1992), Black-and-White, 30 minutes.

Producer, Edward Hersh; executive producer, Peter Kunhardt.

Excerpts from the audiotape of the Richard Meryman interview sessions used for his *Life* magazine article of August 3, 1962.

The Marilyn Files (Syndicated, 1992), Color, 120 minutes.

Production company, Producers Video Inc.; executive producers, Melvin Bergman, William Speckin; co–executive producers, Stan Corwin, Andrew Ettinger; director, Bill Foster; (from Robert Slatzer's book of the same name) hosts, Bill Bixby, Jane Wallace.

Presented as a two-hour live show from Hollywood.

Marilyn: The Last Word (Paramount TV, 1993), Color, 57 minutes.

Producers, Joe Tobin, Peter Herdrich; directors, Joe Tobin, Paul Nichols; writer, Peter Brennan; hosts: Barry Nolan, Terry Murphy.

A re-creation of the last day of Marilyn's life. Stephanie Anderson plays an attractive and vulnerable Marilyn. A veritable who's who of Marilyn conspiracies.

We're told that Marilyn was declared a national security risk because she'd discussed "nuclear issues" with the Attorney General and the President of the United States. But that apparently didn't scare the CIA, because they "set up" busy Marilyn for a sexual liaison with President Sukarno of Indonesia—they wanted to film the dirty deed and use it to destroy Sukarno.

Mata Hari Marilyn!

Marilyn Monroe, Life After Death (Showtime Cable, 1994), Color, 90 minutes.

Executive producers/screenwriters, Gordon Freedman, Anthony Greene.

Shown theatrically in 1995, very briefly, in a version fifteen minutes longer. Featuring the photographs of Milton Greene.

Marilyn, The Mortal Goddess (A&E Cable, 1996), Color, 120 minutes.

Producers, Kim Egan, Torrie Rosenzweig; executive producer, Kevin Burns; writers, Kevin Burns, Jeff Scheftel, and Andy Thomas.

This is probably the best documentary yet on Marilyn, if only because it's the longest. You get many of the same old clichés, but the two hours does have its rare nuggets.

Chapter 10

Pretenders to the Throne

◆

A Quiz on All the *Other* Blondes

There'll never be another like Marilyn . . . but it didn't hurt to try.
See how many would-be Marilyns you can match to their
descriptions. (Some names may be used more than once.)

a. Lola Albright

b. Carroll Baker

c. Brigitte Bardot

d. Angie Dickinson

e. Diana Dors

f. Dixie Lee Evans

g. Joy Harmon

h. Arline Hunter

i. Adele Jergens

j. Hope Lange

k. Joi Lansing

l. Jayne Mansfield

m. Beverly Michaels

n. Marion Michaels

o. Cleo Moore

p. Barbara Nichols

q. Sheree North

r. Kim Novak

s. Roxanne Rosedale

t. Stella Stevens

u. Greta Thyssen

v. Barbara Valentin

w. Mamie Van Doren

x. Yvette Vickers

1. "The poor man's Monroe," the star of *Apple, Knockers and Coke Bottle*.
2. "The German Brigitte Bardot."
3. Director John Huston's original choice for Angela Phinlay in *The Asphalt Jungle*.
4. "The only sex symbol Britain has produced since Lady Godiva."
5. She teased *Cool Hand Luke* (Warner Bros.–7 Arts, 1967) and every guy on the chain gang.
6. Born Vera Jayne Palmer in Bryn Mawr, Pennsylvania.
7. She was one of Clark Gable's four leading ladies in *The King and Four Queens* (United Artists, 1956).
8. Broadway's *Hazel Flagg*, Twentieth Century–Fox thought they would use her to threaten contract star Marilyn into being more cooperative.
9. A *Playboy* centerfold, she was born in Hot Coffee, Mississippi.
10. A *Playboy* centerfold, and a cult favorite as *Reform School Girl* (American-International Pictures, 1957).
11. She got the role Marilyn wanted—a southern child bride.
12. Her given name was Diana Fluck.
13. She brought French films out of the art house and into mainstream movie theaters.
14. "The Marilyn Monroe of Burlesque."
15. She played Marilyn's mother in a movie.
16. She had to darken her blonde hair so she wouldn't detract from Marilyn.
17. *Variety* labeled her "a road-company Marilyn Monroe," which haunted her screen career.
18. She played Eve to Martin Milner's Adam (and Mickey Rooney was the Devil).

19. Blonde bombshell of TV game show *Beat the Clock*.

20. Blonde sexpot of TV sitcom *The Bob Cummings Show*.

21. Starred in the Hugo Haas cult classic *Pickup* (Columbia, 1951).

22. Starred in the Hugo Haas cult entry *Bait* (Columbia, 1954).

23. "Miss Lake Michigan," she jumped into San Francisco Bay in her big screen hit.

24. Miss Denmark of 1951, she starred in *Terror Is a Man* (Valiant, 1959).

25. "The German Jayne Mansfield."

26. Starred in the movie *Bigfoot* (Gemini-American, 1972), written and directed by Robert Slatzer—who says he was married to Marilyn for several days in 1952.

27. Campaigned to be governor of Louisiana, but lost.

28. Fast-talking Tony Curtis wanted her to be "real nice" to a client.

29. Displayed her body in *Playboy* magazine.

ANSWERS ON PAGE 357

Chapter 11

The Great Marilyn Trivia Challenge

◆

Part Two

21. In *The Asphalt Jungle*, Marilyn played Angela Phinlay, mistress to the crooked lawyer played by Louis Calhern. What does Angela call him?

22. A friend/supporter of Marilyn's coined the words "beefcake" and "sneak preview" and called Lana Turner "the Sweater Girl." Name him.

23. Name the actor who starred opposite the real Marilyn—then, years later, starred opposite a blonde actress portraying Marilyn. Second clue: In the first film he played a cowboy; in the second, he played Robert Kennedy.

24. What is the name of the movie Tom Ewell takes Marilyn to see in *The Seven Year Itch*?

25. Marilyn was once part of an all-star lineup that included Ella Fitzgerald, Maria Callas, Peggy Lee, Jimmy Durante, Henry Fonda, Harry Belafonte, Mike Nichols, Elaine May, and Jack Benny. Of course, Marilyn stole the show—doing what?

26. What singer was the most important influence on Marilyn's vocal art?

27. With her salary, how could Marilyn afford that brand-new (1953 or 1954) black Cadillac convertible with red leather interior?

28. What happened at the Clifton Motel in Paso Robles, California, on the night of January 14, 1954?

29. In which movie did Marilyn's character not have a name?

30. Who was "Zelda Zonk"?

31. What did Marilyn do in 1955 that prompted the FBI to start compiling a file on her?

32. In 1956, Marilyn performed a scene from Eugene O'Neill's play *Anna Christie* at the Actors' Studio. O'Neill described the character's hair in the published text—what color was Anna Christie's hair?

Publicity photo for *The Asphalt Jungle* (1950), a breakthrough film for Marilyn. This is a composite photo: Marilyn shares no scenes with Sam Jaffe, who plays the brains behind the robbery that goes awry. [Photo courtesy of Photofest.]

33. Sondra Blake, Sheree North, and Phyllis Coates each portrayed Gladys Baker, MM's mother, in a movie or a TV movie. What was special about the Gladys portrayed by Phyllis Coates?

34. The publicity for *We're Not Married* emphasized Marilyn and another blonde as America's "dream girls." Who was the other blonde?

35. Name four actors who worked with both Marilyn *and* her on-screen competition Jayne Mansfield.

36. Name Marilyn's two famous appearances at New York City's Madison Square Garden.

37. A year after Marilyn's death, Gregory Peck starred in the popular movie *Captain Newman, M.D.* (Universal, 1964), from a best-selling novel based on one of the most important people in Marilyn's life. Name him. (Hint: He doesn't look anything like Gregory Peck.)

38.
> *Whitey Dear*
> *While I'm still warm*
> *Marilyn*

Marilyn gave this item to Whitey Snyder to remind him of his promise to do her makeup when she died, so she'd look her best. Where is this reminder engraved?

39. Emilio Pucci was which—one of Marilyn's favorite cooks, chauffeurs, or fashion designers?

40. Advanced Trivia:

In 1956, Marilyn was requested to appear at a Royal Command Film Performance in London before Queen Elizabeth II. Marilyn discussed curtsying with Queen Elizabeth, and bicycling with Princess Margaret. The film shown that evening was *The Battle of the River Platte*—a title not known in the United States. Why?

ANSWERS ON PAGE 358

Marilyn's

WORLD

Chapter 12

Highlights of the Life and Career of Marilyn Monroe

1926

June 1: Norma Jeane Mortensen (listed as "Norma Jeane Mortenson" on her birth registration) is born to Gladys Baker Mortensen at 9:30 in the morning at Los Angeles General Hospital, in downtown Los Angeles. (This hospital is now called the L.A. County USC Medical Center.)

June 13: Gladys turns the baby over to a foster family, Albert and Ida Bolender, with whom Norma Jeane lives for seven years, in Hawthorne, a community about twenty-five miles southwest from Los Angeles, near the Los Angeles Airport.

1934

Not yet thirty-two, Gladys Mortensen is sent to a rest home in Santa Monica. Later, she is transferred to Los Angeles General Hospital. Most of the rest of her life will be spent in hospitals.

Gladys's friend and coworker Grace McKee assumes the care and education of Norma Jeane.

1935

June 1: Grace McKee becomes the court-appointed guardian to Gladys and the legal guardian of Norma Jeane.

Grace McKee marries Ervin Silliman Goddard, a cowboy nicknamed "Doc."

1938

November: Norma Jeane is boarded with Ana Lower, an aunt of Grace McKee Goddard. In the future, Marilyn Monroe will name Ana Lower as "the first person in the world I ever really loved. She was the only one who loved and understood me."

1942

June 19: Norma Jeane Baker marries James Dougherty, at the West Los Angeles home of Mr. and Mrs. Chester Howell, friends of Grace Goddard. She wears a white gown given her by Ana Lower; Jim wears a rented tuxedo. The wedding reception is held at the Florentine Gardens nightclub in Hollywood.

1944

April: Norma Jeane gets a job in the Radioplane Company in Burbank (where the Burbank Airport is now).

Autumn: Photographers from the army's First Motion Picture Unit arrive at Radioplane in Burbank to take photos and movies of women on the assembly line, to show their contribution to the war effort. Photographer David Conover asks eighteen-year-old Norma Jeane to pose for him. One of his photos of her appears on the cover of *Yank* magazine in 1945.

1945

February: Norma Jeane quits Radioplane—she believes she has a future as a professional model.

August 2: Norma Jeane drives into Los Angeles, to register with the Blue Book Model Agency, in the Ambassador Hotel, near downtown Los Angeles. Emmeline Snively, the Blue Book owner, is impressed by her looks.

Norma Jeane goes to Frank and Joseph's, a popular beauty salon on Wilshire Boulevard, across from the Ambassador Hotel. Over a six-month period, beautician Sylvia Barnhart supervises the bleaching and straightening of Norma Jeane's hair to a golden blonde.

Andre de Dienes contacts the Blue Book Agency, asking for a model who might pose nude. Snively sends him Norma Jeane, thinking he'll like her fresh look. He photographs her seated in the middle of the road; dressed in an apron, holding a lamb; and in blue jeans and a red blouse. She will not pose nude.

1946

April 26: *Family Circle* magazine features Marilyn on the cover, in a photo by Andre de Dienes. This is her first appearance on a national magazine. Before summer, she will appear on thirty-three magazine covers.

July 19: Norma Jeane is screen-tested on the set of the Betty Grable film *Mother Wore Tights* (Twentieth Century–Fox, 1947). Four of the studio's best technicians participate in Norma Jeane's screen test: cinematographer Leon Shamroy, makeup artist Allan "Whitey" Snyder, director Walter Lang, and wardrobe designer Charles LeMaire. Studio chief Darryl F. Zanuck is not enthusiastic about the test, but defers to the enthusiasm and recommendations of Ben Lyon, director of casting, and Leon Shamroy.

July 23: Norma Jeane is offered a standard six-month contract at $75 a week, with an option to renew at $125. Grace McKee signs the contract as Norma Jeane's legal guardian, for Norma Jeane is still under age (she's only twenty). Ben Lyon and Norma Jeane Mortensen decide on her new name: "Marilyn," after Broadway beauty Marilyn Miller; "Monroe," from the maiden name of Norma Jeane's mother. Marilyn Monroe is officially born.

July 29: Marilyn's name is first mentioned in a Hollywood column: Columnist Hedda Hopper picks up the fabricated story that Howard Hughes had seen Marilyn on a magazine cover and wanted to sign her for pictures.

1947

February: Twentieth Century–Fox renews Marilyn's contract for six months. Several days later she receives her first casting call, for *Scudda Hoo! Scudda Hay!*

1948

February: Marilyn meets Twentieth Century–Fox mogul Joseph M. Schenck. He's sixty-eight, Marilyn twenty-one. He becomes a friend and benefactor, probably in return for sexual favors.

Late February: Schenck asks poker friend Harry Cohn, head of Columbia Pictures, to consider Marilyn for work at his studio.

March 9: Marilyn is signed to a standard six-month contract, at $125 a week. She auditions for the low-budget musical *Ladies of the Chorus*, and is assigned a starring role.

New Year's Eve: At a party given by producer Sam Spiegel, twenty-two-year-old Marilyn meets fifty-three-year-old

Johnny Hyde, executive vice president of the William Morris Agency. For Johnny Hyde, it is apparently love at first sight.

1949

First week of January: Johnny Hyde buys Marilyn's contract and devotes his entire professional time to furthering her career.

May 27: Marilyn signs a release form for Tom Kelley, as "Mona Monroe," and poses nude on a red velvet drape for calendar photos. She is paid $50.

End of October: MGM signs Marilyn to play Angela Phinlay in John Huston's crime melodrama *The Asphalt Jungle*. She is listed only in the end credits, eleventh of fifteen names in this major production.

1950

April: Johnny Hyde takes Marilyn to meet director Joseph L. Mankiewicz at Twentieth Century–Fox. She is signed for *All About Eve*, as Miss Caswell, "a graduate of the Copacabana School of Dramatic Art," and the girlfriend of cynical drama critic Addison DeWitt (George Sanders).

December 10: Johnny Hyde arranges a new screen test at Twentieth Century–Fox. Marilyn portrays a gangster's girlfriend, warning actor Richard Conte of impending trouble.

December 18: Johnny Hyde dies of a massive heart attack, at age fifty-five.

1951

May 11: Marilyn's short-term contract with Twentieth Century–Fox is extended to a new seven-year contract. This is the result of her appearance at an exhibitors' party in the studio commissary, at

Posing for pinup
photos to promote
Love Nest (1951).
[Photo courtesy of
Archive Photos.]

which studio president Spyros Skouras is present. Marilyn shows up late, as usual, but makes her usual electrifying entrance. The excited exhibitors want to know what movies she will be in . . . and soon she is in every movie that has a part for a blonde. Twentieth Century–Fox launches a full-scale star-making operation.

September 8: In the September 8, 1951, issue, *Collier's* magazine features the first full-length national magazine story on Marilyn, entitled "Hollywood's 1951 Model Blonde," by Robert Cahn.

1952

Winter 1951–1952: Arrangements are made for sports hero Joe DiMaggio to meet Marilyn at the Villa Nova restaurant, 9015 Sunset Boulevard. Marilyn is twenty-five at the time; Joe is thirty-seven. They have dinner together almost every night for two weeks. (The Villa Nova later became the Rainbow Bar and Grill.)

March 1: The Twentieth Century–Fox press department learns that the nude on a popular calendar has been identified as Marilyn Monroe.

April 7: Marilyn appears on the cover of *Life* magazine for the first time, photographed by Philippe Halsman, wearing an off-the-shoulder white dress. Marilyn tells *Life* she and columnist-producer Sidney Skolsky are planning a film biography of Jean Harlow.

June 1: As a birthday present, Twentieth Century–Fox announces that Marilyn will be the blonde in the screen version of the Broadway-musical hit *Gentlemen Prefer Blondes.*

August 31: Marilyn makes her live radio debut, on NBC's *Hollywood Star Playhouse,* playing a murderess in the episode "Statement in Full."

September: Marilyn is grand marshal for the Miss America Pageant parade in Atlantic City, New Jersey—and many are shocked by her revealing clothing.

1953

January 21: *Niagara* is released, and launches a star.

March 9: *Photoplay* magazine names Marilyn as "Fastest Rising Star of 1952," in a prestigious ceremony at the Beverly Hills Hotel, 9641 Sunset Boulevard. Marilyn wears William Travilla's gold lamé gown that has comedian Jerry Lewis jumping up and down on a table, and movie queen Joan Crawford fuming. The latter summons the press later and denounces Marilyn's "burlesque show."

June 26: Marilyn and *Gentlemen Prefer Blondes* costar Jane Russell are immortalized in the cement outside Grauman's Chinese Theater, 6712 Hollywood Boulevard.

September 13: Marilyn makes her live television debut on Jack Benny's CBS-TV comedy series show, singing "Bye Bye,

Baby" from *Gentlemen Prefer Blondes*, and successfully performing a comedy sketch with Jack.

December: A new magazine, *Playboy*, appears. Marilyn is shown on the cover, and is featured inside with the Tom Kelley "Golden Dreams" nude photo.

1954

January 14: Marilyn and Joe DiMaggio are married in San Francisco City Hall. She is twenty-eight; he is thirty-nine.

February 2: The newlyweds arrive in Tokyo and are mobbed by thousands of fans. Marilyn is invited to entertain the American troops in Korea.

Starting February 16: Marilyn travels to ten different sites, entertaining over one hundred thousand soldiers and marines.

September 15: As a publicity stunt for the New York filming of *The Seven Year Itch*, Marilyn stands over a subway grating

On her 1954 honeymoon with Joe DiMaggio, Marilyn spent four days in Korea, entertaining American soldiers who carried on like teenage bobby-soxers. "It was the best thing that ever happened to me," she said. [Photo courtesy of Archive Photos.]

Marilyn sang for the soldiers wearing a low-cut dress of plum-colored sequins. She had pneumonia by the time she returned to Japan. [Photo courtesy of Archive Photos.]

at Lexington Avenue and 52nd Street, the breeze billowing up her white pleated dress. Two hundred photographers record the scene, as thousands of ogling spectators watch. Joe DiMaggio is furious.

September 16: Marilyn and Joe return to Los Angeles. Two weeks later, Marilyn files for divorce.

November 5: The famous "Wrong Door Raid" takes place. A private detective hired by Joe DiMaggio, along with DiMaggio, Frank Sinatra, and a squad of men furnished by Sinatra, storm a Hollywood apartment building at 8122 Waring Avenue and break down a door, intending to catch Marilyn in the act with Hal Schaefer—but the goons break down the wrong door.

November 6: Producer Charles K. Feldman gives a dinner party in honor of Marilyn at Romanoff's restaurant in Beverly Hills. The movie industry elite shows up: Samuel Goldwyn, Jack Warner, Darryl F. Zanuck, Claudette Colbert, Doris Day, Gary Cooper, Humphrey Bogart, Irving Lazar, William Holden, and many more.

Marilyn is introduced to her idol Clark Gable, then age fifty-three, and dances with him. They chat about working together.

1955

January 7: Marilyn holds a press conference/party to announce the formation of Marilyn Monroe Productions, in partnership with photographer Milton Greene.

February: Marilyn visits Lee Strasberg, who makes ongoing psychoanalysis a condition of her becoming a member of the Actors Studio.

March 30: Marilyn rides a pink elephant on opening night of the Ringling Brothers and Barnum and Bailey circus at Madison Square Garden, a benefit for Mike Todd's Arthritis and Rheumatism Foundation.

April 8: Edward R. Murrow interviews Marilyn for TV's *Person to Person*, broadcasting live from Milton Greene's Connecticut home.

October 31: The final decree dissolving the Monroe-DiMaggio marriage becomes effective.

The lawyers for Twentieth Century–Fox and Marilyn Monroe Productions finally agree on a contract.

December 12: Marilyn attends the film premiere of *The Rose Tattoo*, and then the party at the Astor Hotel. Jayne Mansfield is photographed looking admiringly at Marilyn. (This photo is in James Haspiel's *Marilyn: The Ultimate Look at the Legend*, page 98.)

1956

February 9: A press conference for *The Prince and the Showgirl* is held at the Plaza Hotel, 768 Fifth Avenue. Marilyn wears a low-cut black velvet dress with thin shoulder straps...one of which obligingly breaks.

February 17: Marilyn performs the barroom scene from Eugene O'Neill's *Anna Christie* at the Actors Studio.

February 25: Marilyn returns to Hollywood after being away for over a year. Facing reporters at the Los Angeles airport, she is asked, "Is this the new Marilyn?" And she replies, "No, I'm the same person—but it's a different suit."

March 12: Norma Jeane Mortensen legally becomes Marilyn Monroe.

June 29: Marilyn and Arthur Miller are married in the Westchester County Court House in White Plains. Not a single member of the press is present.

July 1: A second ceremony—the traditional Jewish marriage rite—is held at the home of Miller's agent, Kay Brown, near Katonah, New York.

Late August: Marilyn learns she is pregnant, but fears she will lose the baby. In the first week of September, she does.

1957

July: Marilyn announces to Miller that she's pregnant. He has never seen her happier or more confident.

August 1: It's an ectopic pregnancy, and she loses the baby. Marilyn takes an overdose of pills. Arthur Miller realizes what is happening and calls for medical help in time.

1958

Late October: Marilyn is pregnant again, while filming *Some Like It Hot* at the Hotel del Coronado, near San Diego, California.

December 16: Marilyn miscarries.

1959

May 13: Marilyn receives Italy's version of Hollywood's Oscar, the David di Donatello Award, as Best Actress in a Foreign Film, for *The Prince and the Showgirl*. The ceremony is held at the Italian Consulate, at 686 Park Avenue, New York City.

Attending the Hollywood premiere of the film *Gigi* (MGM, 1958) at the Paramount Theater on Hollywood Boulevard. [Photo courtesy of Photofest.]

1960

January: On the recommendation of Marianne Kris, her New York analyst, Marilyn begins seeing Dr. Ralph Greenson on an irregular basis.

March: The Foreign Press Association gives Marilyn the Golden Globe Award for Best Actress for *Some Like It Hot.*

End of June: The last month in Los Angeles, before going to Nevada for the filming of *The Misfits*, Marilyn begins seeing psychiatrist Dr. Ralph Greenson five or six times a week.

Last weeks of October: Marilyn asks Arthur Miller to leave their Beverly Hills Hotel bungalow, as they have agreed to divorce.

November 5: Marilyn's costar in *The Misfits*, Clark Gable, has a serious heart attack.

November 16: Clark Gable dies of a heart attack at age fifty-nine. Gossip columns print stories of Marilyn's aggravating behavior on the set of *The Misfits*. Marilyn is despondent. However, no one seems to want to report that Gable insisted upon doing his own stunts for the film, or that he had smoked three packs of cigarettes a day for thirty years.

1961

January: Marilyn and Lee Strasberg propose a television dramatization of *Rain*, the story of Sadie Thompson. Strasberg insists that only he can direct such a production, but NBC holds out for a veteran talent. Marilyn and Strasberg cancel the project.

February: Marilyn reads that Clark Gable's widow blames her for his death. Marilyn tells friend/masseur Ralph Roberts of how close she came to committing suicide.

February 7: Marilyn's analyst Marianne Kris is alarmed by Marilyn's suicidal behavior. She persuades Marilyn to enter the Payne Whitney Psychiatric Clinic, on New York's Upper East Side. Marilyn goes willingly, but does not realize she will be treated as a disturbed patient—she's even locked in a padded room. After three days of panic, she is able to contact Joe DiMaggio, who comes to her rescue.

October 2 or 3: Bobby Kennedy attends a dinner party at Peter Lawford's home, 625 Palisades Beach Road in Santa Monica, at which Marilyn is present. They do not want to let an inebriated Marilyn drive home alone, so Bobby and Edwin Guthman (Special Assistant for Public Information) drive her home.

1962

Late January: At Dr. Greenson's suggestion Marilyn buys a small Spanish hacienda at 12305 Fifth Helena Drive in Brentwood. Also at Dr. Greenson's suggestion, Marilyn hires Eunice

Marilyn's Spanish hacienda at 12305 Fifth Helena Drive in Brentwood. "I felt badly because I was buying a house all alone," she said. Her bedroom is on the right. [Photo courtesy of Patrick V. Miller.]

Murray as her companion and housekeeper. Mrs. Murray, age fifty-nine, a widow, is also there to monitor Marilyn's activities for Dr. Greenson.

March 5: Marilyn receives another Golden Globe Award as "The World's Favorite Female Star." At the presentation, Marilyn is seen to be drunk to the point of embarrassment, but it may be the result of too many prescription drugs—all freely prescribed by both Drs. Greenson and Engelberg (her Los Angeles internist). (Marilyn lives in the Greenson's home at 902 Franklin Street, in Santa Monica. Greenson tells colleagues that he is treating her for schizophrenia.)

March 24: Marilyn and President Kennedy are house guests of Bing Crosby in Palm Springs. She phones masseur Ralph Roberts from the bedroom, asking him professional advice on massaging President Kennedy's back. (Marilyn later tells Roberts and actress Susan Strasberg that this encounter was the extent of their "affair.")

April 23: Production begins on *Something's Got to Give* at Twentieth Century–Fox...but Marilyn says she is sick with acute sinusitis.

April 30: Marilyn appears on the movie set for the first time.

April 31: Marilyn is back in bed with another sinus infection.

May 14, 15, 16: Marilyn works on the sound stage at Twentieth Century–Fox.

May 17: Marilyn leaves for New York, to sing for the President, at a fund-raising birthday celebration at Madison Square Garden.

May 18: In New York, Marilyn receives a breach-of-contract notice from Twentieth Century–Fox, charging her with failure to work and a stern warning of dire consequences to follow. She is outraged.

May 19: Marilyn sings "Happy Birthday, Mr. President," at the JFK birthday gala at Madison Square Garden.

May 23: Marilyn films a swimming sequence, wearing a flesh-colored bikini. She suggests that she be photographed nude, for publicity.

June 1: Marilyn's thirty-sixth birthday. During this day, she gives what will turn out to be her final performance in a motion picture, acting in a scene with Wally Cox and Dean Martin.

June 8: A meeting is held at which Dr. Greenson assures Twentieth Century–Fox executives that he can get Marilyn back to the studio. It is academic, as the studio has (the day before, June 7) fired Marilyn and filed a lawsuit against Marilyn Monroe Productions.

June 9: The Saturday newspapers show director George Cukor with actress Lee Remick, hired as Marilyn's replacement. Again, the act is academic, as Twentieth Century–Fox, in their anger, forgot that Dean Martin has cast approval, and he refuses to proceed with *Something's Got to Give* without Marilyn.

June 23–July 12: Marilyn has three photo sessions with photographer Bert Stern, on assignment from *Vogue* magazine.

June 29–July 1: Marilyn spends these three days with photographer George Barris, on assignment from *Cosmopolitan* magazine, posing on the Santa Monica beach and at a home in North Hollywood.

July: Marilyn continues to see analyst Dr. Greenson daily. Internist Dr. Hyman Engelberg visits Marilyn almost daily, to give her "youth shots" which often make her speech rapid and disjointed.

July 4, 5, 7, and 9: Richard Meryman interviews Marilyn for *Life* magazine. This will be her last interview.

July 8: Joe DiMaggio visits Marilyn in Brentwood.

July 20: According to Donald Spoto's *Marilyn Monroe, The Biography*, Marilyn has yet another operation at Cedars of Lebanon to alleviate her chronic gynecological problems.

Saturday, July 28–Sunday, July 29: The weekend at Cal-Neva.

(Versions 1, 3, 4, and 5 are summaries; version 2 is a direct quote.)

VERSION #1 (Donald Spoto, *Marilyn Monroe: The Biography*)

Marilyn goes with the Peter Lawfords to the new Cal-Neva Lodge in Lake Tahoe to see Frank Sinatra perform. She asks Joe DiMaggio to meet her there. She and Joe keep a low profile, to prevent any discord between Joe and Sinatra, who are no longer friends.

That weekend, Marilyn and Joe decide to remarry. On Sunday evening, the twenty-ninth, she returns to Los Angeles, and Joe heads for San Francisco.

VERSION #2 (Fred Lawrence Guiles, *Legend: The Life and Death of Marilyn Monroe*)

Marilyn is admitted to Cedars of Lebanon Hospital in Beverly Hills under an alias, because she is having a pregnancy aborted. The cover story given out at the time by the office of publicist Arthur Jacobs is that Marilyn has spent that weekend with the Lawfords in Lake Tahoe. It is likely that not even housekeeper Mrs. Murray knows the truth.

VERSION #3 (Anthony Summers, *Goddess: The Secret Lives of Marilyn Monroe*)

Marilyn is tense during the weekend. She complains to a friend that she is being pressured to go to Peter Lawford's parties, which are really orgies. Frank Sinatra has photos showing Marilyn in utter disarray.

Joe DiMaggio, still trying to help Marilyn, takes a room at a nearby motel. An employee of the Cal-Neva Lodge tells of seeing Marilyn, near dawn, staring up the hill at Joe...who stands in the driveway, staring back.

VERSION #4 (Kitty Kelley, *His Way: The Unauthorized Biography of Frank Sinatra*)

Marilyn tries to commit suicide on this weekend, but manages to contact the Cal-Neva operator in time to be rushed to the hospital to have her stomach pumped. Peter Lawford reports that Frank Sinatra was so mad at Marilyn for her suicide attempt that he just snarled at everyone.

VERSION #5 (Sam and Chuck Giancana, *Double Cross*)

A distraught Marilyn goes to Cal-Neva, where she drinks herself into near oblivion. She pours out her heart to Mafia head Sam "Mooney" Giancana, telling him Bobby Kennedy refuses her phone calls.

Giancana has sex with Marilyn—has had her many times, pleased that he can take whatever the Kennedys might have. Giancana has had Marilyn's body. Soon he will have her life.

July 30: Marilyn and Dean Martin discuss costarring in a comedy to be called *I Love Louisa*, at Twentieth Century–Fox.

July 31: Marilyn has the final fittings of a new gown by Jean Louis—but is it for theater-going or for a wedding?

August 1: Twentieth Century–Fox agrees to hire Jean Negulesco to replace George Cukor as director of *Something's Got to Give*, when production resumes. Marilyn is delighted: Negulesco directed one of her better films, *How to Marry a Millionaire*.

Twentieth Century–Fox signs Marilyn to a new contact with a salary of $250,000 per picture, more than twice her current salary.

August 2: Marilyn goes to Dr. Greenson's home for a morning session, and he comes to her house for an afternoon therapy session.

These last three photos are cited as evidence that Marilyn wouldn't have killed herself—because she seemed so relaxed, confident, and happy.

These photos are costume and makeup test shots for the unfinished 1962 movie *Something's Got to Give*. [Photos courtesy of Photofest.]

"The close-up . . . as she slowly turns her head has all the essence of the myth that was Marilyn."
—Richard Whitehall, *Films and Filming,* September 1963. [Photo courtesy of Photofest.]

August 3:

- Marilyn has a morning session with Dr. Greenson.

- Dr. Engelberg arrives to give her an injection.

- She has a thirty-two-minute phone call with poet Norman Rosten.

- She calls Jean Louis about her new dress.

- Songwriter Jule Styne calls from New York, to propose a screen musical version of the play and film *A Tree Grows in Brooklyn.*

- Publicist Arthur Jacobs calls to set up a meeting with director J. Lee Thompson.

- Marilyn has an afternoon session with Dr. Greenson.

- Marilyn has dinner with personal publicist Pat Newcomb and Peter Lawford at La Scala restaurant in Beverly Hills.

- Mrs. Murray goes home for the night. Pat Newcomb stays over at Marilyn's.

August 3: The new issue of *Life* magazine contains the interview with Richard Meryman, "Marilyn Lets Her Hair Down About Being Famous."

August 3: Gossip columnist Dorothy Kilgallen prints an item that Marilyn is seeing "a handsome gentleman" with "a bigger name than Joe DiMaggio."

August 4–Saturday:

- Photographer Lawrence Schiller arrives to discuss the semi-nude photos from *Something's Got to Give.*

- Dr. Greenson arrives after lunch and spends six hours with Marilyn.

- Dr. Greenson tells Mrs. Murray to take Marilyn for a walk on the beach. The two women go to Peter Lawford's home.

- Back home at Fifth Helena, Marilyn declines Peter Lawford's dinner invitation for that night.

- Ralph Roberts calls. Dr. Greenson answers the phone, says Marilyn is not there.

- Dr. Greenson calls Dr. Engelberg to come give Marilyn an injection to help her sleep, but Engelberg refuses.

- Approximately 7:00–7:15 P.M.—Greenson departs, leaving Marilyn alone with Mrs. Murray.

- Approximately 7:00–7:15 P.M.—Joe DiMaggio, Jr., calls, and Marilyn is alert and in good spirits.

- 7:40–7:45 P.M.—Peter Lawford calls, still hoping Marilyn will come for dinner—but she's disoriented, almost inaudible. Lawford, alarmed, calls producer Milton Ebbins (vice president of Lawford's production company)...who calls Marilyn's lawyer Mickey Rudin (8:25)...who calls Eunice Murray (8:30), who says Marilyn is fine.

- 10:00–10:30 P.M.—Publicist Arthur Jacobs is contacted at the Hollywood Bowl (where he is attending a concert with the Mervyn LeRoys and actress Natalie Trundy) and told that Marilyn is dead.

- 11:00 P.M.—Lawford calls agent and close friend Joe Naar (who lives just a half mile from her) to check on Marilyn...but Rudin calls Ebbins who tells Naar that all is fine, that Dr. Greenson has given Marilyn a sedative.

August 5–Sunday:

- 1:00 A.M.—Lawford telephones producer friend William Asher, asking him to go check on Marilyn.

- 1:30 A.M.—Rudin calls Ebbins who calls Lawford, to say that Marilyn is dead, that Rudin and Dr. Greenson found her dead at midnight.

- 5:00 A.M.—Pat Newcomb is told by Mickey Rudin that Marilyn is dead.

- 5:30 A.M.—Marilyn's body is covered with a pink woolen blanket, loaded into a Ford panel truck and taken to the Westwood Village Mortuary.

- 8:00 A.M.—She is taken to the city morgue in downtown Los Angeles.

- 10:30 A.M.—Deputy coroner Dr. Thomas Noguchi completes his autopsy and files his preliminary report.

Joe DiMaggio sends a telegram to Marilyn's half-sister Berniece Miracle, in Florida, asking her whether she will help with the funeral arrangements.

August 6–Monday: Joe DiMaggio claims Marilyn's body from the morgue. She is taken back to the Westwood Village Mortuary on Glendon Avenue.

August 7–Tuesday: Joe DiMaggio calls upon three of Marilyn's longtime associates and friends to prepare Marilyn's body for the funeral. Her personal makeup man Whitey Snyder agrees to apply Marilyn's makeup, but he can't do it sober. Her personal wardrobe supervisor Marjorie Plecher Snyder dresses Marilyn in a favorite green Pucci dress. Her personal hairstylist Agnes Flanagan does Marilyn's hair.

August 8–Wednesday: Marilyn is interred in a crypt at Westwood Memorial Cemetery, at 1218 Glendon Avenue, off Wilshire Boulevard.

(Also see Part 4, Chapter 22, "Marilyn's Biographies" for an extensive list of books on Marilyn's life.)

Who Was at the Funeral?

Joe DiMaggio decreed that there would be only a few relatives and friends at Marilyn's funeral—no studio executives, no reporters, and no photographers. Those who attended were

1. Joe DiMaggio, ex-husband.
2. Joe DiMaggio, Jr.
3. Berniece Miracle, Marilyn's half-sister.
4. Reverend Floyd Darling, of the First Southern Baptist Church in Santa Monica—a local minister picked out of the phone book to help Berniece through the pressures of the funeral.
5. Enid Knebelkamp, sister of Marilyn's legal guardian Grace Goddard.
6. Sam Knebelkamp, Enid's husband.
7. Erwin "Doc" Goddard, former husband of Grace Goddard, with wife Anne.
8. Lee Strasberg, acting teacher.
9. Paula Strasberg, acting coach.
10. Sydney Guilaroff, hairdresser friend.
11. Allan "Whitey" Snyder, Marilyn's personal makeup man.

12. Marjorie Plecher (Mrs. Snyder), Marilyn's wardrobe supervisor.

13. Ann "Nana" Karger, mother of Fred Karger, Columbia Pictures vocal coach.

14. Mary Karger Short, sister of Fred Karger.

15. George Solotaire, lifelong buddy of Joe DiMaggio.

16. Pat Newcomb, Marilyn's personal press secretary.

17. Eunice Murray, Marilyn's housekeeper.

18. Rudy Krautzky, Marilyn's driver, from Carey Limousine Service.

19. Inez Melson, Marilyn's business manager, also Gladys's guardian.

20. Pat Melson, husband of Inez.

21. Agnes Flanagan, Marilyn's personal hairdresser.

22. Florence Thomas, Marilyn's former housekeeper.

23. Aaron Frosch, Marilyn's New York lawyer.

24. Milton Rudin, Marilyn's Los Angeles lawyer.

25. May Reis, Marilyn's personal secretary.

26. Ralph Roberts, Marilyn's personal masseur.

27. Dr. Ralph Greenson, Marilyn's Los Angeles psychiatrist.

28. Hildi Greenson, Mrs. Ralph Greenson.

29. Dan Greenson, son of Dr. and Mrs. Ralph Greenson.

30. Joan Greenson, daughter of Dr. and Mrs. Ralph Greenson.

The Unabridged Marilyn also lists mime/acting coach Lotte Goslar and hair stylist Pearl Porterfield. It does not list Reverend Darling. Marilyn's former housekeeper Florence Thomas is mistakenly identified as a friend of Berniece Miracle.

The Service

The service was held in the small chapel of the cemetery.

An organist played a selection from Tchaikovsky's Sixth Symphony, "The Pathétique," music of lamentation. This was followed by "Over the Rainbow" from *The Wizard of Oz*.

Dr. A. J. Soldan, a Lutheran pastor of the Village Church of Westwood, conducted the services, reading from the Book of Amos: "How wonderfully she was made by her Creator."

Lee Strasberg spoke: "She had a luminous quality—a combination of wistfulness, radiance, yearning—that set her apart and yet made everyone wish to be a part of it, to share in the childish naiveté which was at once so shy and yet so vibrant."

The Pallbearers

Whitey Snyder and Sydney Guilaroff, plus four employees of the cemetery: Allen Abbott, Ronald Hast, Leonard Krisminsk, and Clarence Pierce.

The Flowers

The 1930s movie legend Jean Harlow had requested it of her movie-star lover, William Powell, and he complied, so Marilyn asked it of Joe DiMaggio—that he send flowers for her gravesite. For twenty years, between August 1962 and September 1982, Joe had six red roses delivered three times a week. The flowers were from Parisian Florists, 7528 Sunset Boulevard, in Hollywood.

Joe stopped the roses after twenty years because he felt the money could be put to better use, such as donations to the children's charities Marilyn had favored.

Robert Slatzer, who claims he was once married to Marilyn, held a press conference at Marilyn's crypt in 1982. He announced that he would pick up where Joe DiMaggio left off, having roses delivered three times a week. Furthermore, Slatzer said he was establishing a trust fund to ensure uninterrupted delivery even after his own death.

Delivery of the roses was stopped after a year.

Who Keeps Marilyn Company in Westwood Memorial

1. Grace McKee Goddard, Norma Jeane's legal guardian.
2. Ana Lower, Grace's aunt—"The first person I ever really loved."
3. Natalie Wood, actress–child star in Marilyn's first screen appearance, *Scudda Hoo! Scudda Hay!*
4. Andre de Dienes, photographer of the young and beautiful Marilyn.
5. Dean Martin, actor, costar of her last, unfinished film, *Something's Got to Give.*
6. Darryl F. Zanuck, mogul who masterminded the greatness of Twentieth Century–Fox.
7. Richard Conte, actor who costarred in Marilyn's second screen test.
8. Eve Arden, actress who appeared in *We're Not Married.*
9. Jim Backus, actor who appeared in *Don't Bother to Knock.*
10. Estelle Winwood, actress who was featured in *The Misfits.*
11. Peter Lawford, actor, Kennedy brother-in-law. (Lawford's ashes were removed in 1988, after a dispute over funeral costs.)
12. Truman Capote, writer, New York friend.
13. Franz Planer, cinematographer on *Something's Got to Give.*
14. Guy Hockett, owner of Westwood Memorial Cemetery and coroner's representative. He went to Marilyn's home to claim her body.

15. And one of these days, Hugh Hefner, publisher who featured Marilyn in the first issue of his *Playboy* magazine. Hefner owns the crypt next to Marilyn's.

"You know where the poor darling is buried? You go into this cemetery past an automobile dealer and past a bank building, and there she lies, right between Wilshire Boulevard and Westwood Boulevard, with the traffic moving past."

—*director George Cukor*

Chapter 13

The Great Marilyn Trivia Challenge

◆

Part Three

41. What man directed Jean Harlow and Lana Turner and Marilyn Monroe?

42. When Marilyn wrote her name in wet cement at Grauman's Chinese Theater in Hollywood, on June 26, 1953, she dotted her *i* with a special addition—which was quickly stolen. What was it?

43. What do the theater-lobby scene of *All About Eve*, *The Fireball*, Marilyn's second screen test at Twentieth Century–Fox, in 1950, with Richard Conte, and *Hometown Story* all have in common?

44. In her first official screen appearance, Marilyn is glimpsed walking behind two females. She calls out, "Hi, Rad!" The first actress starred as Marilyn Miller in a 1949 film, and also costarred with Marilyn in a 1951 film. Who is she? Marilyn made a screen test with the husband of the second actress. Remember who she is?

45. Who was Marjorie Stengel?

46. To whom did Marilyn say, "Please don't make me look like a joke"?

47. Marilyn said, "For the first time in my life, I had the feeling that the people seeing me were accepting and liking me." What was the occasion?

48. On December 2, 1990, the *Los Angeles Times* noted that in *Something's Got to Give* Marilyn had her first screen role as a mother. True or false?

49. Marilyn owed a debt of gratitude to...Ronald Reagan. For what?

50. When screenwriter I. A. L. Diamond came up with the title *Some Like It Hot*, the producers had to clear it with Paramount Pictures, because this title had been used for a 1939 screen comedy. Who starred in that earlier film?

51. By the way, what do Diamond's initials I. A. L. stand for?

52. During the filming of *Let's Make Love*, Marilyn and Arthur Miller stayed in bungalow number 21 at the Beverly Hills Hotel. Her costar Yves Montand and his actress wife Simone Signoret were in bungalow number 20. An equally famous couple was said to be in bungalow number 19. Who were they?

53. As if Marilyn didn't have enough emotional and physical problems, she also suffered from agoraphobia, which is...?

54. Marilyn often said she used to imagine that Clark Gable was her father. Who did she imagine as her mother?

55. *Darling, I Am Growing Younger* is the original title for what Monroe film?

56. Why might you go out of your way to see *Riders of the Whistling Pines*, a 1949 Gene Autry western?

57. Trick question: In which film was Marilyn a fairy?

58. Joe DiMaggio was automatically excommunicated from the Roman Catholic Church when he married Marilyn. Why?

59. Lee Strasberg was Joe DiMaggio's second choice to deliver the eulogy at Marilyn's funeral. Who had been his first choice?

60. In *Niagara*, what was it about Rose that first attracted George Loomis?

ANSWERS ON PAGE 360

Chapter 14

Cast of Characters in the Life of Marilyn Monroe

◆

A Biographical Directory

Casey Adams

A character actor with goofy mannerisms. Born in 1917, he was Jean Peters' oblivious husband in *Niagara*, and a *Life* magazine photographer at the rodeo in *Bus Stop*.

While filming *Niagara* on location in New York, Adams says, Marilyn stood naked in her hotel window while crowds of men collected below. Late at night she'd rush into his room and jump into bed with him, pleading, "Don't do anything but just hold me!" (Patrick Agan, *The Decline and Fall of the Love Goddesses*)

Gladys Baker

The mother of Norma Jeane Baker who in time became the star Marilyn Monroe.

Gladys was born Gladys Pearl Monroe, the daughter of Della May and Otis Elmer Monroe, in 1902. At fourteen, Gladys married twenty-six-year-old businessman John Newton Baker. They had two children. After four years of marriage, Gladys filed for divorce; John Baker took custody of the children.

Gladys married again, in 1924, to Martin Edward Mortensen, a meter man for the gas company. She left him after only four months, then ten months later found out she was pregnant.

The birth certificate of the baby girl identified her as Norma Jeane Mortenson. Almost immediately, Gladys put the baby in the care of a foster family... and left her there for the first seven years of her life.

Gladys reclaimed the little girl and they lived together in Hollywood for a short time. However, when Gladys began withdrawing from the world, she was put in a rest home, and then a hospital, and then a state mental hospital. She would spend much of her life in hospitals or homes for the emotionally disturbed.

Gladys died in a Florida nursing home in 1984 at the age of eighty-two.

Jose Bolanos

A handsome young writer Marilyn met in Mexico in February 1962. She invited him to escort her to the Golden Globe Awards, and paid for his plane ticket to Los Angeles.

After her death, Bolanos said that he and Marilyn had planned to be married.

Albert and Ida ("Aunt Ida") Bolender

Norma Jeane's first foster parents. She was brought to them when she was two weeks old, and lived there for seven years, in their modest four-room bungalow in Hawthorne, California. Albert was a postman, while Ida was a foster mother who raised her wards with a strict regard for religion.

The Bolenders were interviewed for the 1966 ABC-TV documentary *The Legend of Marilyn Monroe*, which was reissued in 1991 as *Portrait: Marilyn Monroe*.

Frank A. Capell

A right-wing fanatic who published *The Strange Death of Marilyn Monroe* in 1964, an almost unreadable attack on Communism, the Kennedys, and Marilyn Monroe. Capell says that Bobby Kennedy used his "personal Gestapo" to cover up Marilyn's murder.

Jeanne Carmen

The clipping file on Jeanne Carmen in the research library of the Academy of Motion Picture Arts and Science, has an early photo from a New York newspaper listing her as "Jeanne Carmen of Queens." She's the "granddaughter of a Comanche Indian chief" in the *Cleveland Plain Dealer* of May 1, 1950. *TV Guide* of January 1–7, 1958, describes her as "a large and imposing twenty-six-year-old Hollywood blonde out of Paragould, Arkansas." And the *Los Angeles Examiner* of May 3, 1959, says that "Jeanne Carmen and her twin brother were left considerable wealth when their Texas oilman father died."

An interview in *Ladies' Home Journal* of August 1991 describes Jeanne as Marilyn Monroe's confidante and next-door neighbor. When Marilyn died, she said, "I was just devastated. And I thought, How come I didn't see it coming? Why didn't I go over that night and maybe we could have talked and it might not have happened? We were supposed to play golf that day, and I know she was really looking forward to it." (Can you imagine Marilyn Monroe wearing golf shoes?)

Finally, *Coasters* magazine of Newport Beach, California (May 23, 1994) says Jeanne was Marilyn's best friend. "They were look-alike dolls whom you could hardly tell apart, except that Jeannie had the much larger upper torso. Together, they cut wide swaths through Rodeo Drive and the Las Vegas strip." Jeanne has written a tell-all memoir, 596 pages long, in which she reveals inside stuff on Marilyn and Jack and Bobby Kennedy, and Jeanne's own seven-year relationship with one of the most famous people in the world. (Now there's one-upmanship for you!) Jeanne has rejected a $50,000 advance for the book. Aw, shucks.

The Men Who Murdered Marilyn by Matthew Smith (1996) has a full-page photo of Jeanne Carmen.

Paddy Chayefsky

Acclaimed playwright and screenwriter Paddy Chayefsky (1923–1981) had a turbulent relationship with Marilyn Monroe.

Chayefsky first came to public attention with *Marty* (1953), a TV drama of two plain and lonely people in the Bronx. The 1955 film adaptation won Oscars for Chayefsky, star Ernest Borgnine, director Delbert Mann, and for Best Picture. His first Broadway play, *Middle of the Night* (1956), starred Edward G. Robinson and Gena Rowlands, and was highly praised. Marilyn told Chayefsky she wanted to star in the screen version for her own production company. She kept Chayefsky dangling for months until Arthur Miller apparently rejected it. (When *Middle of the Night* was finally filmed, in 1959, it starred Fredric March and Kim Novak.)

The angry Chayefsky sat down and wrote *The Goddess*, a downbeat screenplay which painted a grim portrait of Marilyn. Monroe actually expressed interest in making the film, but Kim Stanley starred in the 1958 entry. The unhappy Chayefsky-Monroe relationship is described at length in Shaun Considine's biography *Mad as Hell: The Life and Work of Paddy Chayefsky*.

Michael Chekhov

Michael Chekhov (1891–1955) was a noted actor, director, and drama coach. He was the nephew of Russia's foremost playwright Anton Chekhov (1860–1904).

Born in St. Petersburg, at nineteen he began studying with Konstantin Stanislavsky at the Moscow Art Theater. For two decades he acted leading roles in Shakespeare, Gorky, and Chekhov.

He fled the Bolshevist revolution to join Max Reinhardt, with whom he spent ten years touring the Continent. In 1935, he came to America with a Moscow Art Theater group, and stayed. In 1943, compatriot Gregory Ratoff directed Chekhov in a screen test in which he performed his uncle's sketch "I Forgot." MGM signed him on the basis of this audition.

He played character roles in Hollywood films for fourteen years. He was nominated for an Oscar for his performance as the psychiatrist who helps Ingrid Bergman in Hitchcock's *Spellbound* (RKO, 1945). As a drama coach, his students included Gregory Peck, Joan Caulfield, Yul Brynner, Hurd Hatfield, Cornel Wilde, and Jack Palance (who introduced Marilyn to him.) His book *To the Actor: On the Technique of Acting*, first published in 1953, is still widely studied.

In autumn of 1951, Marilyn began private lessons with the kindly Michael Chekhov. He instructed her in the methods of the Moscow Art Theater, which were not as extreme then as they would become under Lee Strasberg at the Actors Studio. It was Chekhov who first encouraged Marilyn to study the role of Grushenka, for a film version of Dostoyevsky's *The Brothers Karamazov*.

She told journalist W. J. Weatherby (in *Conversations with Marilyn*) of a class project where she played Cordelia to Chekhov's King Lear: "He gave the greatest performance I have ever seen."

In Marilyn's first will, made in 1956, she left $10,000 to the actor's widow. In her last will, written in 1961, a trust fund was established to provide Mrs. Chekhov a minimum of $2,500 a year. The Russian-born Xenia Julie Chekhov died in Los Angeles on December 22, 1970, at age seventy-three, without ever receiving any benefit from Marilyn's estate—because of legal complications and a reported lack of funds to hire the necessary legal advice in the matter.

Jack Clemmons

Acting watch commander at the West Los Angeles police station on August 5, 1962, he received a call at 4:25 A.M. that Marilyn Monroe was dead. He went to investigate, and was the first police officer at the scene. He found Dr. Greenson and Dr. Engelberg in the bedroom with Marilyn. Mrs. Murray, the housekeeper, was running the washing machine.

Clemmons visited the Marilyn Remembered Fan Club many years later, and told how he sensed the presence of other people in the house. Maybe Bobby Kennedy.

Montgomery Clift

"He's the only person I know who's in worse shape than I am."

—*Marilyn Monroe*

Montgomery Clift's life had the makings of legend, along the lines of Marilyn and James Dean, but it never happened. Maybe it was just too sad.

Clift's mother grew up in the family of a drunken Germantown, Pennsylvania, steelworker. At eighteen she discovered she was an abandoned child of southern aristocracy. She was able to marry wealth and raised her own children as if they were exiled royalty.

An unusually handsome boy, Clift made his Broadway debut at fourteen. At nineteen he acted with the Lunts, Broadway theater royalty, who almost adopted him.

In Hollywood, he established his screen persona as the tormented outsider in *A Place in the Sun* (Paramount, 1951). In 1956, a car crash destroyed his handsome face and his spirit. Biographer Patricia Bosworth (*Montgomery Clift*) termed his death "the longest suicide in Hollywood history, he crushed his life and career under an avalanche of booze, pills and inexplicable anguish."

As with the film's other stars, Montgomery Clift played himself in *The Misfits*, and was even given lines referring to his damaged face.

Marilyn and Monty Clift were longtime friends by the time they did *The Misfits*. They leaned on each other emotionally.

Clift died in 1966, forty-six years old but looking far older.

Harry Cohn

A cofounder—but the real boss—of Columbia Pictures. Cohn (1891–1958) was ruthless and vulgar, and probably the most hated man in Hollywood during the Golden Age of the film studios.

However, he was so flamboyant, so outrageous, you had to love him. His creed was, "I don't have ulcers, I give them!" Cohn is the model for the mogul in *The Godfather* (Paramount, 1972) who finds his horse's head in bed with him.

Cohn put Marilyn in *Ladies of the Chorus* as a favor to Twentieth Century–Fox executive Joseph M. Schenck, but apparently didn't put her under contract because she said no to an intimate weekend on Cohn's yacht.

Arthur Miller's *Timebends* has a wonderful account of Harry Cohn as monster. Bob Thomas's *King Cohn* is one of the most readable of all Hollywood biographies.

Jack Cole

Dancer/choreographer/friend who choreographed Marilyn's dance numbers in *Gentlemen Prefer Blondes*, *River of No Return*, *There's No Business Like Show Business* (the "Heat Wave" number), and *Let's Make Love*. At Marilyn's insistence, Cole worked with her, without credit, on the "Running Wild" number in *Some Like It Hot*.

According to *Unsung Genius*, Glenn Loney's biography of Jack Cole (1911–1974), the dancer worked behind the scenes with Marilyn, "helping her develop her sensuous walk and breathlessly sexy mode of speaking." Loney also says, "He understood how to give her bits of business which could work—and which were right for her screen personality."

The manner in which Marilyn and Jack Cole worked together was unusual. During actual filming, Cole would stand beside the camera and perform the number—while Marilyn copied him in an exact, mirror-image rendition of the dance. So while she seemed to be looking at the camera when she danced, she was actually following the off-camera movements of Jack Cole.

Jack Cole was one of dance's most influential choreographers. He devised the jazz-influenced style synonymous with American show-dancing, and which influenced Jerome Robbins, Michael Kidd, Bob Fosse, Michael Bennett, and Ron Field.

Films for which he created the dances include *Kismet* (MGM, 1944, uncredited), *Tonight and Every Night* (Columbia, 1945), *Gilda* (Columbia, 1946), *Down to Earth* (Columbia, 1947), *On the Riviera* (Twentieth Century–Fox, 1951), *Meet Me After the Show* (Twentieth Century–Fox, 1951), *The Merry Widow* (MGM, 1952), *Three for the Show* (Columbia, 1955), *Gentlemen Marry Brunettes* (United Artists, 1955), *Kismet* (MGM, 1955), and *Les Girls* (MGM, 1957).

If for nothing else, Cole will be remembered for Rita Hayworth's seductive dance in *Gilda*, as she sings "Put the Blame on Mame."

Joan Crawford

"Kids don't like [Marilyn]...because they don't like to see sex exploited."

—Joan Crawford

She started out as a rival to Clara Bow with her anything-for-fun flapper roles in the movies of the 1920s. Over the decades she graduated from a suffering, sacrificing heroine of pulp drama and romances to a mature femme fatale, and on to a woman menaced by handsome young men. She became a STAR, a legend in her own mind. And after her death she became a camp classic. Born in 1904, she died in 1977.

For a *Photoplay* awards dinner in 1953, Marilyn wore a body-hugging, attention-grabbing gold lamé gown, without underwear. Joan Crawford was outraged and told the world about it. (There were retaliations of repeated gossip of Joan's career in stag films.) The gown, designed by Travilla for *Gentlemen Prefer Blondes*, became known as "the Joan Crawford gown."

Another rumor worth mentioning is that Joan's hostility was aroused when Marilyn rejected her sexual advances. This incident is recounted in Fred Lawrence Guiles' biography *Legend*, page 200.

George Cukor

A Hollywood film director (1899–1983) usually included on the lists of the great ones. Cukor directed Marilyn in *Let's Make Love* and began *Something's Got to Give*. They were all smiles in public, but insiders had a far different view.

James Spada (*Monroe: Her Life in Pictures*):

According to Nunnally Johnson, who wrote the screenplay of *How to Marry a Millionaire* and who had worked with Marilyn on a version of *Something's Got to Give* with which she was quite happy, Marilyn's chronic illness and frequent failures to report to work were the result of her fears and misgivings about George Cukor. The director was not happy with the script and made changes, with which Marilyn disagreed. She felt frustrated and helpless and was afraid that a repeat of the *Let's Make Love* fiasco would ensue.

George Cukor [Nunnally Johnson claimed he loathed Marilyn] later said of Marilyn, "There may be an exact psychiatric term for what was wrong with her, I don't know—but truth to tell, I think she was quite mad. The mother was mad, and poor Marilyn was mad...."

The best of Cukor: *What Price Hollywood?* (RKO, 1932), *Dinner at Eight* (MGM, 1933), *Little Women* (RKO, 1933), *David Copperfield* (MGM, 1935), *Camille* (MGM, 1937), *Holiday* (Columbia, 1938), *The Women* (MGM, 1939), *The Philadelphia Story* (MGM, 1940), *Adam's Rib* (MGM, 1949), *A Star Is Born* (Warner Bros., 1954), and *My Fair Lady* (Warner Bros., 1964).

Tony Curtis

Born in 1925, Tony Curtis's early career in movies was as a "baron of beefcake," but he gradually established himself as an actor of range and depth in *Sweet Smell of Success* (United Artists, 1957), *The Defiant Ones* (United Artists, 1958), *Some Like It Hot* (United Artists, 1959), *Spartacus* (Universal, 1960), and *The Boston Strangler* (Twentieth Century–Fox, 1968).

The making of *Some Like It Hot* has been well documented. In his book *Tony Curtis: The Autobiography*, he describes the difficulties of working with Marilyn—that she had lost all control, from too much alcohol or pills and was "emotionally devastated." It took forty-seven takes for her to knock on a door and say, "It's me, Sugar." Another scene took fifty-nine takes. Tony

Marilyn sings "Running Wild," while playing her ukulele and shaking her rhythm section, in *Some Like It Hot* (1959). A true classic. [Photo courtesy of Photofest.]

Curtis said that making love to Marilyn Monroe was "like kissing Hitler" . . . and later protested that too much was made of the remark.

Tony Curtis also starred in Nicolas Roeg's film version (a Zenith Production in association with the Recorded Picture Company, 1985) of the play *Insignificance*, in which he portrays a Joseph McCarthy–type senator who seduces a Marilyn Monroe–type actress.

Joe DiMaggio

The great ball player, and the second husband of Marilyn Monroe.

He was born November 25, 1914, in Martinez, northern California, the eighth of nine children. His parents were Sicilian immigrants, his father a fisherman. Joe and older brother Vince and younger brother Dom were all passionate about baseball.

Vince was signed by the minor-league San Francisco Seals. Joe joined him on the playing field the following year. Shortly after, the brothers moved on to the majors, Joe with the Yankees, Dom with the Red Sox, while Vince had a long career in the National League. Joe went into the record books, and into legend, in 1941 when he hit in an incredible fifty-six consecutive games.

In early 1952, Joe saw a photo of Marilyn posing with two Chicago White Sox players, one of whom he knew. He called to ask, "Who's the blonde?"

Joe's courtship of Marilyn lasted about two years, 1952 and 1953; their marriage lasted nine months, from January to September 1954. There were many reasons the marriage didn't work—mainly, unreconcilable differences in what each wanted from life and from marriage. They seemed to grow closer in later years, and there was speculation that Marilyn and Joe were planning to remarry at the time of her demise.

At Marilyn's death, Joe stepped in and took charge (with Marilyn's half-sister Berniece Miracle). He refused to let her funeral become a Hollywood circus, allowing only a small group of Marilyn's friends and associates to attend the service.

Joe ordered that six red roses be delivered three times a week to Marilyn's crypt in Westwood, California. He stopped them after twenty years, reasoning that the money could be put to better use by the children's charities that Marilyn had helped support.

James Dougherty

Marilyn's first husband, born in 1921, he was the boy next door who used to drive her home from Van Nuys High School, where she was in the tenth grade.

In December 1941, Jim Dougherty took Norma Jeane Baker to a Lockheed Aircraft company dance. By March of 1942 they were going steady. They were engaged by that May and married on June 19.

Dougherty joined the merchant marines in 1943. When he returned home from his World War II duties, Norma Jeane was well on her way to becoming a pinup model, and her own woman. The Doughertys were officially divorced in September of 1946.

In June 1950, Jim Dougherty, now a police officer, was assigned to keep the crowds behind the barricades at Grauman's Egyptian Theater in Hollywood for the premiere of *The Asphalt Jungle*. He looked for Marilyn but she never appeared on the scene.

In 1984, he retired and moved to Maine with his third wife.

Dougherty told his story of life with Marilyn in *The Secret Happiness of Marilyn Monroe*, published in 1976, and appears prominently in many of the Marilyn documentaries. He usually tells the story of how Norma Jeane cooked peas and carrots together because she liked the color combination. Dougherty announced a second book, one that would address all the nonsense and myths about his famous ex-wife, but it hasn't appeared yet.

Hyman Engelberg

Marilyn's Los Angeles physician, recommended by her psychiatrist Dr. Ralph Greenson.

Engelberg freely wrote prescriptions for barbiturates that were not controlled as strictly then as they would be later.

On the night/morning of Marilyn's death, August 5, 1962, Marilyn's housekeeper, Eunice Murray, called Dr. Greenson who called Dr. Engelberg, who pronounced Marilyn dead. It was Engelberg who summoned the police.

Dixie Lee Evans

"The Marilyn Monroe of Burlesque," she imitated Marilyn's speech and mannerisms in slightly risqué adaptations of scenes from several of Marilyn's movies.

Dixie discontinued her Marilyn act as Monroe's personal problems became publicly known. "I refused to impersonate a sick girl."

Tom Ewell

Tom Ewell (1909–1994) was born in Kentucky, studied acting at the University of Wisconsin, and made his Broadway debut in 1934. He starred in *The Seven Year Itch* and *Will Success Spoil Rock Hunter?* on Broadway and repeated the roles in the movie versions, with Marilyn Monroe and Jayne Mansfield respectively. Though an unlikely leading man and not at all handsome, nevertheless he held his own with the two blonde bombshells.

Agnes Flanagan

Hairdresser at Twentieth Century–Fox, she did Marilyn's hair for *The Fireball*, and they became lifelong friends. Marilyn found a nurturing mother figure in her. Flanagan died in 1985.

There are photos of Agnes Flanagan and Whitey Snyder fussing over Marilyn in the George Barris photo collection *Marilyn*. The second Barris book, *Marilyn: Her Life in Her Own Words*, has a color photo of Agnes and Whitey.

It was Agnes Flanagan who arranged Marilyn's hair for the open-casket funeral at Westwood Memorial Cemetery.

Clark Gable

"She makes a man proud to be a man."

—*Clark Gable*

Over a long screen career, the leading ladies of Clark Gable (1901–1960), "The King," included Vivien Leigh, Greta Garbo, Joan Crawford, Claudette Colbert, Ingrid Bergman, Norma Shearer, Lana Turner, Ava Gardner, and the two blondes, Jean Harlow and Marilyn Monroe.

At one point, young Norma Jeane Mortensen thought Clark Gable was her father, confusing him with a photo her mother had on the wall, probably of Stanley Gifford (who worked with Gladys Baker at Consolidated Film Industries and had an affair with her).

On November 4, 1954, agent Charles Feldman gave a party for Marilyn, on completion of principal photography for *The Seven Year Itch*, and invited Hollywood royalty. Marilyn met Clark Gable for the first time. They danced and discussed working together.

Marilyn and Clark Gable next met in 1960, in the miserable summer heat of Nevada, to film *The Misfits*. It was a nightmare for Marilyn, with her marriage to Arthur Miller disintegrating into public fights, and with her growing dependence on barbiturates.

Perhaps the main impulse that kept Marilyn going was that she was acting with Clark Gable, the man she had envisioned as being her father. Gable, in turn, had tremendous compassion for Marilyn. He felt she was worth the delays and frustration—that when she did finally show up on the set she was magic.

Clark Gable had a heart attack on November 5, 1960, the day after *The Misfits* was completed, and died on November 11. The fifty-nine-year-old Gable had insisted upon doing his own stunts for *The Misfits*, and had been a three-pack-a-day smoker for thirty years. But there was gossip that Gable's pregnant widow blamed his death on Marilyn's exasperating behavior. In May of 1961, Gable's widow invited Marilyn to the christening of the baby John Clark Gable. Marilyn took this as a sign that she was not blamed.

Look at the photo in this book (page 35) in which Marilyn sits beside Clark Gable at a pre-*Misfits* luncheon. You could write a book around the expression on her face.

Jay Garnett

A film director whose career spanned half a century, Garnett (1894–1977) directed many of the top stars: Clark Gable and Jean Harlow in *China Seas* (MGM, 1935), Marlene Dietrich and John Wayne in *Seven Sinners* (Universal, 1940), and Lana Turner in *The Postman Always Rings Twice* (MGM, 1946).

He directed Marilyn in the Mickey Rooney roller-skating movie *The Fireball*, which he cowrote with novelist Horace McCoy.

Garnett published his autobiography *Light Your Torches and Pull Up Your Tights* in 1973. He writes of approaching Joseph M. Schenck to back *The Fireball*; Schenck agreed to put up the $50,000 front money and to release the film through Twentieth Century–Fox, where he had been chairman of the board and was now an executive producer.

Garnett makes no mention of Marilyn Monroe being part of the *Fireball* deal...but she *was* Schenck's girl at the time.

Sam "Mooney" Giancana

The mobster who once claimed to have controlled America. Conspiracy theorists agree that Giancana had *something* to do with the murder of Marilyn—either in connection with Joseph Kennedy, or J. Edgar Hoover and his FBI, or the CIA, or the State Department, or maybe even aliens... *Or* on his own, to get even with Joseph Kennedy or Hoover or the CIA or the State Department or the aliens.

Jeanne Carmen, a sometime actress who claims she was Marilyn's roommate and best friend (though no one in Marilyn's circle had ever heard of her) says she and Marilyn had lunch with Giancana three times.

The book *Double Cross* has Giancana and MM in the bedroom together at the Cal-Neva Lodge on the weekend before Marilyn's death. The documentary *Marilyn: The Last Word* also puts them there together.

Giancana's constant companion at this time was Phyllis McGuire, of the McGuire Sisters, one of America's most popular female singing groups.

C. Stanley Gifford

The father of Marilyn Monroe . . . or the man most likely to be her father.

Gifford worked with Gladys Baker at Consolidated Film Industries in Hollywood, in 1925, and had an affair with her. It ended when she told him she was pregnant. Her baby, the future Marilyn Monroe, was born on June 1, 1926.

During one of the brief periods in which Norma Jeane and her mother lived together, Gladys Baker hung one small photo in the bedroom. It was of a handsome man with a broad face and a mustache—Stanley Gifford. But Norma Jeane thought it was Clark Gable. She started telling school friends that Clark Gable was her father.

There is a snapshot of Gifford in both of the Fred Lawrence Guiles biographies, *Norma Jean* and *Legend*.

Eleanor "Bebe" Goddard

Norma Jeane Mortensen's foster sister. In 1940, Bebe came to Van Nuys to live with her father Ervin "Doc" Goddard, his new wife Grace Goddard, and Grace's ward Norma Jeane. The two fourteen-year-old girls became close friends.

Bebe had survived a dreadful childhood, being shunted from one foster home to another, growing up in abusive, miserable conditions. Struggling actress Marilyn Monroe was inspired to borrow the pathetic stories she had heard from Bebe, passing them off to reporters as her own sad childhood—apparently to win sympathy and to get her name in the magazines.

In April of 1942, Doc Goddard was promoted to a job in West Virginia. Grace and Bebe would go with him, but they could not afford to bring Norma Jeane with them. She remained in Los Angeles.

Norma Jeane and Bebe corresponded and occasionally spoke on the phone; Norma Jeane visited her in the fall of 1944.

In the summer of 1945, Grace and Doc Goddard moved back to California. Bebe Goddard didn't return until August 1951.

The last time Bebe saw Marilyn was in early 1956, just before Marilyn left Los Angeles for a new life in New York.

Grace McKee Goddard

"The great manager of Norma Jeane's life."

—*Donald Spoto*

Gladys Baker and Grace McKee (born 1895) were coworkers and good friends at Columbia Pictures: Gladys was a film splicer, Grace a supervisor. When Gladys was institutionalized in 1934, Grace stepped in and took charge of Gladys's daughter, eight-year-old Norma Jeane.

On June 1, 1935, Grace McKee became Norma Jeane's court-appointed guardian. To meet the guardianship requirements of the state of California, Norma Jeane was placed in the Los Angeles Orphans Home in Hollywood for a six-month period, which stretched into two years. Just after her eleventh birthday, Grace reclaimed Norma Jeane and took her home to Van Nuys, a community in the San Fernando Valley, about ten miles from Hollywood.

When Twentieth Century–Fox signed newly-named Marilyn Monroe to a standard six-month contract, on July 23, 1946, Grace signed the contract as Norma Jeane's guardian—at twenty, the actress was still legally underage.

On September 28, 1953, Grace McKee Goddard committed suicide with an overdose of the barbiturate phenobarbital, after suffering for years from chronic alcoholism and crippling strokes. She was buried in Westwood Memorial Cemetery, near the UCLA campus. Less than nine years later, Marilyn herself would be buried there.

Betty Grable

"I'm not envious of Marilyn. There's room for us all."

—*Betty Grable*

Twentieth Century–Fox had four great blonde stars over the decades: Shirley Temple and Alice Faye, popular in the 1930s and 1940s... replaced by Betty Grable in the 1940s and early 1950s... to be replaced by Marilyn Monroe in the 1950s. By then, the studio system was tottering on its last legs.

Marilyn became a legend, but Betty Grable (born in 1916) probably had the greatest popular appeal, with her peaches-and-cream complexion that was just made for the Technicolor cameras, her gorgeous figure, and her friendly, easygoing style. She was the industry's highest-paid star during the World War II years, when the GIs chose her as their number one pinup girl.

Before Marilyn's nude calendar photo created a sensation, the most familiar pinup in the world might have been the 1942 photo of Betty Grable in a white one-piece swimsuit, smiling coyly over one shoulder at viewers admiring her shapely legs and rear end.

Grable asked Twentieth Century–Fox head Darryl F. Zanuck for *Gentlemen Prefer Blondes* but the new blonde, Marilyn

Monroe, got the coveted role of Lorelei Lee. When the two costarred in *How to Marry a Millionaire*, blonde bitchiness on the set was anticipated but never happened. On July 1, 1953, Betty Grable tore up her studio contract... and Marilyn moved into her Star Building dressing room.

Then irony moved into the picture, when Marilyn refused to do *How to Be Very, Very Popular*, and Grable was asked to replace her. It was Grable's last film. She had had enough.

She segued into Las Vegas acts and productions of *Hello, Dolly!* Audiences were cheering her Million Dollar Legs even after she became a grandmother. She died in 1973.

Lauren Bacall seems to be telling Marilyn that the night is hers—the November 10, 1953 premiere of *How to Marry a Millionaire*—but Marilyn already knows it. [Photo courtesy of Archive Photos.]

Dr. Ralph Greenson

The big question mark in the last two years of Marilyn's life. Marilyn started seeing Los Angeles–based psychiatrist Dr. Ralph Greenson on the recommendation of Marianne Kris, her New York analyst. In June 1960, before she filmed *The Misfits*, Monroe was seeing Dr. Greenson five or six times a week. When she came back to Los Angeles from the nightmare of *The Misfits*, she saw him seven days a week, at his home.

In March of 1962, Marilyn was living with the Greenson family—the doctor, his wife Hildi, and their college-student children Dan and Joan. Greenson told his colleagues he was treating her for schizophrenia. When the doctor went to Europe on vacation, in June, he was summoned home to treat an emotionally deteriorating Marilyn.

In the last weeks of her life, Marilyn saw Dr. Greenson almost daily, at her house or at his. On Saturday, August 4, 1962, the psychiatrist spent six hours at Marilyn's home. At some point during that night, the housekeeper Eunice Murray called Dr. Greenson...who found Marilyn dead.

There are many questions about the nature of Dr. Greenson's relationship to Marilyn that will probably never be answered. The only time he spoke up was in 1973, in response to Norman Mailer's controversial biography, *Marilyn*. *The Chicago Daily News* printed a brief story ("Marilyn's Doctor Says Mailer Lied" by Arthur J. Snider) on Greenson's interview with *Medical Tribune* on October 30, 1973:

> "Marilyn Monroe's psychiatrist, speaking out after eleven years of silence, said the actress is 'vilified and lied about' in Norman Mailer's biography, *Marilyn*. Dr. Ralph H. Greenson of Beverly Hills, California, said Mailer was '100 percent wrong' in his intimations that Miss Monroe may have had an affair with President Kennedy or his brother, Robert; that she

may have been murdered and that the CIA may have had a hand in her death.

"'The Mailer book vilified and lied about her,' Greenson said in an interview with *Medical Tribune*, a publication for physicians.

"'It's wrong to connect her death with any sort of political intrigue. I want to discredit Mailer. He distorts, makes innuendoes about her sexual life and suggests that unethical things were done to her by doctors. They're a bunch of lies.'

"Greenson said he had remained silent because professional ethics did not permit him to talk about confidential relations with a patient.

"'But I could not keep silent to what I know are false and demeaning inaccuracies,' he said in the interview.

"Miss Monroe's suicide in 1962 came as a surprise to him, Greenson said, because she had been making progress in coping with her emotional problems.

"He had agreed to try to help her because she had made several suicide attempts before, he said."

Jean Harlow

The movie-star idol of the young Norma Jeane was born in 1911.

Jean Harlow eloped (from Kansas City) at sixteen, with a young businessman. They headed for Los Angeles where she found work as a film extra, and then appeared in comedy shorts produced by Hal Roach. Howard Hughes cast her in his aviation epic *Hell's Angels* (United Artists, 1930), which made her a big-screen name.

She appeared in *The Public Enemy* (Warner Bros., 1931) and *Platinum Blonde* (Columbia, 1931), and the public responded to this "coarse, flashy, whorish sexpot" (Ephraim Katz, *The Film Encyclopedia*). Then MGM signed her in 1932 and transformed her into a subtle actress with a flair for comedy. She became a superstar, appearing opposite Clark Gable, Spencer Tracy, and William Powell. Her hits at MGM include *Red Dust* (1932), *Bombshell* (1933), *Dinner at Eight* (1934), *China Seas* (1935), and *Libeled Lady* (1936).

Harlow became ill during the filming of *Saratoga* (1937), and was hospitalized for uremic poisoning. She died on June 7 of cerebral edema, at age twenty-six.

There are many striking similarities between Jean Harlow and Marilyn Monroe. Some of the most notable:

- Both left high school at sixteen to get married.
- Both used their mothers' maiden names professionally: Norma Jeane Baker became Marilyn Monroe; Harlean Carpenter became Jean Harlow.
- Both had three husbands.
- Both posed nude, and in revealing costumes, and preferred to dress without underwear.
- Both lived, at one time, on North Palm Drive in Beverly Hills.
- On January 30, 1937, Harlow left the filming of *Personal Property* to go to Washington, D.C., to appear at a birthday ball for President Franklin D. Roosevelt—which made the studio furious. On May 18, 1962, Marilyn left the filming of *Something's Got to Give* to go to New York City to sing at President John F. Kennedy's birthday celebration—which made the studio furious.
- Clark Gable costarred in their final films: with Harlow in *Saratoga* (1937), and with Marilyn in *The Misfits* (1961).
- After Harlow's death, actor William Powell, to whom she had been engaged, arranged for flowers to be delivered weekly to her grave. After Marilyn's death, ex-husband Joe DiMaggio arranged for roses to be delivered to her grave three times a week.

Howard Hawks

One of Hollywood's major directors, Hawks (1896–1977) directed Marilyn in the comedy *Monkey Business* and in the musical
Gentlemen Prefer Blondes. He was one of many who lost patience
with Marilyn's emotional insecurities and her on-the-set delays,
yet *Blondes* emerged as one of Marilyn's most purely enjoyable
films. She never seemed so relaxed, so assured, or to be getting
so much pleasure from performing.

Talking about the major stars he'd worked with, Hawks said,
"They weren't all great actors, but they were great personalities.
That's what I prefer. A great personality illuminates the screen.
Monroe's problem was that many directors handled her as if she
were real. She wasn't. She was only comfortable in unreal roles."

**Marilyn in a white
version of the pink
gown from *Gentlemen
Prefer Blondes*. She
wears it here for the
premiere of *Call Me
Madam* (1953).
[Photo courtesy of
Archive Photos.]**

Hedda Hopper

She was a powerful and flamboyant Hollywood gossip columnist for twenty-eight years, her chief competition being the formidable Louella Parsons. Marilyn was mentioned first in Hedda's column, on July 29, 1946, and they were sympatico for a long time. But maybe Hedda (1890–1966) became uncomfortable with Marilyn's flagrant sexuality, because they drifted apart and Louella became Marilyn's supporter in the gossip columns.

Arline Hunter

"The poor man's Monroe," a model who resembled Marilyn. She was *Playboy*'s August 1954 Playmate of the Month, and also posed for other girlie magazines in the 1950s. Her official film credits include *Revolt in the Big House* (Allied Artists, 1958), *Sex Kittens Go to College* (Allied Artists, 1960), and *Madison Avenue* (Twentieth Century–Fox, 1962).

Somewhere around the time Marilyn was posing for Tom Kelley, in the late 1940s, Arline Hunter appeared in a short nudie film called *The Apple, Knockers and the Coke Bottle*, in which she sensuously rolls an apple and a bottle over her bare breasts.

In 1970, the footage showed up in a stag film compilation called *Hollywood Blue*, with the subject identified as Marilyn Monroe. James Haspiel, longtime friend of Marilyn's, was reported in *Variety* to be waging a one-man battle to set the facts straight.

Apple, Knockers ... reemerged in 1974, with New York underground filmmaker Bruce Conner repeating the footage to the sound of the real Marilyn singing "I'm Through With Love." The Conner film, called *Marilyn Times Five*, was featured in a New York City program called "Homage to Marilyn Monroe." James

Haspiel was co-coordinator. *Film Quarterly*, Spring 1974, quoted Conner: "[Norman] Mailer has speculated that this may not be Marilyn because the breasts are so large, but I have written him a long letter arguing that she is real."

Arline Hunter's image showed up again in 1989, when early boyfriend Ted Jordan published *Norma Jean: My Secret Life with Marilyn Monroe*. The book contains two nude photos which Jordan says he took of Marilyn; others identify the model as Arline Hunter, in photos from *Playboy*.

John Huston

"I had no idea that she would go so far so fast."
—*John Huston*

Screenwriter, director, producer and actor, John Huston (1906–1987) led too colorful a life—too *busy* a life—to take up much space here. There are numerous solid books about him, plus his autobiography published in 1980.

Marilyn's breakthrough film was *The Asphalt Jungle*, and, as everyone has pointed out, her last completed movie, *The Misfits*, was also directed by Huston.

Huston narrated the 1966 ABC-TV documentary *The Legend of Marilyn Monroe*.

He said that Marilyn had been his first choice for *Freud* (Universal, 1962), for the role of the patient played eventually by Susannah York. Marilyn said she couldn't do it because her analyst (Margaret Hohenberg) said that *her* own analyst (Anna Freud, daughter of Sigmund) didn't want the movie to be made.

Johnny Hyde

Johnny Hyde (1895–1950) was vice president of the William Morris Talent Agency in Los Angeles and therefore one of the most powerful players in the business. Though a sickly man, and barely five feet tall, he was widely respected in the industry.

On New Year's Eve, 1948, Johnny Hyde met Marilyn Monroe at a party in Los Angeles hosted by film producer Sam Spiegel. Hyde was in love with Marilyn before the night was over.

The besmitten Johnny Hyde left his wife and four sons and devoted his remaining life to Marilyn and her career. In October of 1949, Marilyn was signed for *The Asphalt Jungle*. In April 1950, she signed for *All About Eve*. Johnny got her the Royal Triton television commercial, and a feature story in *Photoplay*.

Johnny begged Marilyn to marry him, promising she would be rich after his death—which could be soon, as he had a serious heart condition. (He was fifty-three at the time, Marilyn twenty-two.) Marilyn refused; she loved Johnny, but not that way. He died of a massive heart attack on December 18, 1950. His final words were a call for Marilyn.

Marilyn always gave credit to Johnny Hyde for her movie success.

Ted Jordan

"'God, Eddie,' she said, breathlessly, 'isn't fucking just the greatest thing that ever was?'"

—*Ted Jordan (Eddie was his real first name)*

A claimant who insists he and Marilyn were once lovers, Jordan tells his story in *Norma Jean: My Secret Life with Marilyn Monroe*, and in various tabloids. In 1945–1946, Marilyn was one of Emmeline Snively's models at the Blue Book Agency in the Ambassador Hotel, and Jordan was a lifeguard at the Lido Club just behind the Ambassador (in another version it's the Roosevelt Hotel). Anyway, they were lovers and then friends right up to the end.

Jordan says Marilyn had an affair with stripper Lili St. Cyr. Jordan had an affair with Lili and married her. He reports the three of them went to bed together.

Jordan's book has two nude photos he says he took of Marilyn, but the model has been identified as Arline Hunter in *Playboy* photos.

Ted Jordan says that Marilyn called him twice on the night she died. "Sensing that something wasn't right," he called her back and actor-friend Peter Lawford answered her phone.

The 1996 HBO movie *Norma Jean and Marilyn*, featuring Ashley Judd and Mira Sorvino, was loosely based on Jordan's book. Josh Charles portrayed the young Jordan.

Fred Karger

Columbia Pictures vocal coach, composer, and conductor in 1948, when Marilyn was signed to costar in that studio's *Ladies of the Chorus*.

Karger (1916–1979) taught Marilyn how to sing, but also introduced her to good music and books.

Marilyn moved in with Karger—who lived in West Hollywood with his mother, his daughter, his divorced sister, and her children—but he wouldn't marry Monroe. She called him her first love (slighting her first husband Jim Dougherty), but he didn't think she was made for marriage.

Karger's mother became a mother figure and lifelong friend to Marilyn. Ann Karger (1886–1975) and her sister Effie had been members of a vaudeville act known as the Conley Sisters. Ann retired from showbiz to marry Max Karger, an early motion picture executive.

There is a photo of Fred Karger in Susan Doll's *Marilyn: Her Life and Legend*, page 61, with his second wife, actress Jane Wyman.

Elia Kazan

"[Marilyn was a] simple, eager young woman, a decent-hearted girl whom Hollywood brought down, legs parted."

—*Elia Kazan*

A director noted for both stage and screen productions. He had affairs with Marilyn while she was married to Joe DiMaggio (1954), and also while she was wed to Arthur Miller (1956–1960).

Marilyn wrote in a letter, "Kazan said I was the gayest girl he ever knew and believe me, he has known many. But he loved me for one year and once rocked me to sleep one night when I was in great anguish."

Dr. Leon Krohn

Marilyn's gynecologist in Los Angeles. While some accounts claim that Marilyn had as many as a dozen abortions, Dr. Krohn insisted that Marilyn never had a single one.

Peter Lawford

A breezy, romantic British-born star with a lot of natural charm, he was part of the MGM stock company in the 1940s and early 1950s.

He was also part of Frank Sinatra's "Rat Pack" gang, and a brother-in-law of President John F. Kennedy. He reportedly procured women, including Marilyn Monroe, for the President's pleasure.

Peter Lawford (1923–1984) plays a prominent part in many of the conspiracy claims surrounding Marilyn's death—including ones that say he cleaned up the incriminating evidence after her murder. And there are claims that say he and Bobby Kennedy personally did the dirty deed. (See Part 4, chapter 23, "How Did Marilyn Die?")

Peter Levathes

"[Levathes] wore the look of a permissive parent who had given his child a loaded gun to play with, and had then been shot with it."

—*screenwriter Walter Bernstein*

Darryl F. Zanuck was production chief for Twentieth Century–Fox for twenty-two years. When he left in 1956 to become an independent producer, he was replaced by Buddy Adler, who died in 1960. A committee replaced Adler with Robert Goldstein...who was kicked out by outside financial experts. He was in turn replaced by Peter Levathes, who had been an attorney and an advertising man. Levathes was captain of the sinking ship when *Something's Got to Give* started giving way. Levathes is the man who fired Marilyn Monroe for not showing up for work.

Film director Jean Negulesco described Levathes as "a tall, dark man, nervous and with the faraway look of a man with responsibilities beyond his understanding or ability."

Joshua Logan

"She is the most completely realized actress since Garbo."

—*Joshua Logan*

Broadway and film director, and playwright (1921–1988), he turned to directing film seriously only in the mid-1950s, with *Picnic* and *Bus Stop*. Logan had not wanted to direct Marilyn, until Lee Strasberg assured him that Marlon Brando and Marilyn Monroe were the two greatest actors with whom he'd ever worked. Logan later became one of the most vocal champions of Marilyn's acting abilities, calling her "one of the greatest talents of all time."

Ana Lower

Marilyn spoke of Ana Lower to Maurice Zolotow for his book *Marilyn Monroe*: "She changed my whole life. She was the first person in the world I ever really loved and she loved me . . . . She showed me the path to the higher things of life and she gave me more confidence to myself. She never hurt me, not once. She couldn't. She was all kindness and all love. She was good to me."

Ana Lower (1880–1948) was an aunt of Norma Jeane's legal guardian, Grace McKee Goddard. She was a caring, grandmotherly type, a Christian Science practitioner who read the Bible to inmates in the local jail, in West Los Angeles. In November of 1938, Norma Jeane was boarded with her while she went to school at nearby Emerson Junior High. Ana Lower's health began failing in 1940, so Norma Jeane returned to the Goddards' in Van Nuys, in Los Angeles' San Fernando Valley

Natasha Lytess

"She needed me like a dead man needs a casket."

—*Natasha Lytess*

Most books on Marilyn Monroe talk of how Marilyn antagonized her movie directors by insisting that her drama coach Natasha Lytess (and later Paula Strasberg) be present on the set to advise her. In *The Fifty Year Decline and Fall of Hollywood*, Ezra Goodman presents Natasha's side of the story:

"Lytess told me that Monroe put her on the spot with directors and studios . . . by insisting that she be on the set with her and guide her, acting-wise, from behind the camera. This aroused resentment on the part of many directors and did not help Lytess professionally. The gray-haired Lytess said: 'I worked with her on every line, every gesture, every breath, every movement of the eyes. I worked on all her dances and songs. Marilyn wouldn't move without me.

"I introduced her to books...I gave her the things I believe in myself as I would give them to my little daughter. She was like a child.'"

Fred Lawrence Guiles fills in some of Natasha's dramatic background, in his Marilyn biography *Legend*: Natasha Lytess was part of the exodus of Jewish and other intellectuals fleeing the coming Nazi storm in 1930s Europe. She came to the U.S. with her lover, the novelist Bruno Frank, and their young daughter. Frank died in 1945. Her years with stage director Max Reinhardt in Europe opened doors for her, and she became head of the drama department at Columbia Pictures. On March 10, 1948, she was introduced to starlet Marilyn Monroe.

Although ill for a number of years, Natasha Lytess outlived Marilyn. Lytess died in 1964.

Joseph L. Mankiewicz

Movie director, producer, writer (1909–1993). One of Hollywood's best. At the urging of superagent Johnny Hyde, Mankiewicz signed Marilyn for the role of Miss Caswell in *All About Eve* at Twentieth Century–Fox. It became the breakthrough role for Monroe.

Mankiewicz's principle memory of Marilyn is of the remarkable number of takes she required for her scene. He also commented on her aloneness: "Throughout our location period in San Francisco, Marilyn would be spotted...dining alone. Or drinking alone. We'd always ask her to join us, and she would and seem pleased, but somehow she never understood or accepted our unspoken assumption that she was one of us. She remained alone. She was not a loner. She was just plain alone."

When Mankiewicz was prepping his film version of the Broadway hit musical *Guys and Dolls* (MGM, 1955), Marilyn expressed an interest in the role of Adelaide (created on the stage by Vivian Blaine). Mankiewicz kept Marilyn's interest a secret from producer Samuel Goldwyn (who surely would have taken her up on it) because Mankiewicz was fighting for Blaine.

The Mankiewicz filmography also includes *The Ghost and Mrs. Muir* (Twentieth Century–Fox, 1947), *A Letter to Three Wives* (Twentieth Century–Fox, 1949), *No Way Out* (Twentieth Century–Fox, 1950), *The Barefoot Contessa* (United Artists, 1954), *Suddenly, Last Summer* (Columbia, 1959), and *Cleopatra* (Twentieth Century–Fox, 1963).

Jayne Mansfield

Jayne Mansfield is not too far behind Marilyn Monroe in terms of lasting appeal—which is remarkable when all her excesses are taken into account and it is remembered how little merit there is in her screen work. The weight of growing public scorn would have crushed a weaker person.

She was born Vera Jayne Palmer, in 1933, in Bryn Mawr, Pennsylvania. Married at sixteen and a mother at seventeen, she attended drama classes in Texas and later at UCLA, driven to become a movie star.

She consciously and sometimes successfully imitated Marilyn: She registered with Emmeline Snively's Blue Book Model Agency. She modeled for pinup calendars. She gave interviews and told everyone she wasn't wearing underwear. She did a screen test for Paramount, and one for Warner Bros., both using a scene from *The Seven Year Itch*.

Her career breakthrough came when she showed up at a Florida publicity junket for the Jane Russell film *Underwater!* (RKO, 1955), displaying her abundant figure in a skintight red swimsuit—she was 40–24–36 to Marilyn's 38–23–36.

Her real break came when she appeared on the Broadway stage, featured in the George Axelrod comedy *Will Success Spoil Rock Hunter?* She later repeated the role—a dizzy Marilyn Monroe blonde—in the 1957 screen version of the play.

Jayne posed in the nude for *Playboy* magazine, but it didn't work for her as it had for Marilyn. Columnist Hedda Hopper criticized her: "She'll be a long time living down those nude photos. Marilyn Monroe could get by with posing in the altogether—on Jayne it's just not very pretty." (*Photoplay*, August 1963)

The gossip machine would have us believe that Jayne Mansfield also followed Marilyn into involvement with the Kennedy brothers and with the Mob—with Peter Lawford as the go-between. C. David Heymann's *A Woman Named Jackie* describes Jayne as having "a more realistic view of men than her more celebrated rival." Lawford is quoted: "She had the best body in Hollywood, long legs, large firm breasts and a minuscule waistline. But she couldn't make it with a man unless she was bombed."

Jayne's career was in decline by the mid-1960s, when she was killed in a freak car accident near New Orleans, in 1967.

Dean Martin

Marilyn's costar in the ill-fated *Something's Got to Give*. He was the former singing partner of comedian Jerry Lewis, one of the most popular teams ever—it lasted for ten years and sixteen movies. Martin was also a charter member of Frank Sinatra's famed Rat Pack.

Twentieth Century–Fox signed Lee Remick to replace Marilyn, but Dean Martin pointed out that he had costar approval, and that he had signed to star with Marilyn. *Only* Marilyn.

Marilyn was very touched by his loyalty, and they discussed doing another project together. However, time ran out for her. Born in 1917, Dean Martin died in 1995.

Inez Melson

The calm, protective Inez Melson was Marilyn's business manager from 1952 to 1962. She also acted as conservator to Marilyn's mother Gladys Baker, even visiting her in various hospitals. She testified in Marilyn's divorce from DiMaggio that she had seen Joe push Marilyn away.

Inez Melson contested Marilyn's will, claiming that beneficiaries Lee Strasberg and Marianne Kris had used undue influence in being named as such in the will.

There is a photo of Inez Melson at Marilyn's funeral on page 152 of John Kobal's *Marilyn Monroe, A Life on Film*. She died in 1986.

Arthur Miller

"She's got more guts than a slaughterhouse."

—*Arthur Miller*

Acclaimed playwright, novelist, and screenwriter, Arthur Miller was born in New York in 1915. His Pulitzer Prize–winning play, *Death of a Salesman* (1949), made his reputation. *The Crucible* (1953) and *A View from the Bridge* (1955) solidified it.

Marilyn wed Arthur Miller, her third husband, on June 29, 1956, in White Plains, New York; and again, in a traditional Jewish marriage rite, on July 1, in upstate Katonah, New York. They were fighting in front of others by the beginning of 1958. During their marriage, Marilyn became pregnant twice but miscarried each time.

Miller began writing the screenplay for *The Misfits*, from his short story, as a gift or a tribute to his wife. As their marriage soured, the screenplay reflected the couple's misery. Miller wrote lines for Marilyn to say that she might have said in real life. Marilyn felt betrayed. Their imminent divorce was announced on November 11, 1960.

In February of 1964, less than two years after Marilyn's death, Arthur Miller's autobiographical play *After the Fall* was produced in New York City. In this critically-condemned drama, the Arthur Miller character admits finding the Marilyn character near death from an overdose of sleeping pills—and feels grateful that his ordeal with her is almost over.

In 1990, after nearly thirty years of marriage to his third wife, photographer Inge Morath, Arthur Miller still couldn't shake Marilyn out of his mind. He wrote an original screenplay for the movie *Everybody Wins*. Debra Winger stars as "an unfathomable woman, a beauty abused yet noble, a liar and near-psychopath who overpowers men and then slips away, unreachable, tormented, tormenting.... It is the Marilyn of Miller's autobiography." (David Denby, *New York* magazine, February 5, 1990)

Berniece Miracle

Marilyn's half-sister (same mother, different fathers), Berniece was born in 1919, in the beach community of Venice, California, the daughter of Gladys Monroe and John Baker. Gladys filed for divorce in 1921, and, two years thereafter, John Baker took Berniece and her brother Jack and moved to Kentucky.

Seven years later, Gladys gave birth to Norma Jeane (father unknown). The two sisters met for the first time in 1944, when eighteen-year-old Norma Jeane visited her foster sister Bebe Goddard in West Virginia, and then went to Tennessee to see half-sister Berniece.

Berniece visited Marilyn in New York in 1961, and Marilyn visited her in Florida when she went there to see ex-husband Joe DiMaggio.

The following year, Joe DiMaggio summoned Berniece to California to help him with Marilyn's funeral arrangements.

In her book *My Sister Marilyn*, Berniece notes that her last name, Miracle, should be pronounced as to rhyme with tire (page 80).

Robert Mitchum

Screen tough-guy Robert Mitchum (1917–1997) knew Marilyn when she was Norma Jeane Dougherty, as he worked with her husband Jim at Lockheed Aircraft factory in Van Nuys, California. Years later, he costarred with Marilyn in *River of No Return*, a western that did little for either of their careers, but did create a long-lasting bond between the two actors.

Robert Mitchum was interviewed continually after Marilyn's death in 1962. He appeared in many of the documentaries, usually recounting the same stories. And yet, over thirty years later, Mitchum's name is in the introduction to Matthew Smith's book, *The Men Who Murdered Marilyn*—with an alarming story no one had heard before. Mitchum recalls the night of May 19, 1962, when Marilyn was to sing "Happy Birthday" to "Mister President."

> "She came up to my hotel room and told me that she was not going to Madison Square Garden. I convinced her that she must go and took her down to the lobby into a swarm of Secret Service agents. Later she called me and seemed anxious to talk to me. For some shallow and selfish reason I regarded her concern as trifling and begged off. I never saw her again.
>
> "After her death I had a long luncheon with [Monroe publicist] Pat Newcomb in Washington, D.C., at which time she told me, 'Marilyn *really* wanted to talk to you.' I have never shed the guilt I felt at hearing that."

Raise your hand if you believe in this story.

Yves Montand

French actor (1921–1991) who had a highly publicized affair with Monroe, while starring opposite her in the Hollywood musical *Let's Make Love*. The coupling was scandalous, because both parties were married to others at the time: Marilyn to Arthur Miller, Montand to French actress Simone Signoret.

Earl Moran

One of the great pinup illustrators. Vargas, Petty, and Moran made pinup illustration a respectable and collectable art form.

Earl Moran hired Marilyn from the Blue Book Agency in 1946. She posed for him off and on for the next four years. He usually took photos of her, which he used as reference for his pinup illustrations.

Forty years later, in January 1987, *Playboy* magazine published some of Moran's nude photos of Marilyn.

Evelyn Moriarty

"Friends were the most important thing to Marilyn."

—*Evelyn Moriarty*

Marilyn's stand-in—with her same five-foot-five-and-a-half-inch height and coloring—on *Let's Make Love*, *The Misfits*, and the unfinished *Something's Got to Give*. The two became good friends. After Marilyn's death, Evelyn became one of her champions, always quick to set the record straight.

Evelyn had been working as an Earl Carroll showgirl when director George Cukor hired her for *Let's Make Love*.

She says that she never saw any evidence that Marilyn was involved with the Kennedys. And she never saw or heard of "ex-husband" Robert Slatzer until years after Marilyn's death.

Evelyn can be seen in published photos from the birthday party on the set of *Something's Got to Give*, looking very much like Marilyn.

Eunice Murray

When Marilyn began sessions with the psychiatrist Dr. Ralph Greenson, he recommended that she hire a friend of his, fifty-nine-year-old Eunice Murray, as her housekeeper and companion.

Marilyn's friends right away saw the situation, but it took Marilyn awhile to understand it—that Mrs. Murray was there as Dr. Greenson's agent, to report back to him on Marilyn's behavior.

On the night of August 4, 1962, an alarmed Mrs. Murray called Dr. Greenson, who rushed over and found Marilyn dead. What was it that alarmed Mrs. Murray? She told different, conflicting stories, and couldn't explain why. She even said, "I wouldn't swear to my version at all."

Patricia Newcomb

Marilyn's personal press representative, she was with Marilyn on the day she died. There are many who feel that Patricia Newcomb *knows what really happened.*

The unofficial (but carved-in-stone) take is that the Kennedys supposedly earned Newcomb's silence by giving her a job in the U.S. Information Agency after Marilyn's death.

Thirty years later, Pat Newcomb responded to this allegation to syndicated columnist Liz Smith, on March 10, 1992:

> "The Kennedys never gave me a dime, never offered me anything, and never made a job available to me! On the afternoon of the night Marilyn died, I had been with her, but her psychiatrist advised me to go home, because he wanted to talk to

her. I did go home and was awakened at four in the morning by the lawyer Mickey Rudin. He told me Marilyn was dead— an overdose. I rushed to Marilyn's house. It has been printed that I saw her body, but I never did. The press was there, and I *did* become overwrought and yell at them, calling them 'vultures.' Then I went home, knowing no more about how Marilyn had died than anyone else.

"I spent the next forty-eight hours tied to my phone, fielding calls from all over the world, saying to reporters what I believed to be true—that Marilyn had died of an accidental overdose. It could easily have happened. I have never believed she meant to kill herself. Everybody who knew her in that last year knows she was in just about the best physical shape of her life. She was also in a positive mood then, except for small things."

Dr. Thomas Noguchi

Coroner and chief medical examiner of Los Angeles County in 1962; a forensic pathologist, he combines medical science with detective skills. He conducted the autopsies on Marilyn Monroe, Sharon Tate, Robert Kennedy, six members of the Symbionese Liberation Army, John Belushi, and many others.

He says that the medical evidence plus Monroe's psychological profile all indicate suicide. (See Part 4, Chapter 23, "How Did Marilyn Die?")

Sir Laurence Olivier

Olivier is usually identified as the greatest actor of our time. Born in Dorking, England, in 1907, the son of a clergyman, he was knighted in 1947, and in 1971 became the first actor honored with the title "Lord."

He married actresses Jill Esmond (1930–1940), Vivien Leigh (1940–1960), and Joan Plowright (from 1961 until his death in 1989).

He played Shakespeare and won Oscars, he played great romantic dramas (*Wuthering Heights*, United Artists, 1939; *Rebecca*, United Artists, 1940; *Lady Hamilton*, United Artists, 1941), and he made more than his share of movie rubbish. He excused himself by saying, "Nothing is beneath me if it pays well. I've earned the right to damn well grab whatever I can in the time I've got left."

He was probably slumming when he agreed to *The Prince and the Showgirl*, not suspecting what lay in store for him. But Marilyn won again, with a lovely performance, while Olivier gave perhaps the worst film performance of his career.

Sir Larry and Marilyn did not get along during the making of this film in England. He writes of being humiliated by her rudeness (*Confessions of an Actor*), and she was devastated by *his* rudeness (Colin Clark, *The Prince, the Showgirl and Me*).

Fred Otash

"Mr. O"—a "colorful Hollywood private eye"—Fred Otash was allegedly involved in the wiretapping of Marilyn in 1961—hired by the Mafia, Jimmy Hoffa, maybe even Joe DiMaggio. Take your choice. And on August 5, 1962, actor Peter Lawford hired him to "to remove anything incriminating" to JFK and RFK from Marilyn's home.

As a private eye, he prowled Hollywood in a chauffeured Cadillac full of "little sweeties," and worked for celebrity lawyers like F. Lee Bailey, Jerry Geisler, and Melvin Belli, and both major political parties. His detective career ended in 1959 when he was convicted of conspiracy to drug a racehorse.

He once told the *Los Angeles Times* that he never discussed his activities because "I didn't see any purpose in getting involved...I'm not getting paid. I'm not writing a book."

At the time of his death, however, in 1992, he had just written a book, titled *Marilyn, Kennedy and Me* (which has yet to appear). A four-pack-a-day smoker, Otash was said to have died of natural causes.

Louella Parsons

One of the most powerful Hollywood columnists, back when they had power, Louella (1880–1972) was an early promoter and defender of Marilyn. When Marilyn wore Travilla's curve-hugging gold lamé gown to an awards dinner, Joan Crawford called a press conference to denounce Marilyn's "burlesque show." Marilyn responded by appearing on Louella's national radio show. The thing that hurt the most, said Marilyn at her most disarming, was that she'd always admired Miss Crawford for being such a wonderful mother—"Who better than I knows what that means to homeless little ones?"

May Reis

Marilyn's secretary in New York, 1957–1960. She had been secretary to director Elia Kazan, and then to Marilyn's future husband, playwright Arthur Miller.

Journalist friend W. J. Weatherby described May Reis as "a small, mild woman, respected for her loyalty to liberal causes even when they were lost causes."

There is a photo of May Reis with Marilyn in Jim Spada's *Monroe: Her Life in Pictures*, page 172.

Ralph Roberts

Marilyn's physical therapist. A tall, handsome, soft-spoken southerner, Roberts was always on call to give Marilyn a massage to help her sleep.

He had met Marilyn at the Lee Strasbergs' in 1955 as an acting student and friend of the family. Roberts had performed on Broadway in *The Lark* with Julie Harris and Boris Karloff in 1955, and had trained the actor who played the masseur (a character based on himself) in the Broadway production of *Will Success Spoil Rock Hunter?*

Truman Capote quotes Marilyn (in "A Beautiful Child") referring to Roberts as "practically my sister"—another reason to question Capote's honesty per his descriptions of Marilyn.

Norman Rosten

Poet, novelist. Photographer Sam Shaw first brought Marilyn to the Rostens' apartment in Brooklyn Heights in 1955, to get out of the rain. Norman Rosten and his wife Hedda became two of Marilyn's closest friends. In her will, Marilyn left $5,000 for the education of the Rostens' daughter, Patricia.

The son of Russian immigrants, Rosten was raised in Coney Island and lived in Brooklyn most of his life. He began writing at Brooklyn College, where he won a playwriting scholarship to the University of Wisconsin. He published several volumes of poetry, two novels, several plays, and magazine pieces. He wrote the screenplay for Arthur Miller's *A View from the Bridge*, a drama set on the Brooklyn waterfront.

In 1973, Norman Rosten published *Marilyn: An Untold Story*, a personal memoir. "We saw her with her hair down when she was relaxed and funny, lonely and depressed. It's the story of Marilyn reduced to human size, the opposite of myth." Rosten told Marilyn's story at greater length in *Marilyn Among Friends*, with two hundred photos by Sam Shaw.

Rosten published three Marilyn poems under the umbrella title of *For Marilyn Monroe*. Here is the one called "Sunday Morning."

Who killed Norma Jean?
  I, said the City,
  As a civic duty
I killed Norma Jean.

Who saw her die?
  I, said the Night,
  And a bedroom light,
We saw her die.

Who caught her blood?
  I, said the Fan,
  With my little pan,
I caught her blood.

Who'll make her shroud?
  I, said the Lover,
  My guilt to cover,
I'll make her shroud.

Who'll dig her grave?
  The Tourist will come
  To join in the fun.
He'll dig her grave.

Who'll be chief mourners?
  We who represent
  And lose our ten percent,
We'll be chief mourners.

Who'll bear the pall?
    We, said the Press,
    In pain and distress,
We'll bear the pall.

Who'll toll the bell?
    I, screamed the Mother,
    Locked in her tower,
I'll pull the bell.

Who'll soon forget?
    I, said the Page,
    Beginning to fade,
I'm first to forget.

Jane Russell

Buxom leading lady; Marilyn's costar in *Gentlemen Prefer Blondes*. The press printed all the obvious stories about "the battle of the bulges" and the anticipated cat fights, but Jane and Marilyn fooled them by becoming friends.

Jane Russell was studying acting with the great Maria Ouspenskaya, when her chest and other measurements came to the attention of Howard Hughes, who was looking for someone as well-endowed as she was for his Billy the Kid movie *The Outlaw* (United Artists, 1943).

Born in 1921, Jane survived the years of corny bosom jokes and proved she had staying power.

Hal Schaefer

Twentieth Century–Fox musical director, he worked with Marilyn on *Gentlemen Prefer Blondes* (1953), *River of No Return* (1954), and *There's No Business Like Show Business* (1954). She

Marilyn is Vicky, the hat-check girl who wants to be a singer, in *There's No Business Like Show Business* (1954). Donald O'Connor joins the Navy because he thinks she doesn't love him. [Photo courtesy of J. C. Archives.]

saw that he received screen credit for *Show Business*—an achievement so highly regarded that he was loaned to Warner Bros. to work with Judy Garland on *A Star Is Born* (but without credit) that same year.

In July of 1954, Hal Schaefer tried to kill himself, apparently over complications from his affair with Marilyn. The details have never emerged.

Joseph M. Schenck

One of the giants of the motion picture industry, and a cofounder of Twentieth Century–Fox. At the time Schenck was introduced to Marilyn Monroe, in 1947 or 1948, Schenck was in his late sixties; his title at Twentieth Century–Fox then was executive producer. He was known to take an interest in attractive women, and to help them professionally, in return for "considerations." He brought Marilyn to the attention of poker buddy Harry Cohn, head of Columbia Pictures, who cast her in the low-budget musical *Ladies of the Chorus*.

Joseph M. Schenck (1878–1961) was born in Rybinsk, Russia. The family went to New York when Joseph was thirteen. He went to work in a drugstore and later bought it.

Joseph and his brother Nicholas went into the entertainment business, catering to holiday crowds at Paradise Park in upper New York. They did so well they bought Palisades Park in New Jersey. There they met Marcus Loew, and the three went into business together: real estate, vaudeville, nickelodeons, motion pictures.

In his earlier moviemaking years, Schenck had under contract Evelyn Nesbitt Thaw, Fatty Arbuckle, the three Talmadge sisters, and Buster Keaton. He married the beautiful Talmadge sister, Norma (1897–1957). They separated in 1926, but he continued to manage her silent-movie career until the introduction of sound ended it.

Leon Shamroy

"She got sex on a piece of film like Jean Harlow."

—*Leon Shamroy*

One of the great Hollywood cinematographers. Leon Shamroy (1901–1974) shot Marilyn's first screen test, at Twentieth Century–Fox, in July 1946. Shamroy's enthusiasm helped convince studio head Darryl F. Zanuck to sign the newcomer. Later, Shamroy was cinematographer for *There's No Business Like Show Business*.

In his long career, Shamroy collected twenty-one Oscar nominations and won four—for *The Black Swan* (Twentieth

Century–Fox, 1942), *Wilson* (Twentieth Century–Fox, 1944), *Leave Her to Heaven* (Twentieth Century–Fox, 1946), and *Cleopatra* (Twentieth Century–Fox, 1963).

Frank Sinatra

This singer, actor, and living legend was born in 1915. He and Marilyn were romantically involved over a period of time, but the relationship apparently worked better as a strong friendship.

Sinatra first met Marilyn and started dating her in late 1953, when they were to costar in *Pink Tights*, a remake of Betty Grable's 1943 film, *Coney Island*. Marilyn chose to go on suspension rather than do the film, and the project was permanently shelved.

There were various other projects with Marilyn and Sinatra as the dream cast (see Part 2, Chapter 8, "The Films of Marilyn Monroe"), but it wasn't meant to be.

Sidney Skolsky

The popular Hollywood columnist who covered the Hollywood scene from Schwab's drugstore on Sunset Boulevard. He was an early friend and promoter of Marilyn. He had known 1930s movie star Jean Harlow and saw that the two actresses had similar goals and ambitions.

Born in New York in 1905, Skolsky had produced *The Al Jolson Story* (Columbia, 1946) with Larry Parks, and *The Eddie Cantor Story* (Warner Bros., 1953) with Keefe Brasselle. He and Marilyn planned a film biography of Jean Harlow; they were discussing it the week of her death.

Skolsky's 1975 memoir, *Don't Get Me Wrong—I Love Hollywood*, has a sizable chapter on Marilyn. Sidney had the endearing quality of being shockable. He was shocked when Marilyn returned from her honeymoon to Joe DiMaggio and told him she was going to marry Arthur Miller. Sidney was shocked, and sad, when Marilyn told him of her affair with the President. Skolsky died in 1983.

Robert F. Slatzer

No one familiar with Marilyn Monroe had ever heard of Robert F. Slatzer until 1974, when he published *The Life and Curious Death of Marilyn Monroe*. Since then there's no avoiding the man. He appears in all the interview shows, the investigative series, and the television documentaries about Marilyn, identified as her ex-husband, lover, longtime confidant.

His books claim that Robert Kennedy was involved in Marilyn's death. In turn, they inspire other books which repeat his claims, and these books in turn create more television documentaries. Slatzer's own story of his alleged marriage to Marilyn became a TV movie (*Marilyn and Me*). He starred in his own reenactment of Marilyn's last days (*The Marilyn Files*). He hired a detective to investigate Marilyn's death—which produced books by the detective.

It was Slatzer who came up with the infamous "press conference": Marilyn told Slatzer (and no one else) that she was calling a press conference for August 6, 1962, to "blow the lid off this whole damn thing," to tell the world that the Kennedys had promised to marry her and then reneged. She was also going to reveal state secrets that the Kennedys had told her about nuclear testing, and plots to kill Castro, et cetera.

It is this improbable press conference that becomes the heart of the conspiracy theories: Marilyn had to die because she was going to stand before the television cameras and discredit the Kennedys and reveal secrets they had told her about plans to kill world leaders, and about nuclear testing.

So she had to be silenced. Over and over, Slatzer growls, "She was a little girl that knew too much."

There seems to be no limit to what Slatzer seemingly knows about Marilyn. In 1996 he held his own press conference and this time revealed that Marilyn had to die because she knew about the government cover-up of "the Roswell incident"— when a flying saucer crashed in the desert outside Roswell, New Mexico, in 1947; the government supposedly has hidden the incredible truth from the world.

In 1993, Donald Spoto published *Marilyn Monroe: The Biography*, which contains an enormous amount of research and fact-finding that earlier biographies of Marilyn had not attempted. Spoto deals at length with Slatzer's assorted claims and, to many people, effectively counters them all.

However, apparently it's too late.

The books and the documentaries and the wild claims keep coming. (See Part 4, Chapter 7, "How Did Marilyn Die?" for details on these claims.) Add it up and you'll see that the murder and cover-up of one frail little woman involved hundreds of people—the Los Angeles Police Department, major government agencies, the Mafia, the media, the telephone company, everyone who was close to Marilyn, every ambulance company in Santa Monica.

And now...flying saucers.

It's enough to make you call your own press conference.

Emmeline Snively

She operated the Blue Book Model Agency in Los Angeles, which groomed young ladies for modeling and the movies. She saw the possibilities in Norma Jeane and quickly found work for her.

She called upon her agent friend Helen Ainsworth to arrange a meeting for Norma Jeane at Twentieth Century–Fox.

Emmeline Snively is interviewed for the 1962 CBS-TV documentary *Marilyn Monroe, Why?* and in the 1966 ABC-TV documentary *The Legend of Marilyn Monroe* (aka *Portrait: Marilyn Monroe*).

Allan "Whitey" Snyder

Veteran Twentieth Century–Fox makeup artist who did Marilyn's makeup for her initial screen test, in July 1946. He later became a mentor, teaching her makeup techniques, and was one of her closest friends.

Marilyn made Whitey promise "when I die or anything like that," that he would make her look good. And he said, "Sure, bring the body back while it's warm." She gave him a money clip inscribed *"Whitey Dear: While I'm still warm—Marilyn."* (There's a photo of the money clip on page 210 of Lawrence Crown's *Marilyn at Twentieth Century–Fox*.)

When it came time, on August 7, 1962, Whitey made her look good, but he needed a bottle of gin to help him get through the ordeal.

There is a photo of Whitey with Marilyn in the Norman Rosten–Sam Shaw book *Marilyn Among Friends*, on page 23. There are photos of Whitey Snyder and Agnes Flanagan with Marilyn in both of the George Barris photo collections (*Marilyn*; *Marilyn: Her Life in Her Own Words*).

Lee Strasberg

Easily the most controversial individual in Marilyn's life. Love him or shoot him. As a famed acting coach and mentor, he encouraged Marilyn's passion to be a serious actress. He was a friend and father figure (but virtually ignored his own talented daughter, Susan). He and wife Paula helped shape Marilyn's strong screen performances in *Bus Stop, The Prince and the Showgirl,* and *Some Like It Hot.*

However:

Donald Spoto succinctly describes the influence and control of the Strasbergs which, along with that of Marilyn's psychoanalyst Marianne Kris, was keeping Marilyn in a childlike dependence, dwelling on the past without giving her direction into the future. "She was going nowhere very quickly—at least partly because she had not one but two therapists; in reality, she needed not to be enclosed within a prison of self-examination but freed from it." (Donald Spoto, *Marilyn Monroe: The Biography*)

Secondly, Lee Strasberg made outrageous financial demands on Marilyn Monroe Productions (i.e., Marilyn Monroe). For *Bus Stop*, Lee insisted that Paula Strasberg be paid $1,500 per week for coaching Marilyn—more than any other crew member. For *The Prince and the Showgirl*, he demanded $2,500 per week for Paula plus expenses and overtime. Marilyn quickly agreed to his demands. Donald Spoto bluntly refers to Strasberg's "Method-acting portrayal of Sammy Glick"—a name synonymous with greed.

Thirdly, the Strasbergs spoke of Marilyn someday playing Lady Macbeth, but at the same time they kept her from projects which might have been good for her.

For example, in 1961, Marilyn and Strasberg proposed a TV dramatization of *Rain*, the story of Sadie Thompson—a role that had been portrayed memorably by Tallulah Bankhead, Joan Crawford, Rita Hayworth, and others. However, Strasberg insisted on directing. When the network held out for a more experienced TV director, Strasberg canceled the project.

Also, film producer Martin Jurow spoke with Marilyn about the upcoming movie production of *Breakfast at Tiffany's*. Marilyn insisted she was the only one to play Holly Golightly. Within forty-eight hours, the Strasbergs advised Jurow that Monroe would not be available, that they would not have her play a lady of the evening.

Lee Strasberg (1901–1982) was born Israel Strassberg in Poland. The family emigrated when he was seven, so he grew up on the Lower East Side of New York. He studied improvisation with Richard Boleslavsky, a student of the Russian acting theorist Konstantin Stanislavsky (1865–1938). In 1931, Strasberg cofounded The Group Theater, which produced plays that reflected the problems of contemporary society. The actors and directors who got their start here include Elia Kazan, Stella Adler, John Garfield, Lee J. Cobb, and Franchot Tone.

In 1947, The Actors Studio debuted, bringing with it the much-debated and -maligned Method, by which an actor prepares for a role by digging into his own subconscious. The Actors Studio was founded by Elia Kazan, Cheryl Crawford, and Robert Lewis; Strasberg joined it a year later and soon became the guiding force there.

Strasberg made his screen acting debut in *The Godfather Part II* (Paramount, 1974).

He was married three times: to Nora Z. Krecaun, Paula Miller, and Anna Mizrahi, his widow.

Paula (Miller) Strasberg

"I think we're doing Paula a disservice. For all we know, she's holding this picture together."

—*John Huston, discussing* **The Misfits**

Paula replaced Natasha Lytess as Marilyn's on-set acting coach. Paula was born in 1911 and died in 1966. She was Marilyn's guiding force in *Bus Stop*, *The Prince and the Showgirl*, *Some Like It Hot*, *Let's Make Love*, and *The Misfits*.

There is a photo of Marilyn with the Strasbergs in which Paula actually looks attractive, on page 180 of James Spada's *Monroe: Her Life in Pictures*.

There is an amazing description of Paula in sycophancy to
Marilyn, in *The Prince, the Showgirl and Me* by Colin Clark
(pages 102–3).

David Wayne

David Wayne shared screen credit with Marilyn in four films—
more than any other actor: *As Young as You Feel, We're Not
Married, O. Henry's Full House*, and in *How to Marry a Millionaire*. Marilyn thought of him as an old friend and a good-luck
token.

Wayne (1914–1995) was a versatile actor, appearing in film,
TV, and theater, and was the first recipient of a Tony Award for
acting, as the leprechaun in the Broadway play *Finian's
Rainbow* (1947). He won a second Tony for the Broadway play
The Teahouse of the August Moon (1954), as the clever Sakini.
In addition to his movie credits, he appeared in several TV
series in the 1970s.

Billy Wilder

The genius film director who probably did the most with and for
Marilyn—he cowrote and directed two of her best films, *The
Seven Year Itch* and *Some Like It Hot*. He also helped immortal-
ize her, with a steady stream of hilarious and sardonic stories
over the years about the extreme difficulties of working with her
on a studio set. (For some of his comments see Part 1, Chapter
3, "The Best Things Others Said.")

Wilder was born in Vienna in 1906. He studied law for a
year and then abandoned it to become a reporter. He wrote
screenplays on the side, and collaborated on the scripts of
numerous features. Being Jewish, he left Germany in 1933
ahead of the Nazi takeover.

In collaboration with various writers—Charles Brackett, Raymond Chandler, I. A. L. Diamond—he produced a long list of critical and commercial hits. These include *Double Indemnity* (Paramount, 1944), *The Lost Weekend* (Paramount, 1945), *Sunset Boulevard* (Paramount, 1950), *Ace in the Hole* (Paramount, 1951), *Witness for the Prosecution* (United Artists, 1958), and *The Apartment* (United Artists, 1960).

Darryl F. Zanuck

Hollywood mogul, the hardworking genius behind the success of Twentieth Century–Fox...but actually he had little to do with Marilyn Monroe's success.

Zanuck (1902–1979) entered the movie business in 1923 as a screenwriter at Warner Bros., where his screenplays for Rin Tin Tin helped make the canine a movie star. By 1928, he was in charge of production. He resigned from Warner Bros. in 1933 and started a new company, Twentieth Century Pictures, with movie executive Joseph M. Schenck. In 1935, they merged with Fox, with Zanuck as chief of production for the new company.

From 1935 to 1952 (when he became an independent producer), Zanuck was the guiding force behind Twentieth Century–Fox's exceptional output of movies—historical dramas, westerns, musicals, social dramas—all made with attention to strong screenplays and high technical polish.

Marilyn Monroe made her first screen test for Twentieth Century–Fox in July 1946. Zanuck was not especially impressed, but deferred to the enthusiasm of cinematographer Leon Shamroy and studio talent director Ben Lyon. Marilyn was signed to a standard six-month contract, which was later renewed for six more months. Then she was dropped from the roster.

In 1950, agent/lover Johnny Hyde arranged for Marilyn's second screen test. Zanuck felt that the only suitable role available was that of a secretary in *As Young as You Feel*.

Everything changed in May 1951, when Marilyn made one of her traffic-stopping entrances at a film exhibitors' party in the studio commissary. Zanuck was not present, but Spyros Skouras, president of Twentieth Century–Fox, was. When the shouting died down, the exhibitors wanted to know in what films the blonde bombshell was going to be featured.

Zanuck had no choice. He ordered that Marilyn be put in every available movie that had a part for a blonde. Ironically, despite Zanuck's indifference, Marilyn was going to be a star.

Yet even after the stunning three-in-a-row success of *Niagara*, *Gentlemen Prefer Blondes*, and *How to Marry a Millionaire*, Zanuck refused to renegotiate her contract—Jane Russell was paid $150,000 for *Blondes*, and Marilyn received only $15,000.

Next she was cast in the mediocre western, *River of No Return* and the interminable musical *There's No Business Like Show Business*. The projects that were announced for her were even less appetizing. After *The Seven Year Itch*, Marilyn walked away from the studio, went to New York, and formed Marilyn Monroe Productions with photographer Milton Greene—she had to in order to save herself professionally.

After heated legal hassles that finally gave Marilyn the contract and the respect she deserved, she returned to Twentieth Century–Fox in February 1956. Zanuck resigned a month later...and didn't return until 1962, the year Marilyn was fired by the studio.

It has been suggested that Zanuck had no interest in Marilyn's career because of prior claims on her body. Zanuck was an advocate of the casting–couch route to stardom—and Marilyn had already sought aid and protection from executive Joseph M. Schenck, and talent agent Johnny Hyde. When Zanuck met Marilyn, she was already "Joe Schenck's girl" and "Johnny Hyde's girl."

Always a good sport with the photographers, Marilyn displays the latest in skiwear: swimsuit plus fur gloves and boots. An arcade card from 1947. [Photo courtesy J. C. Archives.]

Connie Gilchrist as Madame Adelaide and her traveling "showgirls"—Marion Marshall, Joyce MacKenzie, Marilyn Monroe, and Barbara Smith, in *A Ticket to Tomahawk* (1950). [Photo courtesy of Photofest.]

Marilyn makes her show-stopping entrance in *Niagara* (1953), as cheating wife Rose Loomis, wearing a dress the color of sin. [Photo courtesy of Photofest.]

Marilyn competes with Niagara Falls, and wins, in this publicity pose for *Niagara* (1953). [Photo courtesy of Photofest.]

Marilyn's most purely enjoyable performance, as gold digger Lorelei Lee in *Gentlemen Prefer Blondes* (1953). Jane Russell plays her level-headed friend Dorothy. [Photo courtesy of Photofest.]

A sexy pinup from 1953, probably a publicity photo for *Niagara*. [Photo courtesy of Photofest.]

Marilyn reclines to make a phone call, the better to fill the Cinemascope screen in *How to Marry a Millionaire*. [Photo courtesy of J. C. Archives.]

Monroe and Russell, as Lorelei and Dorothy, dress for dinner in *Gentlemen Prefer Blondes*. [Photo courtesy of Photofest.]

Publicity fun for *How to Marry a Millionaire* (1953), a romantic comedy about three models determined to marry money. [Photo courtesy of Photofest.]

Marilyn sings "Diamonds Are a Girl's Best Friend," wearing a gown by Travilla that's a marvel of engineering. [Photo courtesy of Photofest.]

"All you want is my money," Marilyn tells husband Rory Calhoun in the Cinemascope western *River of No Return*. Robert Mitchum costarred. [Photo courtesy of Photofest.]

After three hits in a row—*Niagara, Blondes, Millionaire*—Fox cast Marilyn in a western, *River of No Return* (1954). She sings four songs, so it's not a total waste. [Photo courtesy of J. C. Archives.]

A scene from the musical tribute to Irving Berlin, *There's No Business Like Show Business* (1954), which Marilyn had to do to get *The Seven Year Itch.* Here she tempts Donald O'Connor. [Photo courtesy of J. C. Archives.]

Tom Ewell looks on as Marilyn enjoys the breeze heard 'round the world, in *The Seven Year Itch* (1955). [Photo courtesy of Photofest.]

Top left: Putting on a happy face for the cameraman: Marilyn with costar Tony Curtis on the set of *Some Like It Hot* (1959). [Photo courtesy of J. C. Archives.]

Top right: The second film of Marilyn Monroe Productions: *The Prince and the Showgirl*. Marilyn more than held her own with costar Laurence Olivier. [Photo courtesy of Photofest.]

Left: Don Murray as the virginal cowboy, Bo, woos Marilyn as Cherie the chantoozie, in *Bus Stop* (1956). [Photo courtesy of Photofest.]

Zanuck didn't get there first and so wasn't interested.

(Also see Part 4, Chapter 22, "Marilyn's Biographies," for an extensive list of books on Marilyn's life, by topic.)

Chapter 15

Marilyn's "Escorts to Immortality"—or Making Love to the Camera

◆

A Biographical Directory to Marilyn's Still Photographers

"No other famous movie actress is so scattered or blank on the screen. If that seems too dismissive, look instead at the authority she had and the pleasure she took in stills."

—*David Thomson, Film Comment (September-October 1982)*

"She talked about these photography sessions [with Richard Avedon] the way other actors talk about their films."

—*Simone Signoret, Nostalgia Isn't What It Used To Be*

Slim Aarons

He photographed Marilyn wearing a deep red negligee with a black lace wrapper, surrounded by stacks of fan mail. The photo first appeared in *Town and Country* magazine in 1952.

Slim Aarons was born in New Hampshire. He was a photographer for *Yank* magazine during World War II. He later became a society photographer, and then covered Hollywood for *Life* magazine.

Interview magazine featured him in the September 1981 issue. His memory of Marilyn was not favorable: "Marilyn was always available for anything. She loved photographers in those days. She knew that they could help her."

Eve Arnold

Although born (in 1913) and raised in America, Eve Arnold became one of England's most notable photojournalists. Her work appears mainly in the London *Sunday Times*. She is a member of Magnum, the cooperative of international photographers.

She spent considerable time with Marilyn, and published a selection of her Marilyn photos in *The Unretouched Woman*, in 1976. In 1987, she published *Marilyn Monroe: An Appreciation.* Eve Arnold writes:

> "Our quid pro quo relationship, based on mutual advantage, developed into a friendship. The bond between us was photography. She liked my pictures and was canny enough to realize that they were a fresh approach for presenting her—a looser, more intimate look than the posed studio portraits she was used to in Hollywood."

Eve Arnold had six photo sessions with Marilyn:

- In Mount Sinai, Long Island, 1952, with Marilyn reading James Joyce's *Ulysses*, in an abandoned children's playground. Also, Marilyn in leopard skin, crawling through muddy marsh grass like a primal, predatory animal. This is this author's nomination for the dumbest MM photo ever.

- Marilyn's one-day trip to Bement, Illinois, in 1955, to help the town celebrate its Abraham Lincoln centenary.
- The 1956 press conference for *The Prince and the Showgirl* at the Plaza Hotel. A dress strap conveniently broke.
- Two months on the set of *The Misfits* in 1960, as a Magnum photographer.
- Studio session, Los Angeles, 1960: Marilyn in a white two-piece swimsuit, looking tired.
- 1961: Marilyn with her hairdresser Kenneth, for a *Good Housekeeping* story on him.

Richard Avedon

Born in 1923 in New York, the son of Russian immigrants, he had his first Rolleiflex when he was eighteen. He spent World War II taking portraits of his fellow servicemen. After the War, he enrolled in classes taught by Alexey Brodovitch, art director of *Harper's Bazaar* and a great teacher of photography.

By 1944, Avedon was married to a beginner model, and working for *Harper's Bazaar*, then under the editorship of Diana Vreeland. In his work, he pioneered the use of the stark white background. He began violating the "no manipulation" rules of photography, cropping images, altering everything.

Avedon shot publicity photos for *The Prince and the Showgirl*, photographing Marilyn in feathers on a sofa (pages 186–7, *Marilyn and the Camera*). *Marilyn by Moonlight* has an unretouched shot from this session which shows more of Marilyn than in the official photos.

Over an eight-week period in 1958, in New York City, Avedon photographed Marilyn as the "Fabled Enchantresses." This striking color photo essay of Marilyn as Theda Bara, Clara Bow, Marlene Dietrich, Lillian Russell, and Jean Harlow appeared in the special entertainment issue of *Life*, December 22, 1958.

Ernest Bachrach

Chief portrait photographer at RKO, Bachrach shot publicity photos of Marilyn for *Clash by Night*. Bachrach's photo of Marilyn in a black lace negligee is widely reproduced, but often credited to others. *Marilyn Monroe unCovers* features it on pages 142–4.

Bachrach was born in New York City, in 1899. He studied with professional photographers while still in high school. He entered the film industry as a "still man" with the Famous Players–Lasky studio on Long Island in 1920. It was young Bachrach who introduced the notion of taking scene "stills" while the players were in action, thus saving thousands in production costs. The system was quickly adopted for use throughout the industry.

William DeMille brought Bachrach to Hollywood in 1925 to institute his system in the Paramount studios. Assigned to the Gloria Swanson unit, he became her favorite photographer and made most of the portraits of this star which appeared during the height of her fame.

When RKO was organized in 1927, Bachrach was hired as head of the still-camera department and chief portrait photographer.

Ed Baird

He marketed two 5"x7" Marilyn photos in 1973, advertising them in various collectors' publications. The photos are of a smiling Marilyn, in white sweater and light shorts, with a shoulder bag.

In a letter accompanying the photos, Baird tells of a 1944 war-bond golf tournament at a Los Angeles country club, with "stars" in attendance. He asked the beautiful young blonde if he could take her picture. He looked at the photos many years later and recognized the model.

The photos were probably taken later than 1944; they could have been taken at the August 1947 celebrity golf tournament at Cheviot Hills Country Club, in West Los Angeles, when Marilyn was caddy for actor John Carroll. In 1944, Marilyn was living in North Hollywood and working at the Radioplane Company factory in nearby Burbank. Besides, she was not a blonde until the winter of 1945.

James Haspiel's *Young Marilyn* has a similar photo (page 15) which may be by Baird, or perhaps by a better photographer.

Baron

Marilyn posed for this British photographer in the summer of 1954. *Marilyn and the Camera* reproduces one of his photos on pages 122–3.

George Barris

A photojournalist whose work has appeared in a number of the top national magazines. On June 29, 30, and July 1, 1962, Barris photographed Marilyn for *Cosmopolitan*, on the beach at Santa Monica, and at a friend's home in North Hollywood. After Marilyn's death, Barris moved to Paris, where he lived for twenty years.

Some of the Barris photos were published in Norman Mailer's *Marilyn* in 1973, but most of them were not widely seen until 1986, when he collaborated with Gloria Steinem on *Marilyn*. This book featured forty-four color and eighty-five black-and-white photos to illustrate Gloria Steinem's biographical essays.

In 1955, Barris published another selection of the 1962 photos in *Marilyn: Her Life in Her Own Words*, with Marilyn's as-told-to memories.

Cecil Beaton

The British-born Cecil Beaton (1904–1980) was a self-taught photographer, specializing in royalty, English eccentrics, movie stars, rock stars, and slim young boys. He also designed sets and costumes, and won Academy Awards for *Gigi* (MGM, 1958) and *My Fair Lady* (Warner Bros., 1964).

Cecil Beaton photographed Marilyn for *Harper's Bazaar* in February of 1956. He wrote of her:

> "Miss Marilyn Monroe calls to mind the bouquet of a fireworks display, eliciting from her awed spectators an open-mouthed chorus of wondrous 'Ohs' and 'Ahs.' She is as spectacular as the silvery shower of a Vesuvius fountain; she had rocketed from obscurity to become our post-war sex symbol—the Pinup girl of an age. And whatever press agentry or manufactured illusion may have lit the fuse, it is her own weird genius that has sustained her flight."

Beaton took one of Marilyn's favorite photos: lying on a bed, hands over chest, holding a dark carnation. This is on page 256 of Norman Mailer's *Marilyn*, page 169 of *Marilyn and the Camera*, and on the cover of Guiles's biography *Norma Jean*. *Marilyn and the Camera* also has Marilyn puffing on a flower stem pretending it is a cigarette (page 170).

Antony Beauchamp

One can't get a better description of Antony Beauchamp than that on the dust jacket of Beauchamp's autobiography *Focus on Fame*:

> "Fame came quickly to Antony Beauchamp and it came in many ways. As a distinguished photographer of beautiful women and society personalities, as the son-in-law of Sir Winston Churchill, and as the producer and director of popu-

lar television shows such as *Fabian of the Yard*, he became well known to millions on both sides of the Atlantic.

"He was thirty-nine when, in August 1957, his suicide wrote a tragic and untimely final chapter...."

Beauchamp came to Hollywood in the early 1950s to photograph new faces, and talent agent Johnny Hyde told him about someone he should meet. He photographed Marilyn in a homemade bikini, "two broad yellow ribbons held together by string." His photos are among the most memorable, and sexiest, of the early Monroe.

Bruno Bernard (Bernard of Hollywood)

"Mine is clean-cut erotic photography."

—*Bruno Bernard*

Bruno Bernard Somer (1912–1987) held a doctorate in criminal psychology from a German university, but fled the country before World War II broke out. He had planned to go to Brazil but saw the movie *San Francisco* (MGM, 1936) and changed his mind. He settled in Los Angeles and opened the Bernard of Hollywood studio at 9055 Sunset Boulevard.

He specialized in glamour portraits and pinups, and was publicity photographer for the Palm Springs Racquet Club for fifty years. He lamented that pinup photography had degenerated into "gynecological" pictures.

Marilyn Monroe unCovers reproduces magazine covers with early Marilyn by Bernard—for *Teen-Age Diary Secrets* (page 13), *Personal Romances* (page 20), and *Prevue* (page 33), five covers of Marilyn in the red *Niagara* dress (pages 34, 35, 39), and in the two-piece white swimsuit (page 94).

Susan Bernard put together a collection of her father's Marilyn photos, thirty in color, almost one hundred in black-and-white, in *Bernard of Hollywood's Marilyn*.

Bruno of Hollywood

To clear up any confusion: Bruno of Hollywood was Anthony J. Bruno, born in Boston. He went to Hollywood in 1919, opened a studio on Hollywood Boulevard, stayed fifteen years, and then went back East, opening a studio in Carnegie Hall.

There is no record of Bruno photographing Marilyn, but who says he didn't? The "lost photographs" are sure to turn up one of these days.

John Bryson

Born in Texas in 1923, Bryson was a still photographer and cinematographer for military training films in World War II. He is mainly associated with *Life* magazine, working as a correspondent or bureau chief, picture editor, or contributing photographer. He was movie unit photographer, and location photographer for *The Brothers Karamazov* (MGM, 1958), *Ben-Hur* (MGM, 1959) and others. He photographed John F. Kennedy for the 1960 presidential campaign posters.

Marilyn prepares for a 1952 photo session at the beach. [Photo courtesy Archive Photos.]

Bryson photographed Marilyn on the set of *Let's Make Love*, for a pictorial feature in *Paris-Match* and for an eleven-page cover feature in *Life*.

His widely reproduced shot of Marilyn being fussed over by Hollywood makeup artists and hairdresser Sydney Guilaroff is on page 270 of *Masters of Starlight*, and on page 185 of Norman Mailer's *Marilyn*. The Mailer book also features Bryson's Marilyn photos on pages 148, 176, 179, and 182–3.

Bill Burnside

A Scottish photographer in Los Angeles, he first photographed Marilyn in February 1946. One familiar series from 1948, often uncredited, has Marilyn frolicking on the beach in Santa Monica, California, wearing red shorts and a blue T-shirt.

Tom Caffrey

He was showcased in the January 1955 *Screen Album* magazine photo feature: "Ten great photographers present MY GREAT-EST PORTRAIT."

Tom Caffrey of Globe Photos found Marilyn seated on a sound-stage, wearing a white bathrobe, quietly studying her lines in a room full of noisy confusion. When she looked up he took a lovely head shot, no expression on her face but an inherent smile.

Leo Caloia

Marilyn and the Camera reproduces an unusual color photo of Marilyn, taken by Leo Caloia at the Ambassador Hotel in Los Angeles in 1946. She was one of seven models for a radio talk show on photo-artistic techniques.

Janice Anderson's *Marilyn Monroe* has a photo of Leo Caloia photographing Marilyn (page 18).

Cornell Capa

The brother of world-famous photographer Robert Capa, Cornell was born Kornel Friedmann in Budapest, Hungary, in 1918. He emigrated to the U.S. in 1937. He was a *Life* photographer from 1946 to 1967, and has been with the Magnum cooperative since 1955. Capa's photographs are described as "clear direct statements about the living."

He was one of the photographers from the Magnum cooperative, each of whom spent two weeks on location with *The Misfits* in 1960.

Norman Mailer's *Marilyn* represents Capa's work with a large head shot of Clark Gable and tearful Marilyn in profile (pages 198–9).

Jack Cardiff

An English cinematographer, born in 1914, noted for his work with color. He made his reputation with the extraordinary color films of the London-based filmmaking team of Michael Powell and Emeric Pressburger: *A Matter of Life and Death* (aka *Stairway to Heaven*) (British, 1946), *Black Narcissus* (British, 1946)—for which he won an Oscar—and *The Red Shoes* (British, 1948).

Cardiff's autobiography, *Magic Hour*, has a twenty-page chapter devoted to Marilyn.

She had been told he was the best in his field, so she asked for him for *The Prince and the Showgirl*. Cardiff says that when he first showed up on the set she acted like a little girl who had just received a special Christmas gift.

An art lover, Cardiff photographed Marilyn with his still camera in a manner to evoke Renoir. One of his photos is reproduced on the cover of *The Unabridged Marilyn*: it's a head shot delicately enhanced by hand coloring, with reddish hair blowing across her face, hiding one eye, on a background of cloudlike white. Seven other Cardiff photos of Marilyn are reproduced in the same book.

Jock Carroll

This Canadian photographer was a photojournalist for Canada's *Weekend* magazine for over twenty years. His photos of Marilyn, taken on location for *Niagara*, show her relaxed and lovely and friendly. Carroll died in 1995; his Marilyn photos were not rediscovered until 1996, when they were published in the book *Falling for Marilyn: The Lost Niagara Collection*. One of Carroll's color photos is on a magazine cover reproduced in *Marilyn Monroe unCovers*, page 131.

Carroll also published photo books on the Olympics and on pianist Glenn Gould. He wrote *The Shy Photographer*, a comic novel featuring a character based on Marilyn.

William Carroll

After David Conover met and photographed Norma Jeane Mortensen at the Radioplane Company factory, in the autumn of 1944, he introduced her to his photographer friend William Carroll.

Carroll operated a film-processing and -printing laboratory in Los Angeles. He paid Conover's friend $20 for a day's modeling on the beach at Malibu, the photos to be used as a display for his company. He unpacked the photos many years later and recognized his now-legend model. Ninety-eight color slides and seven black-and-white prints were sold at auction in 1988.

Marilyn and the Camera reproduces a Carroll color photo, Norma Jeane wearing a red sweater and white shorts with suspenders.

Henri Cartier-Bresson

He photographed Marilyn on *The Misfits* set in 1960, as part of
the Magnum team of photographers.

A man who sought invisibility—for the sake of his photographs—he taped an unprecedented interview on his experience, saying, "I was struck as by an apparition in a fairy tale."

Cartier-Bresson, born in 1908, is often cited as the greatest
living photographer. *Marilyn and the Camera*, page 211, shows
you his genius with a black-and-white photo of Marilyn in gentle repose. Of all the *Misfits* photos, none show a Marilyn this
soft, this lovely.

Edward Clark

He was a photojournalist who spent nearly six decades covering
history around the world. Clark photographed Marilyn in late
1950, at the request of Twentieth Century–Fox publicist Roy
Craft. In 1991, Clark offered a limited-edition portfolio contain-
ing ten 11"x14" photos of Marilyn for $4,495. Individual prints
were offered at $495.

The images shown were those of a photojournalist, not a
glamour photographer.

David Conover

He was an army photographer assigned by his superior officer,
Ronald Reagan, to take photos of the women on the home front
for the men who weren't. He went to the Radioplane company in
Burbank, in autumn of 1944, where he took the first commercial
photos of Norma Jeane Dougherty.

A Conover photo of Norma Jeane appeared on *Yank*, her first
magazine cover. In the summer of 1945, Conover and Norma
Jeane went on a photo safari around the California countryside,

taking many photos (most of them now lost), which ended with them "doing what comes naturally."

Conover (1919–1983) published *Finding Marilyn* in 1981, with a color cover photo and a dozen black-and-whites. Some years after his death, Conover's widow sold fifty-three Marilyn negatives at auction. A Canadian investment group bought them, restored them, and sold them as limited-edition prints— the first time most of the photos had ever been seen in color.

Henri Dauman

He photographed Marilyn as she arrived for the premiere of *Some Like It Hot* in March 1959. His photo is on page 197 of *Marilyn and the Camera*.

Bruce Davidson

A Magnum photographer, born in 1933, Davidson took the photos of MM and Arthur Miller with Yves Montand and Simone Signoret, during the filming of *Let's Make Love*. (A different photo of the Millers and the Montands dining together appears in Norman Mailer's *Marilyn*, pages 180–81.)

He also took his two-week turn on the set of *The Misfits*. Eleven of his photos appear in *Magnum Cinema*.

Andre de Dienes

"Marilyn's success would not have come about if she had not cooperated so whole-heartedly with many photographers. In fact, no girl can succeed in this business unless she poses for any Tom, Dick and Harry photographer." —*Andre de Dienes*

Born in Transylvania (now Romania), he taught himself photography. He came to America in 1938, with the help of

Esquire's Arnold Gingrich, and opened a studio in New York City. Independent film producer David O. Selznick brought him to Hollywood in 1944 to photograph Ingrid Bergman. He later moved there permanently.

De Dienes (1913–1985) was a noted photographer of nudes, publishing twenty-four books on the subject.

He took many photos of Marilyn from 1945 to 1949. Some rate them the best ever taken of Marilyn. His involvement with Marilyn Monroe is documented in his book *Marilyn, Mon Amour.*

Masters of Starlight features the radiant color photo of Marilyn which he called "the sexiest picture I ever made" (page 247). There is also a small photo of de Dienes taken by Marilyn (page 246).

In 1993, Lincoln Mint announced a twenty-four-karat-gold–fitted boxed coffee table book of de Dienes's Marilyn photographs, to sell for $600. The story goes as follows.

> "After she died…de Dienes, apparently inconsolable, buried his negatives in his Los Angeles backyard and vowed they would never be exploited. More than twenty years later, and near death, de Dienes claimed he was visited by Marilyn in a vision and 'guided' by her spirit, he recovered the photographic originals and began the Herculean task of restoring the precious negatives."
> —*New York Newsday, April 30, 1993*

At this writing, the $600 baby is yet to appear. But it's a nice tale, in any case.

Nat Dillinger

One of Hollywood's old-timers, born in 1911, Dillinger spent many years photographing the stars, mostly in candid shots. He headed the Hollywood bureau of World Wide Photos, was on staff at MGM, and worked for King Features Syndicate. His photos have appeared in many national magazines.

In his collection *Unforgettable Hollywood*, Dillinger features two Marilyn photos: in 1947, age eighteen, playing tennis; and in 1953, hugging comedian Danny Thomas at a benefit in Beverly Hills.

Alfred Eisenstaedt

"The father of photojournalism" was born in Poland in 1898. He received his first camera when he was thirteen. He grew up in Germany and became a button salesman. His first professional assignment was photographing Thomas Mann accepting his Nobel Prize in 1929, in Stockholm.

After photographing dictators-in-the-making Adolf Hitler and Benito Mussolini, Eisenstaedt saw the bleak future on the Continent, and emigrated to the United States. He began his lifelong association with *Life* magazine, for which he recorded many of this century's most significant events and people.

Eisenstaedt pioneered candid portrait photography, usually done in natural light. He photographed Marilyn in Hollywood, in 1953, on her patio. She is wearing white pants, and a black turtleneck top. The most familiar shot of the session has her with one hand on left hip, the other on her right thigh, looking into the camera. (It is in *Marilyn and the Camera*, page 87.)

Glenn Embree

American Photo, "Those Who Knew Her," May-June, 1997:

"Embree started his career in films as a set designer for MGM, but soon switched to still photography. The California native opened his own photography studio and shot virtually all the female stars at MGM and Paramount. He also did fashion, portrait, and other types of editorial photography. During World War II, he was stationed in India and China as a photo reconnaissance officer in the Army Air Corps. After the war he returned to Hollywood photography, did extensive advertising photography, and also shot television films and industrial shorts."

Embree is represented in the Marilyn issue of *American Photo* by a photo of a seminude Marilyn, from the swimming-pool sequence in *Something's Got to Give.*

John Engstead

His career began in Paramount Pictures' publicity department when, without permission, he appointed himself art director for a photo session with Jean Harlow. The photos were a success; by 1929 Engstead was Paramount's art supervisor, in charge of all stills. He went independent in 1941.

Engstead (1909–1983) photographed Marilyn only once, for a 1947 fashion shoot: she is wearing a strapless white gown, holding her arms up. It's in *Marilyn and the Camera*, page 37.

In his 1978 photo collection *Star Shots*, Engstead writes, "Her pretty face was all that impressed me and I still wonder what transformed this sweet young thing into the superstar and sex symbol of a generation."

Elliott Erwitt

A Magnum photographer, he was part of the team assigned to cover the making of *The Misfits* on location in Nevada.

Erwitt photographed the familiar group shot: Marilyn seated in front, legs crossed, wearing Jean Louis's white dress with red cherries; Clark Gable and Montgomery Clift are on either side of her. Director John Huston stands behind Marilyn, actor Eli

Wallach sits on a ladder. In the back, husband/screenwriter Arthur Miller stands on a stepladder, while producer Frank Taylor stands under it. Norman Mailer's *Marilyn* has this famous group shot in color (page 187).

Born in Paris in 1928, Erwitt studied filmmaking before turning to still photography. His work is notable for its offbeat humor.

Ed Feingersh

Marilyn spent the last week of March 1955 in New York City. On March 24, she attended the Broadway debut of Tennessee Williams' *Cat on a Hot Tin Roof* with photographer Milton Greene. On March 30, she rode a pink elephant at a benefit given by the Ringling Brothers and Barnum and Bailey Circus in the old Madison Square Garden building on Eighth Avenue.

New York photojournalist Ed Feingersh covered this week, on assignment from *Redbook* magazine to shoot "A Day in the Life of Marilyn Monroe." Only a few of the photos appeared in

Candid shot of Marilyn preparing for a photo session. Probably from 1952. [Photo courtesy Archive Photos.]

the magazine. The rest of the shots were discovered after Feingersh's death. One hundred of the photos were published in *Marilyn: March 1955.*

The photos show Marilyn primping before the mirror, at the theater, at a party at El Morocco, reading the show-business trade papers, riding the subway with Dick Shepherd, at Costello's restaurant, in a mood at the hotel, a trip to Elizabeth Arden's beauty salon, a costume fitting for riding an elephant.

The collection includes "the Chanel photo," which is the author's nomination for the definitive Marilyn photo—for all it says about Marilyn and sexuality and America's infatuation with the woman: The outrageousness of the quart-size bottle of Chanel. The abandonment with which she splashes it on. The languorous fingers at her cleavage. The peek at the perfect bosom below the fingers. The superfluous dress strap that's fallen away. The metallic glints from the gold lamé dress. The otherworldly quality of the impossible silver-white hair. And, finally, the immense pleasure and satisfaction Marilyn takes in seeing this vision of perfection reflected in the mirror.

This is the one photo to have if you could have only one.

John Florea

He began as a news photographer for the *San Francisco Examiner.* As a staff photographer for *Life* magazine, 1943–1946, he covered World War II in Europe (both VE day and VJ day), and the motion-picture industry. He became a movie director by watching the directors he photographed, beginning with industrial films. He directed seven feature films, and more than three hundred television shows, winning an Emmy for a 1974 ABC-TV *Afterschool Special.*

Florea photographed Marilyn in 1953, wearing pink long-john underwear, before a fireplace (*Masters of Starlight*, page 191).

The September 1951 *Esquire* has a terrific color gatefold from the long-john session: an unbuttoned bust shot, Marilyn lying on a fur rug.

Another familiar Florea photo is of a reclining, sultry Marilyn, her breasts spilling out of her swimsuit top. It's on pages 104–5 of *Marilyn and the Camera*. It's also on the cover of Matthew Smith's *The Men Who Murdered Marilyn*, incorrectly attributed to Sam Shaw.

Allan Grant

A *Life* magazine photographer based in Los Angeles, the last to shoot Marilyn Monroe—probably on July 9, 1962—for the Richard Meryman interview in the August 3, 1962, *Life* magazine.

Grant also did the terrific photo of Jayne Mansfield in a swimming pool surrounded by dozens of Mansfield dolls.

Milton Greene

Marilyn: "Why, you're nothing but a boy!"
Milton: "Well, you're nothing but a girl!"

Born in New York, in 1922, Milton Greene began taking photos at age fourteen. He was apprenticed to photojournalist Elliot Elisofon, and then was assistant to fashion photographer Louise Dahl-Wolfe. Along with Avedon, Beaton, Penn, and Parkinson, Greene is credited with making fashion photography a fine art. A number of his fashion photos are collected in *Of Women and Their Elegance*.

Marilyn and Milton Greene met in 1953 when he came to Los Angeles to photograph her for a *Look* magazine cover story. In November 1954, Greene took Marilyn back to New York with him; at the end of the year they announced the formation of Marilyn Monroe Productions, to make motion pictures starring her.

Greene quit his job, mortgaged his home to cover Marilyn's expenses, and became her Svengali; he is credited with making *Bus Stop* and *The Prince and the Showgirl* critical successes.

Then Arthur Miller persuaded Marilyn that she no longer needed Milton—and suddenly the photographer was scorned by the woman to whom he had devoted considerable talent, time, and money. The partnership ended in bitterness—Marilyn's lawyers bought out Milton's stock in Marilyn Monroe Productions for $100,000, his entire remuneration for two years of work.

Marilyn later admitted to Milton Greene's wife Amy that "Arthur was taking away the only person I ever trusted, Milton," but that she felt powerless to withstand her husband. In other accounts, Milton was exploiting Marilyn for his own ambition. He also encouraged her use of pills and alcohol.

Milton Greene returned to work as a photographer, but the madness of Marilyn's world had done its work. He became bitter and disillusioned, as his dependence on alcohol and drugs increased. He died in 1985.

Milton's Marilyn was published in 1994, a collection of photos taken from 1953 to 1956. Marilyn was never again so beautiful, so sexy, so appealing.

Ernst Haas

"[*The Misfits*] was like being at your own funeral."

—*Eve Arnold*

He was one of the Magnum photographers on the set of *The Misfits* in 1960. Eve Arnold quotes Haas in *Marilyn Monroe: An Appreciation*:

"'All the people who were on the film were misfits—Marilyn, Monty, John Huston, all a little connected to catastrophe, Gable not saying much, just himself being Gable.

"'It showed how some stars are like stars in heaven that are burned out. The light is still traveling, but the star is gone.

They were actors playing out the allegory, then seeing it in life. It was like being at your own funeral.'"

One picture is worth a thousand words: Norman Mailer's *Marilyn* has a Haas photograph of Arthur Miller with Marilyn's empty chair beside him. *Magnum Cinema* has Haas photos of the horse-roping sequence. *Marilyn and the Camera* offers two photos from this sequence.

Ernst Haas (1921–1986) was born in Vienna. His widely published photos showing the aftermath of World War II earned the admiration of Robert Capa, who invited him to join the distinguished Magnum photo cooperative.

He became known for his photojournalism, and his innovative use of color. Haas photographed the original "Marlboro Man" cigarette campaign, and was special stills photographer for the movies *Hello, Dolly!* (Twentieth Century–Fox, 1969) and *Little Big Man* (National General, 1970).

Philippe Halsman

"With every step her derriere seemed to wink at the onlooker."

—*Philippe Halsman*

He had three encounters/photo sessions with Marilyn, the results all published in *Life* magazine.

- In 1949, he made "screen tests" of eight studio starlets, with a photo series of Marilyn showing her range of emotions.
- Marilyn's first *Life* cover portrays her seductively in a white dress. *Marilyn and the Camera* features a contact sheet with twelve photos plus a full-page photo for the *Life* session.
- In 1955, Halsman had fun with his "jumping" photos, saying that a person jumping cannot control his muscles or his expressions, so the real person is revealed. *Marilyn and the*

Camera has two jumping photos, pages 190–1. Norman Mailer has them on pages 72–3.

The Unabridged Marilyn notes that Halsman later produced a film about Marilyn's life.

Halsman (1906–1979) was born in Riga, Latvia, and emigrated to America in 1940. He studied electrical engineering but taught himself photography.

Bob Henriques

A Magnum photojournalist, Henriques photographed Marilyn in New York during the filming of *The Seven Year Itch*. Four of these photos—of Marilyn leaning out a window waving at the crowd below—appear in *Magnum Cinema*, on pages 122–3. An

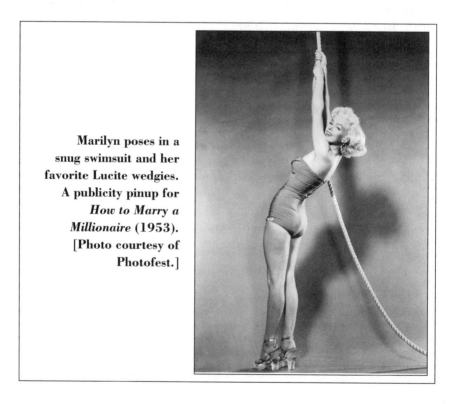

Marilyn poses in a snug swimsuit and her favorite Lucite wedgies. A publicity pinup for *How to Marry a Millionaire* (1953). [Photo courtesy of Photofest.]

atmospheric shot of Marilyn applying makeup appears in the Norman Mailer book, page 93.

An off-camera Henriques photo is in the Marilyn issue of *American Photo*, May-June 1997, which says that he left photography in the late 1960s, opened a wax-products factory in Jamaica, and now lives in Miami.

Potter Heweth (also spelled "Hueth")

He was a friend of David Conover's. Norma Jeane Dougherty posed for him with a Dalmatian, in a sweater and a plaid skirt, in a tight sweater and a pair of slacks, and on a bale of hay. Heweth showed his photos to Emmeline Snively, who ran the Blue Book Model Agency in the Ambassador Hotel, near downtown Los Angeles. Snively sent Norma Jeane a note suggesting that she was wasting her time working in a defense plant.

George Hurrell

"The Rembrandt of photography," he is generally acknowledged as the greatest of the Hollywood portrait photographers.

George Hurrell (1904–1992) opened a photography studio in Los Angeles in 1927. His first celebrity portraits were of movie star Ramon Novarro, and then cinema queen Norma Shearer. MGM's production supervisor Irving G. Thalberg made him head of MGM's portrait gallery from 1930 to 1933, where he created his most famous photos of the MGM greats. He then alternated between having his own studio, to being under contract at Warner Bros. and then Columbia Pictures, to working in various areas of freelance photography.

George Hurrell reported on a 1952 session with Marilyn at his studio: "She did the same routine Harlow did. [She arrived] wrapped in something and, all of a sudden, let it fall. I presume the idea was to get you going. Well, they were exhibitionists."

Joseph Jasgur

Photographer Joseph Jasgur photographed Marilyn in 1946. In the late 1980s, he started telling the story of Marilyn's six toes, and in 1991, he published the photos to prove it: *The Birth of Marilyn: The Lost Photographs of Norma Jean.*

There is a two-page color photo in his book that appears to show just such an abnormality. But turn the pages for the black-and-white photos that clearly show only five toes.

Joseph Jasgur was the official photographer for the legendary Hollywood Canteen, where the stars entertained and served coffee to the American soldiers on leave during World War II. He has a major archive of photos taken at the Canteen.

Tom Kelley

"Marilyn knew that the ['Golden Dreams'] shot was going to be big. It was as if she sensed that something was about to happen in her career."

—*Tom Kelley*

Tom Kelley (1914–1984) began learning photography as a teenager apprenticing in a New York studio. He worked for the Associated Press, assisting veteran photojournalists, and was one of many covering the Lindbergh kidnapping (1932).

He ventured to Hollywood in the early 1930s, was hired by moviemaker David O. Selznick, and began photographing the stars. He worked for nearly five decades, establishing himself as a major artist with photos represented in many galleries and museums.

Kelley will be remembered always for the session he had in his studio, on May 27, 1949, of Marilyn Monroe stretched out nude on a red velvet drape. The "Golden Dreams" photo is one of the most familiar, most widely reproduced images in the history of photography.

- Kelley shot twenty-four nudes of Marilyn that evening: "Golden Dreams" and "A New Wrinkle" being the only two used for calendars. The unused transparencies were either stolen from Kelley's file cabinet, or borrowed by Marilyn and not returned. Another version has Marilyn giving them to Joe DiMaggio as a wedding present.

- Marilyn was identified as "the nude blonde in the calendar" on March 13, 1952. The calendar had first been issued for 1951, without anyone spotting Marilyn. But then it was reprinted for 1952—because the image was so popular—and Marilyn's escalating fame in movies and on magazine covers made it inevitable that she would be eventually be recognized.

- Kelley never made a nickel from all the many times the photo appeared in *Playboy*—in its first issue (December 1953) and in many anniversary and special issues since. *Playboy* publisher Hugh Hefner had purchased his print directly from the calendar company.

Douglas Kirkland

Born in Toronto, Canada, he worked at a studio in Niagara Falls taking wedding and passport photos. From 1961 to 1972, he was staff or freelance photographer for an assortment of magazines— *Life, Look, Paris-Match, Stern, Town and Country*—shooting Hollywood celebrities.

He was twenty-six and nervous when he photographed Marilyn in 1962, she being naked under silk sheets and apparently inviting him to join her. The Kirkland color photo, shot from above, of Marilyn lying in bed and clutching a white pillow, is very famous.

Kirkland has published two collections featuring Marilyn: *Light Years* and *Icons*, in which he takes his familiar photographs and experiments with computer-manipulated images.

He laments that photography in the 1990s does not have the slice-of-life truth of 1960s photography, because today's stars routinely have photo approval and decide what the public can see.

Bill Kobrin

He was hired by Twentieth Century–Fox to document the skirt-blowing stunt for *The Seven Year Itch*—when Marilyn stood over a subway grating, letting the breeze blow her white dress up, revealing her panties—while hundreds of invited photographers clicked away.

In 1989, Kobrin exhibited his Marilyn photos in a Simi Valley, California, gallery, offering sets of ten different photos for $10,000 per set.

Kobrin had begun as a messenger for the Associated Press. His first professional photography assignment was the Harlem riots. He also covered the Korean War. At the time of the exhibit, Kobrin operated a photographic consultancy in Los Angeles for television production companies.

Gene Kornman

Gene Kornman was stills and portrait photographer for Harold Lloyd until the screen comedian's semiretirement in the mid-thirties. Kornman then joined the newly formed Twentieth Century–Fox film studio as a portrait photographer. Kornman and coworker Frank Powolny took all the portraits of the lot's stars until Kornman retired in the sixties.

Kornman took the classic photo of Marilyn in the gold lamé gown designed by William Travilla for *Gentlemen Prefer Blondes*. It is on page 143 of John Kobal's *Hollywood Color Portraits*, on page 111 of *Marilyn Monroe and the Camera*, on page 125 of *Marilyn: Her Life and Legend*, ad infinitum. An unfamiliar photo from Kornman's photo session is on the cover of this book.

Earl Leaf

American Photo magazine, May-June, 1997, describes Leaf as one of the more colorful, if lesser known, Marilyn photographers. Leaf (1905–1980) was an ex-cowboy and onetime sailor who went on to a newspaper career in China in the 1930s. By the 1950s he was in Hollywood turning out photos and stories about the town's various celebrities, including the blonde starlet Marilyn Monroe. Leaf saw her at a dull party. She suggested they go live it up somewhere else, but Leaf was green then and said no. His Marilyn pictures were published in the book *Marilyn from Beginning to End* in 1997.

George Miller

He took the photographs for George Carpozi, Jr.'s, interviews with Marilyn, in January 1955, in New York City. The photos appeared in Carpozi's book *Marilyn Monroe: Her Own Story*.

Richard C. Miller

A would-be movie actor, Miller began photographing his fellow actors, and eventually offered his portraits for sale. In 1939, he gave up acting and became a full-time freelance photographer. He declined a union job at Columbia Pictures and remained independent, freelancing for various magazines.

He photographed Norma Jeane Dougherty in 1946, for *True Romance* magazine, as a young bride, wearing her own wedding gown, and holding a prayer book borrowed from the photographer's wife.

Masters of Starlight features the color photo of Marilyn as a bride (page 205), and a small photo of the photographer with Marilyn (page 198). *Marilyn Monroe unCovers* reproduces the *True Romance* magazine cover (page 86). The Marilyn tribute issue of *American Photo* has an unfamiliar color photo of Marilyn: a bust shot, in a swimming pool, looking up at the camera.

In 1959, Miller photographed Marilyn again, for *Some Like It Hot*, in the bosom-revealing black slip she wears in the sleeping-car sequence.

Jimmy Mitchell

This Twentieth Century–Fox staff photographer was on the set of *Something's Got to Give*. He is responsible for the famous images—taken during the wardrobe test shots—of a slim and radiant Marilyn. He photographed Marilyn's on-set birthday party on her last day of work—June 1, 1962—before she was fired from the picture.

Mitchell also photographed Marilyn's nude swim for the movie, along with promoter Lawrence Schiller and William Woodfield. Mitchell sold his rights to Schiller.

Earl Moran

Moran studied illustration at the Chicago Art Institute and at the Art Students' League in New York, in the late 1920s and early 1930s. He became one of the top pinup and glamour artists, along with Vargas and Petty.

He often took photographs of his models as the basis for his illustrations, which were reproduced on calendars and in girlie magazines such as *Flirt*, *Wink*, and *Giggles*. Moran hired Marilyn through the Blue Book Model Agency in Los Angeles; she posed for him periodically from 1946 to 1949.

The January 1987 issue of *Playboy* featured eight nude photos taken by Moran in 1946, as references for his pinup illustrations. Marilyn was nineteen at the time.

Inge Morath

She was one of the nine Magnum photographers who spent two weeks in the heat of Nevada, covering the production of *The Misfits*. She met Marilyn's husband Arthur Miller at the time; they were married after Miller and Monroe were divorced.

Inge Morath said Marilyn was

"…a photogenic phenomenon. The thing about her was you could not photograph her badly if you tried. Once she was ready [to be photographed] she would surpass the expectations of the lens. She had a shimmering quality like an emanation of water, and she moved lyrically."

Marilyn prepares to show photographers around *Photoplay* magazine's "Dream House." This was her first appearance in *Photoplay*, as part of a publicity stunt for *Love Happy* (1949). [Photo courtesy of Archive Photos.]

Inge Morath was born in 1923, in Graz, Austria, and moved permanently to America in 1962.

Inge Morath's *Misfit* photos are in Norman Mailer's *Marilyn*, on pages 189 and 202, and on page 166 of *Magnum Cinema*.

Arnold Newman

He photographed Marilyn with writer Carl Sandburg for *Life* magazine. Some of these photos are in Norman Mailer's *Marilyn* on pages 212, 214, and 217.

Leif-Erik Nygards

He was an assistant for Bert Stern's "Last Sitting" session with Marilyn in July 1962, at the Bel-Air Hotel in Los Angeles. Nygards took the photo of Marilyn, lying on a bed, with her pubic hair visible. *Playboy* magazine published this photo in January 1984 as "the last nude photo of Marilyn."

Frank Powolny

Born in Vienna, he was the son of the court photographer to Emperor Franz Josef. The family emigrated to Nebraska in 1914. Powolny arrived in Los Angeles in 1920, where his first industry job was in a film laboratory.

He was at Fox (later Twentieth Century–Fox) from 1923 until he retired in 1966. He photographed one of the century's most famous images: studio star Betty Grable in swimsuit, hands on hip, her shapely back to us, looking back over her shoulder. It became *the* pinup shot of World War II with GIs.

Powolny (1901–1986) documented every annual Academy Awards ceremony from 1929 to 1963.

Marilyn and the Camera has a number of powerful Powolny photos, including a publicity still for *The Asphalt Jungle*, "prob-

A 1950 publicity photo in the style of George Hurrell, but by Frank Powolny, the Fox staff photographer who shot many of the most famous photos of Marilyn. [Photo courtesy Twentieth Century–Fox/Archive Photos.]

ably by Powolny," of Marilyn in a low-cut black gown, with a weird starburst thing behind her (page 57). Page 58 is a Hurrell-type pose, Marilyn with her head thrown back, blonde hair spilling over the chair.

On page 73 is a sultry 1953 head shot of Marilyn holding a cigarette. (The cigarette has been removed in some reproductions.) Page 77 is a gleaming bare-shouldered Marilyn. Page 79 is one of the top ten Marilyn photos, the "take me if you're man enough" smolder immortalized in Andy Warhol's silk-screen series.

Masters of Starlight, page 114, has a photo of Powolny photographing Marilyn.

He took the last known still photographs of Marilyn on the set of *Something's Got to Give*.

Willy Rizzo

Marilyn and the Camera has a Rizzo color portrait study of Marilyn, taken for *Paris-Match* magazine (Spring 1962).

Lawrence Schiller

He is the colorful and controversial photographer-entrepreneur who photographed Marilyn's nude swim for *Something's Got to Give*, and sold the photos around the world.

Called "the P. T. Barnum of still photography," Schiller is blind in one eye. He makes up for his handicap with his ambition and his knack for being in the right place at the right time. For example, he got the last interview with Jack Ruby (the man who shot Lee Harvey Oswald); he obtained the rights to Death Row murderer Gary Gilmore's story. He published a book on murdered film actress Sharon Tate, based on an exclusive interview with killer Susan Atkins, one of Charles Manson's gang. He also masterminded O. J. Simpson's book *I Want to Tell You*.

Schiller's nude swimming stills are in pages 219–20, and 222–5 of Norman Mailer's *Marilyn*. A Schiller head shot of Marilyn in white fur hat and collar is on page 208. A grief-stricken Joe DiMaggio at his ex-wife's funeral is on page 260.

Sam Shaw

A New York photographer, he was often used by Twentieth Century–Fox for advertising photography.

In 1954, movie coproducer Charles Feldman hired Shaw to document the making of *The Seven Year Itch*. It was Shaw's idea to stage the skirt-blowing publicity stunt in Manhattan for the press. (While many photographers have published photos of Marilyn with her white dress blowing up, the actual photos used to publicize or advertise the Twentieth Century–Fox film are by Sam Shaw, and were taken inside the studio.)

Sam Shaw has published *Marilyn Monroe as the Girl* (a candid picture-story of the making of *The Seven Year Itch*, a 1955 paperback original), *The Joy of Marilyn*, and *Marilyn Among Friends*.

In *Marilyn Among Friends*, on page 79, is the very familiar and wonderful photo of Marilyn dancing with Clark Gable at the party celebrating completion of *The Seven Year Itch*, at Romanoff's in Beverly Hills. In *her* book, Feldman's wife Jean Howard says that she borrowed Sam Shaw's camera and took this photo. So it's also in her photo collection, *Jean Howard's Hollywood*, credited as her photo.

Bert Stern

"She hadn't just scratched out my pictures, she'd scratched out herself."

—Bert Stern

Brooklyn-born Bert Stern started in the mailroom at *Look* magazine, where an art director saw something in the upstart kid and taught him design. Stern was struck by the elegance of *Vogue* magazine, and the notion that photography could be "a way to sort out the junk of the world." He led advertising into a "photographic impressionism," starting in 1953 with his surprising photos for Smirnoff vodka—going to Egypt to photograph the driest of dry martinis at the base of a pyramid.

Stern was at the top of his profession in 1962 when he asked *Vogue* to ask Marilyn if she would pose for him. He wanted to take the definitive photo of Marilyn, and he wanted to photograph her nude.

Fifteen minutes after she arrived (five hours late), she pulled off her sweater (but not her slacks). Stern promised to retouch the scar from her gallbladder operation, knowing he would not. He photographed her through different colored scarves, for twelve hours.

Near dawn, all her clothes were off, and he switched to black-and-white film, photographing her through a black-and-white scarf.

Vogue liked the pictures, but wanted more—they wanted fashion shots. Stern flew back to L.A., and arranged a new three-day session: Marilyn in a chinchilla coat, a white veil, a black wig, black dresses.

Pat Newcomb, Marilyn's personal publicist, reminded Stern that her client had photo approval. So Stern sent Marilyn one-third of the color, and all the black-and-white contact sheets. When they were returned, Marilyn had crossed out over half of them. She used a black marker on the contact sheets, but she had X-ed out the color transparencies with a hairpin, destroying them.

Thirty years later, Stern reclaimed the images with computer technology—in which a computer artist digitally "lifted" the X's off and replaced them with new dots of unblemished skin.

Phil Stern

Born in Philadelphia in 1919, he was both a staff and freelance photographer for numerous newspapers and magazines. In addition, he was the unit photographer for more than two hundred feature films. He was hired by Frank Sinatra to photograph John F. Kennedy's 1961 presidential inauguration, and also photographed screen idol James Dean.

Stern caught an apprehensive Marilyn looking at comedian Jack Benny, at the Shrine Auditorium in downtown Los Angeles, in 1953. This unusual photo is on page 225 of *Masters of Starlight*.

Dennis Stock

This Magnum photographer was part of the diverse group on assignment for *The Misfits* in 1961 (see *Magnum Cinema*, page 57).

Stock was a close friend of screen legend James Dean (1931–1955) and published the photo book *James Dean Revisited* in 1978.

Earl Theisen

This photographer specialized in pinup photos. In the early 1950s, he shot Marilyn wearing a potato sack (after someone said she'd look good in anything).

John Vachon

A *Look* magazine staff photographer for over twenty years, he had over two thousand of his photos published in that journal. The range of his subjects mirrored that of the popular magazine itself, from war to Hollywood celebrities.

Vachon (1914–1975) had an earlier career, from age twenty-four, shooting a pictorial record of the effect of the Depression on rural America, for the Historical Section of the Farm Security Administration.

He photographed Marilyn and boyfriend Joe DiMaggio in 1953 in the Canadian Rockies, when she was filming *Niagara*.

Two of Vachon's Marilyn photos are in the Norman Mailer book, *Marilyn*, on pages 98 and 117.

Seymour Wally

He shot a series of poses of Marilyn with her dog Hugo, circa 1956.

Weegee

Weegee (1899–1968) was born Arthur Fellig, in what is now Poland. He was a self-taught photographer who became famous for his off-guard photos of a colorful and violent New York City.

Marilyn and the Camera has a Weegee photograph of Marilyn puckering up for photographers on arrival at New York's Idlewild Airport in 1955. Weegee later played around with this photo, distorting it and playing other photo lab tricks.

Leigh Weiner

A New York City native, he sold his first magazine photograph while still in high school. From 1949 to 1957, he was a staff photographer for the *Los Angeles Times* and a freelancer for *Life* magazine. From 1957 to 1972, he had his own studio, with the television networks as his principal clients. At the same time, he was a freelance photographer for performing artists, politicians, athletes. His most famous photo may be the surprising shot of French actress Simone Signoret clutching her breasts when she hears she has just won the Academy Award, for *Room at the Top* (Continental, 1959).

Leigh Weiner published *How Do You Photograph People?* in 1982, which contains shots of Marilyn. He self-published *Marilyn: A Hollywood Farewell—The Death and Funeral of Marilyn Monroe* in 1990. In this book he says he also photographed Marilyn in the morgue, that her lips were blue (indicating poison), but that these photos would never be published.

He died in 1993, age sixty-nine, from Sweet's syndrome, a blood disease that resulted from being exposed to radiation when he photographed atomic-bomb tests for *Life* magazine.

Laszlo Willinger

"Even people who had been around and around and around in Hollywood still fell for this 'Help me' pose."

—*Laszlo Willinger*

Born in Budapest, Willinger learned photography from his mother who was a known professional photographer. He opened a studio in Paris, and then Berlin, where over the years he photographed such notables as Marlene Dietrich, Hedy Lamarr, and Sigmund Freud.

He came to America in 1937, and later succeeded George Hurrell as head of the MGM studio portrait gallery. From 1946 to 1954, he had his own photo studio. He worked for forty years with FPG, a New York photo agency.

Laszlo Willinger was interviewed in *L.A. Style* magazine, December 1986:

"When Joan Crawford came into a room, it went quiet. *Everybody* looked. There was something to her. That's what makes a star and Crawford probably understood that better than anyone else. And, when she was in the mood, Marlene Dietrich. Later, Marilyn Monroe and Susan Hayward. I've just run out of names.

"I worked with Marilyn Monroe. A rather dull person. But when I said 'Now!' she lit up. Suddenly, something unbelievable came across. The minute she heard the click of the camera, she was down again. It was over. I said, 'What is it between you and the camera that doesn't show at any other time?' She said, 'It's like being screwed by a thousand guys and you can't get pregnant.'"

Laszlo Willinger (1906–1989) is interviewed in the 1986 feature-length documentary *Marilyn Monroe: Beyond the Legend*, made by the cable TV network Cinemax.

Willinger's photos appeared on many magazine covers. A number are reproduced in *Marilyn Monroe unCovers*: *Foto Parade* (page 94), *Salute* (page 97), *Regal* (page 106), *Scope* (page 119), and *Man to Man* (page 137).

Bob Willoughby

A "specials" photographer hired by magazines, usually *Life* or *Look*, to take special coverage for their exclusive use. He covered over one hundred films, including *A Star Is Born* (Warner Bros., 1954), *Raintree County* (MGM, 1957), *My Fair Lady* (Warner Bros., 1964), and *Catch-22* (Paramount, 1970).

In 1974, Willoughby published *The Platinum Years*, a book of movie-stills coverage, with text by film critic Richard Schickel. In 1993, he published *The Hollywood Special*, a collection of behind-the-scenes photos, all of them fascinating, many quite remarkable. This book includes three photos of Marilyn filming *Let's Make Love*.

Norman Mailer's *Marilyn* includes a Willoughby photo of Marilyn in the *Niagara* red dress at the party given by musician Ray Anthony (page 77). *Marilyn and the Camera* has five more party photos (pages 90–1) and a pensive black-and-white Willinger portrait taken on the set of *Let's Make Love*.

Garry Winogrand

He shot a series of photos of Marilyn for the December 1954 issue of *Pageant* magazine.

Raphael Wolff

In 1946, Wolff hired Norma Jeane Dougherty for a series of Lustre-Creme Shampoo ads ... on condition that she bleach her hair blonde. Norma Jeane reluctantly agreed.

William Read Woodfield

A freelancer, one of three photographers shooting Marilyn's nude swim in *Something's Got to Give* on May 23, 1962.

Jerome Zerbe

Jerome Zerbe (c. 1903–1988) was born in Ohio, graduated from Yale University, and studied art in Paris before turning to photography. During World War II, he was the personal photographer of Admiral Chester W. Nimitz, and recorded the defeat of Japan.

A collection of five hundred Zerbe photos, including two with Marilyn, was published as *Happy Times*, in 1973, with text by Brendan Gill.

> "This country's first—and only—society photographer. For many years he was the official photographer for El Morocco and was instrumental in making it the most famous and successful nightclub on earth. Save for Cecil Beaton and Lord Snowdon in England, no other photographer has ever enjoyed such exceptional entree. A valued guest . . . he has devoted the greater portion of his career to depicting attractive people on delightful occasions."
>
> —*from the dust jacket of* **Happy Times**

◆

The Last "Last" Photos of Marilyn Monroe

May 23, 1962: Marilyn films a swimming sequence for *Something's Got to Give*, wearing a flesh-colored swimsuit. She suggests that she be photographed nude, that it would be good publicity. Freelance photographers Lawrence Schiller and William Read Woodfield join Twentieth Century–Fox staff photographer James Mitchell, shooting the nude Marilyn for an hour.

May: Twentieth Century–Fox staff photographer Frank Powolny—who took dozens of the most familiar photos of Marilyn—takes the last known still photos on the set of *Something's Got to Give*.

June 23–July 12: Marilyn has three photo sessions with photographer Bert Stern, on assignment from *Vogue*.

June 29–July 1: Marilyn is photographed by George Barris, on assignment from *Cosmopolitan*, posing on the Santa Monica beach and in a North Hollywood home.

July 4, 5, 7, and 9: Richard Meryman interviews Marilyn for *Life*. She is photographed by Allan Grant, probably on July 9. The magazine with the interview and photos appears a day or so before Marilyn's death.

AUTHOR'S NOTE:

Marilyn would appear to have been the most willing, generous, and accommodating celebrity of all time in posing for photos with her fans. Amateur snapshots of varying quality—especially from her brief Korean tour in 1954—seem to turn up almost daily. Many of them capture a candid and spontaneous Marilyn every bit as arresting and memorable as the most familiar studio portraits.

(See Part 4, Chapters 18 and 19, for lists of books by Marilyn's photographers and other photo collections.)

Chapter 16

Marilyn in the Tabloids

♦

The Most Outrageous Stories

Our current tabloid sensibility—the world seen as sleaze—has its origins in the Roaring Twenties with the New York *Graphic*, a newspaper that once featured an exclusive photo of Rudolph Valentino entering Heaven. The *Graphic*'s outlandish photos were composited with scissors, glue, a lurid imagination, and an unshakable belief in human gullibility. The computer has largely replaced the scissors-and-glue approach to illustrate apocryphal stories for supermarket tabloids. If computers can turn a raging dinosaur loose on the streets of San Diego, for Steven Spielberg's *The Lost World: Jurassic Park* (Universal, 1997), how simple it must be to put aliens into the company of politicians, and Marilyn Monroe in the arms of Fidel Castro, or another "lover."

Marilyn has been a staple of gossip columns, scandal magazines, and tabloids from the day she made her presence known. She's the subject of more rumors, speculations, and conspiracies—and plain silliness—than any public figure of this century. A favorite tabloid story appeared in the summer of 1997, when, supposedly, the fabled "Four Horsemen of the Apocalypse" were photographed in Arizona, headed this way. But those guys will have to work hard to top some of the stories about Marilyn:

The Chateau Marmont hotel on Sunset Boulevard—self-proclaimed "favorite of the famous." Marilyn and photographer Milton Greene hid out here for ten days in 1949. In 1956, Marilyn had secret weekends here with future husband Arthur Miller while he was supposed to be living in Reno for his divorce. [Photo courtesy of Patrick V. Miller.]

"Marilyn Monroe: The Truth About My Death"
—*The Globe*, April 22, 1980
Startling facts from beyond the grave.

"Marilyn Monroe Is Alive!"
—*The National Examiner*, June 21, 1983
Government agents confine star in insane asylum for twenty-two years.

"Marilyn's Startling New Love Diary Secrets"
—*The National Examiner*, November 22, 1983
She delighted in never wearing underwear.

"Marilyn Was Pregnant with Kennedy's Baby"
—*The National Examiner*, November 7, 1989

"Monroe Made Love to JFK in Bathtub as Peter Lawford Took Pictures"
—*The Star*, June 12, 1990

"Marilyn Monroe Was a Teenage Hooker"
—*The National Examiner*, February 12, 1991
One of her female lovers was another hooker—the notorious Black Dahlia.

"I Murdered Marilyn Monroe"
—*The Weekly World News*, April 30, 1991
Startling deathbed confession.

"Marilyn Was Assassinated by J. Edgar Hoover"
—*Shhh!*—*Globe* Special No. 3, 1991
Gay FBI director was jealous of her affairs with the Kennedys.

"Marilyn Monroe Was a Russian Spy!"
—*The Weekly World News*, September 29, 1992
She romanced JFK and Nikita Krushchev—at the same time.

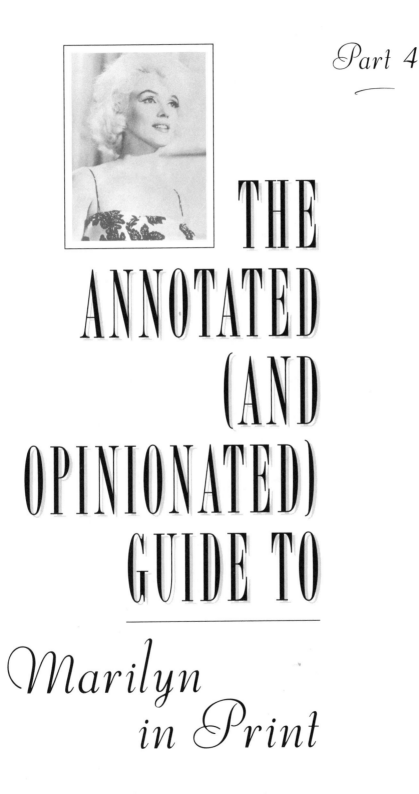

Part 4

THE ANNOTATED (AND OPINIONATED) GUIDE TO

Marilyn in Print

Chapter 17

Marilyn in Her Own Words

(titles listed in chronological order)

- *My Story*, by Marilyn Monroe—an "autobiographical" work ghostwritten by Ben Hecht and others. Unauthorized serialization ran in the *London Empire News*, May 9 to August 1, 1954. First book publication, New York: Stein and Day, 1974.

  *In *Mad as Hell: The Life and Work of Paddy Chayefsky*, author Shaun Considine writes that Ben Hecht spent four months in 1954 ghostwriting Marilyn's memoirs. When the manuscript was completed, Marilyn "wept and wept for joy at what I had written," Hecht told his agent. However, at the insistence of Joe DiMaggio, she refused to allow the book to be published.

  When the book finally appeared in 1974, Milton Greene threatened legal action against anyone who questioned the book's authenticity. Additions had been made to the 1954 version, to make it sound tragically prophetic:

  "Yes, there was something special about me, and I knew what it was. I was the kind of girl they found dead in a hall bedroom with an empty bottle of sleeping pills in her hand."

- "Marilyn's Interview"—with Georges Belmont for October 1960 issue of the French magazine *Marie-Claire*, published in English for the first time in *Marilyn Monroe and the*

Camera. (See Chapter 19, "The Other Photo Collections," for a full description of this book.)

- *As We Are*—a collection of interviews by Henry Brandon, from the London *Sunday Times*: Peter Ustinov, Leonard Bernstein, Frank Lloyd Wright, Walt Kelly, John F. Kennedy, Marilyn Monroe and Arthur Miller. New York: Doubleday, 1961.

  *Note: *Conversations with Henry Brandon* has the same Marilyn interview.

- "Fame may go by and—so long, I've had you"—Richard Meryman's interview with Marilyn, which appeared in *Life* magazine for August 3, 1962—two days before her death. Marilyn asked for the questions in advance, so she had time to think about her answers. Statements from this interview are widely quoted.

  *Same, reprinted in *Life* magazine of August 1992, which also reproduces a contact sheet of MM photos not included in the 1962 issue.

- "A Good Long Look at Myself"—a conversation/interview with Alan Levy which appeared in the August 1962 issue of *Redbook* magazine.

  *Both the Meryman and the Levy interviews are reprinted in the Wagenknecht collection *Marilyn Monroe: A Composite View.*

- *McCall's* magazine, September 1972, featured a selection of Marilyn's poems.

- *Marilyn: An Untold Story*—a memoir by poet friend Norman Rosten, contains some of Marilyn's poems and a few letters. New York: Signet Books, 1973, paperback original.

- *Conversations with Marilyn*—by W. J. Weatherby. Remembered conversations in an Eighth Avenue bar in New York City, with an English journalist who met Marilyn while covering *The Misfits*. New York: Mason/Charter, 1976.

"Sometimes I've got such lousy taste in men . . . . There were times when I'd . . . run into one of these Hollywood heels at a party and they'd paw me cheaply in front of everybody as if they were saying, *Oh, we had her*. I guess it's the classic situation of an ex-whore, though I was never a whore in that sense. I was never kept; I always kept myself. But there was a period when I responded too much to flattery and slept around too much, thinking it would help my career, though I always liked the guy at the time. They were always so full of self-confidence and I had none at all and they made me feel better." (page 144)

"I sometimes felt I was hooked on sex, the way an alcoholic is on liquor or a junkie on dope. My body turned all these people on, like turning on an electric light, and there was so rarely anything human in it." (page 146)

> *Weatherby observes the civil-rights struggle, and wonders why so many blacks identify with Marilyn. A black woman observes, "She's been hurt. She knows what the score is, but it hasn't broken her." Marilyn later describes a secret affair with a young black man (page 129).

- *Marilyn on Marilyn*—compiled by Roger G. Taylor. 128-page hardback, fully illustrated with black-and-white photos. Quotes and comments categorized: "On Childhood," "On Fame," "On Sex," "On Being Late," etc. London: Kwintner Books, 1983.
  > *Same, 1983 Delilah/Putnam edition, New York, quality paperback.
  > *Same, 1988 Comet quality paperback edition. London. (Page 122 has an unfamiliar photo of a nude Marilyn

climbing out of the pool for *Something's Got to Give*...
which turned out actually to be Catherine Hicks from
the TV movie *Marilyn—An Untold Story*.)

- *Marilyn Monroe: In Her Own Words*—edited by Guus
  Luitjers. 7"x10" quality paperback, 128 pages. Profusely
  illustrated with black-and-white photos. New York: Omnibus
  Press, 1991. (Originally published in London.)

- *Marilyn In Her Own Words*—compiled by Neil Grant. A nice-
  ly done oversize 9"x12" pictorial. 64 pages, 58 color and
  black-and-white photos. New York: Crescent Books, 1991.

- *Seductive Sayings: Marilyn Monroe—Her Own Words on Sex,
  Fame, Hollywood, and Marilyn*. Copyright by Herb Boyd. A
  small keepsake/gift book of 30 photos, 58 quotations.
  Connecticut: Longmeadow Press, 1994.

Chapter 18

Marilyn by Her Photographers

Eve Arnold

- *The Unretouched Woman*—photos by Eve Arnold. A photo essay on the lives of women of every economic circumstance—unglamorized, unsentimentalized, unretouched. Includes the *Life* magazine series on Joan Crawford. Marilyn is seen on an unglamorous visit to Bement, Illinois, in 1955, and in a glamour session for *The Misfits* in 1960. 9" x 11" pictorial. New York: Knopf, 1976.

- *Marilyn Monroe: An Appreciation*—by Eve Arnold, who photographed MM on six different occasions over a decade. 10" x 11" pictorial, color and black-and-white photos. New York: Borzoi/Knopf, 1987.

Richard Avedon

"She gave more to the still camera than any actress—any woman—I've ever photographed."

—*Richard Avedon*

- "Fabled Enchantresses"—in the special entertainment issue of *Life* magazine, December 22, 1958, with Avedon's famous photo essay of Marilyn as Theda Bara, Clara Bow,

Marlene Dietrich, Lillian Russell, and Jean Harlow, in full color, costumes, sets. Issue also features essay "My Wife Marilyn," by Arthur Miller.

- *1960 Photography Annual* magazine—with Avedon's Marilyn photos as the "Color Essay of the Year." Avedon tells how he shot the pictures, which took eight weeks.

- *American Photographer* magazine for July 1984—reproducing four of the enchantresses (omitting the Dietrich photo as she had made legal problems), Marilyn as Lillian Russell on the cover. Brief discussion of the photo shoot.

- *The New Yorker* magazine for March 21, 1994—with a fold-out of Marilyn in a sequinned gown, a frieze of unfamiliar photos from a 1957 photo shoot.

George Barris

"The more candid shots show the allure she could project when she wasn't trying to look beautiful."

—*Newsweek, November 10, 1986*

- *Marilyn*—a biography by Gloria Steinem; with photos by George Barris taken in the last few months of Marilyn's life, on the beach in Santa Monica and at a friend's house in North Hollywood. Forty-four color photos, eighty-five black-and-white. New York: Henry Holt, 1986.

- *Marilyn, Her Life in Her Own Words*—as told to George Barris. With over one hundred color and black-and-white photos from the same Malibu–North Hollywood sessions as in his first book. Marilyn supposedly told George her life story as they worked, and George would rush home and write down what he remembered, all of which turns out to be pretty familiar stuff. New York: Henry Holt, 1995.

Antony Beauchamp

She was "just a shy exhibitionist."

—Antony Beauchamp

- *Focus on Fame*—the autobiography of Antony Beauchamp, with sixty-four pages of photographs by the author: Vivien Leigh, Leslie Howard, Ernest Thesiger, Mae West, Sarah Churchill, Audrey Hepburn, Gene Tierney, Grace Kelly, Charles Chaplin, Pier Angeli, and political and social figures of the day. London: Odhams Press, 1958.

    *Marilyn poses in evening gowns, and then asks to be photographed in a homemade bikini: "two broad yellow ribbons held together by a piece of string." It was only then that her true personality emerged—"just a shy exhibitionist." (These photos were widely reproduced: cover of *Movieland*, October 1952; *Photo*, July 1953; *Eye*, August 1953; *Modern Photography*, August 1954; *Male Point of View*, February 1956; *Tab*, December 1956, among others.)

    Beauchamp notices that Marilyn is developing a hint of a German or Austrian accent, and finds the answer in her roommate—Natasha Lytess. He says the accent can be detected in *Niagara*.

Cecil Beaton

- *Cecil Beaton, Photographs 1920–1970*—a retrospective collection, with more than 265 duotone and color photos. Includes the popular shot of Marilyn with the carnation (on the cover of the Guiles bio *Norma Jean*, and a contact sheet with eleven Marilyn photos. New York: Stewart, Tabori and Chang, 1995.

Bruno Bernard

- *Bernard of Hollywood's Marilyn*—images by Hollywood's Great Glamour Photographer. Text and editing by daughter

Susan Bernard. 9"x12" pictorial with thirty color photos, almost one hundred black-and-white. There is argument over whether all the photos here are indeed by Bernard. New York: St. Martin's Press, 1993.

>   *Bernard wrote a serious biography, *Requiem for Marilyn*, published in England in 1986 and difficult to find nowadays.

Jock Carroll

• *Falling for Marilyn: The Lost Niagara Collection*—oversize pictorial, black-and-white photos taken while Marilyn was in town shooting *Niagara* in 1953. Sixty photos, many full- and double-page, Marilyn at work, at play, at rest. Carroll was a photojournalist for the Canadian *Weekend* magazine, in which many of these photos appeared. New York: Friedman/Fairfax, 1996.

>   *Color photos from these sessions have appeared in Canadian Sunday supplements.

David Conover

• *Finding Marilyn*—a romance by David Conover, the photographer credited with discovering Marilyn, in 1945. She was working in a defense plant, when Army photographer Conover showed up to take morale-boosting photos for the boys at war. He says they became lovers and longtime friends. Color cover and twelve black-and-white photos by Conover, plus fifty familiar publicity photos. New York: Grosset and Dunlap, 1981.

• *The Discovery Photos, Summer 1945*—catalogue for the 1991 exhibit and sale of Conover's photos, now painstakingly restored "by a combination of hand-retouching and by computer-driven digital restoration to return the photographs to their original luster," and offered in limited edition printings. 8"x10" booklet with fourteen color photos, five black-and-white. Ontario: Norma Jeane Enterprises, 1990.

*A related video: *Marilyn Monroe: The Early Years* tells the story of the "Discovery" photos, as outlined above. Features interviews with "Joe" Dougherty, Bebe Goddard, Jane Russell, Robert Mitchum, Robert Slatzer, plus reenactments. Ashley Entertainment, 1991, distributed by Maier Communications.

Andre de Dienes

- *Marilyn, Mon Amour*—by Andre de Dienes. He photographed and fell in love with Marilyn when she was an unknown model in 1945. De Dienes's pictures show a fresh and captivating young brunette with a natural smile and grace. 10"x12" pictorial, 113 pages of black-and-white photos, the metamorphosis of a starlet into a magical beauty. New York: St. Martin's Press, 1985.

  "The most stunning, sumptuous photo book available"
  —*The Unabridged Marilyn—Her Life From A to Z*, Riese/Hitchens

Nat Dillinger

- *Unforgettable Hollywood*—a collection of 211 black-and-white photos by Nat Dillinger. Candid photos: the stars at home, eating out, at work, at play. Two photos of Marilyn: in 1947, age eighteen, playing tennis; in 1953, phony hug with Danny Thomas. Also, Jayne Mansfield with Mickey Hargitay, several Clark Gables, Jane Russell as a blonde, many others who figured in Marilyn's life. New York: William Morrow, 1982.

Alfred Eisenstaedt

- *Eisenstaedt's Album: Fifty Years of Friends and Acquaintances*—9"x11" pictorial, more than two hundred black-and-white photos of the most famous faces of the century, together with their handwritten inscriptions to the photographer (which makes it a good autograph reference). Four small photos of Marilyn plus full-page head shot. Also features many who figured prominently in her life. New York: Viking Press, 1976.
   *Reprinted as *Eisenstaedt's Celebrity Portraits*, New York: Greenwich House, 1984.

Ed Feingersh

- *Marilyn: March 1955*—a book of photos by Ed Feingersh documenting a week Marilyn spent in New York: going to the theater, riding the subway, riding an elephant in the circus. Photos rescued by the Michael Ochs Archives, and published here for the first time. Text by Bob LaBrasca. 9"x11" quality paperback. New York: Delta Books, 1990.

Milton Greene

- *Of Women and Their Elegance*—the photographs of Milton Greene, with text by Norman Mailer: "An imaginary memoir... a set of interviews that never took place." Oversize slick pictorial with thirty-six photos of Marilyn, but also Marlene Dietrich, Ava Gardner, Grace Kelly, Sophia Loren, Catherine Deneuve, Audrey Hepburn, and a number of famous fashion models. New York: Simon and Schuster, 1980.

- *Milton's Marilyn*—the photographs of Milton H. Greene. Text by James Kotsilabas-Davis. Directed by son Joshua Greene. Probably the last, and certainly the finest, unpub-

Marilyn and photographer-business partner Milton Greene arrive for the premiere of *East of Eden* (1955). [Photo courtesy of Archive Photos.]

lished photos of Marilyn: 214 color and duotone photos. Marilyn at the zenith of her physical beauty—she never looked so erotic, elegant, or vulnerable, as she did to Milton's unerring eye. 10"x11" size. Printed in Germany by Schirmer/Mosel, the art book publishers. 1994.

Philippe Halsman

• *Hollywood Dreamgirl* magazine, number one, 1955, featuring "Three Encounters With a Love Goddess"—Halsman describes three photo sessions with Marilyn: In 1949, for *Life*, screen-testing eight starlets (these are the familiar range-of-emotion photos); in 1951, when he suggested her for a *Life* cover (her first); and in 1955 when he did another "emotion study" which included the jumping photo. Twelve pages, seven large photos, thirty-six small ones.

An unfamiliar photo from *Bus Stop* (1956), the first film for Marilyn Monroe Productions, and her first chance to show what she had learned from the Strasbergs. [Photo courtesy of Archive Photos.]

• *Philippe Halsman's Jump Book*—"In a jump," Halsman writes, "the subject in a sudden burst of energy, overcomes gravity. He cannot simultaneously control his expressions, his facial and limb muscles. The mask falls. The real self becomes visible." Almost two hundred black-and-white photos of jumping celebrities, with two of Marilyn: alone and with Halsman. Also Brigitte Bardot, Jayne Mansfield, Liberace, et al. New York: Simon and Schuster, 1959.

    *1986 quality paperback reprint by Harry N. Abrams, Inc. New York.

Joseph Jasgur

• *The Birth of Marilyn: The Lost Photographs of Norma Jean* by Joseph Jasgur, text by Jeannie Sakol—10"x12" pictorial, black-and-white and color photos, taken in March 1946, most published here for the first time. A leading celebrity photographer, Jasgur posed Norma Jeane Dougherty in the hills below the Hollywood sign and on Zuma Beach in Malibu. New York: St. Martin's Press, 1991.

*Joseph Jasgur steadfastly maintains that Marilyn had six toes on her left foot. This book contains a two-page color reproduction of the photo that *seems* to show an extra toe, but clearer black-and-white photos in the same book clearly show that she didn't.

Douglas Kirkland

• *Light Years*—three decades photographing the stars. Oversize 12"x16" pictorial, with more than one hundred full- and double-page color photos, with Kirkland's recollections of his encounters with the stars. New York: Thames and Hudson, 1989.

*Marilyn naked under a silk sheet, inviting the photographer to join her: three small photos, full-page photo

February 1956: Marilyn returns to Hollywood after a productive year in New York City. "Is this the new Marilyn?" a reporter asks. "No, I'm the same person—but it's a different suit." [Photo courtesy of Photofest.]

The Ultimate Marilyn

and one double page. Also, Elizabeth Taylor, Brigitte Bardot, Catherine Deneuve, Judy Garland, Jack Nicholson with a burning match in his mouth.

- *Icons: Creativity With Camera and Computer*, by Douglas Kirkland. 10"x10" pictorial with seventy computer-manipulated images in full color, from his famous photographs. Three Marilyn photos. San Francisco: Collins Publishers, 1993.

Earl Leaf

- *Marilyn Monroe, From Beginning to End*, photographs by Earl Leaf, text by Michael Ventura—newly uncovered and mostly unpublished photos by a photographer who had eight sessions with Marilyn, from 1950 to 1962. (The first was May 17, 1950, in the Beverly Hills backyard of agent/lover Johnny Hyde.) Black-and-white photos, fifty-three full-page, twenty-nine smaller. London: Blandford Press, 1997.

    *The text by Michael Ventura is brief but maddening. Can't *any* book on Marilyn be written without dragging in the threatened press conference at which Marilyn was going to denounce the Kennedys (a highly improbable action that only "friend" Robert Slatzer was told about)? Ventura really goes for broke here, describing the secrets the Kennedys had confided to Marilyn as having the power to "change the history of the world." (page 120)

Sam Shaw

- *Marilyn Monroe as The Girl: The Candid Picture-Story of the Making of* The Seven Year Itch—black-and-white photos by Shaw, with a foreword by George Axelrod. New York: Ballantine Books, 1955. Paperback original.

254

*Stanley Kauffmann, editor of this book, wrote of his experiences trying to get Marilyn's approvals in *The American Scholar* magazine, Autumn 1991.

- *The Joy of Marilyn*, photography and commentary by Sam Shaw—9"x11" pictorial, over one hundred black-and-white photos: on the phone, at the beach, on a picnic with Arthur Miller, and life on various film sets including *The Seven Year Itch*. New York: Exeter Books, 1979.

- *Marilyn Among Friends*, photos by Sam Shaw, text by Norman Rosten—two hundred photos, black-and-white and color, many among the most famous of Marilyn: the skirt-blowing shots for *The Seven Year Itch*, in white bathing suit on the beach at Amagansett, shopping in New York City with Arthur Miller, relaxing with Rosten's young daughter, and as the ethereal nymph dancing among the trees. New York: Henry Holt, 1987.

    *Rosten, poet and friend, also wrote *Marilyn: An Untold Story*.

Bert Stern

"Every red-blooded boy in America wanted a few hours alone in a room with Marilyn. I was lucky—I had the camera."

—*Bert Stern*

- *Marilyn Monroe: The Complete Last Sitting*—11"x13" behemoth with quality heavyweight paper, 464 pages with 2,571 color and black-and-white photos—full-page and multiple-image contact sheets—the complete output of three sessions held June–July 1962 for a *Vogue* layout. The first time Marilyn had posed nude since the days of Tom Kelley's red velvet, when she was eighteen. From the great German art-book publisher Schirmer/Mosel, 1992.

*The first edition of this book was published in 1982, in German and French editions, and issued in a slipcase. *The 1992 edition, sans slipcase, was the first time it was available in English.

- *The Last Sitting*—a selection, 110 color and black-and-white photos, full-page and double-page, most previously seen only in contact sheets in the above volume. 10"x12" size. The text, by Bert Stern (an account of the photo sessions) is the same in all editions of this work, English or foreign-language. New York: William Morrow, 1982.

- *The Last Sitting*, introduced by Daniel Dreier—another selection, 101 selected photographs, again with full-page photos previously seen only as small contact sheets. 9"x11" size. Munich: Schirmer Art Books, 1993.

- *Avant-Garde* magazine number 2, March 1968—featuring "The Marilyn Monroe Trip: A Portfolio of Serigraphic Prints by Bert Stern." Twelve pages from *The Last Sitting* silk-screened with the blazing colors of Day-Glo ink for a "phantasmagoric" vision of Marilyn.

- *Eros* magazine for Autumn 1962 (vol. 1, no. 3)—featuring *The Last Sitting* photos, color and black-and-white. This hardcover erotica magazine lasted just four issues: The morality police couldn't get the publisher for the contents of the magazine—constitutional rights and all that—so they sent him to prison for the *advertising* he'd mailed out.

   *This magazine is usually sold only as a set of the four issues. Also, because of the way it's bound, it's rarely found in good condition.

- *American Photo* magazine for November-December 1992—features "The Marilyn Files," in which Stern recounts how Marilyn destroyed photos from *The Last Sitting*, and how a computer artist restored them. Five color photos of Marilyn, including the provocative butt-in-the-air shot that's only a tiny contact print in the main books.

- *Playboy* magazine for January 1984—contains "the last nude photo" of Marilyn, taken by Leif-Erik Nygards, assistant to Bert Stern. This is the photo that shows her pubic hair.

Leigh Weiner

- *Marilyn: A Hollywood Farewell*, a book of photographs by Leigh Weiner—fifty-seven never-before-seen black-and-white photos: mainly the funeral, but also the scene of her death, and three shots of Marilyn as a star. In the brief text, Weiner says that dead Marilyn's lips were blue, indicating poison. Published by the photographer in 1990, Los Angeles.
  *This book was offered in three editions: (1) An unlimited trade edition in cloth cover, acid-free paper, dust jacket, for $85. (2) A limited signed edition of 275 copies, signed by the photographer and by Richard B. Stolley of Time-Life, on archival paper, cloth cover, dust jacket, for $295. (3) A limited deluxe edition, twenty-six lettered copies, signed by Weiner and Stolley, and with two 11"x14" photos from the book, printed and signed by Leigh Weiner, for $3,500.

Bob Willoughby

- *The Hollywood Special*—photos by Bob Willoughby, introduction by Tony Curtis, afterword by Willoughby. A "special" photographer, he was hired to shoot special coverage of films, usually for *Life* or *Look* magazine. This collection is mostly candid, behind-the-scenes photos: Audrey Hepburn,

James Dean, Natalie Wood getting a pie in the face, Silvana Mangano pulling Tony Perkins' hair, etc. Three photos of Marilyn on the set of *Let's Make Love*. New York: Takarajima Books, 1993.

Jerome Zerbe

- *Happy Times*—oversize pictorial, a history of our time in over five hundred photos by society photographer Zerbe, text by Brendan Gill. Featuring Greta Garbo, Charles Chaplin, Steve Reeves, Orson Welles, Jean Harlow, and so on. Two with Marilyn: with Yves Montand, smiling their heads off; and Marilyn with a stuffed-shirt politician. New York: Harcourt Brace Jovanovich, 1973.

Chapter 19

The Other Photo Collections

- *Marilyn*, edited by Lawrence Schiller, with a biography by Norman Mailer—one of the best collections: 109 photos, fifty in color, by twenty-four of "the world's foremost photographers": Eve Arnold, Richard Avedon, George Barris, Cecil Beaton, John Bryson, Cornell Capa, Bruce Davidson, Andre de Dienes, Elliott Erwitt, Milton Greene, Ernst Haas, Philippe Halsman, Bob Henriques, Tom Kelley, Douglas Kirkland, Lee Lockwood, Inge Morath, Arnold Newman, Lawrence Schiller, Sam Shaw, Bert Stern, John Vachon, Bob Willoughby, and William Read Woodfield. New York: Grosset and Dunlap, 1973.

  *Also issued as a Collector's Edition, an unnumbered limited edition, signed by Norman Mailer and Lawrence Schiller, set in a folding box.

- *Marilyn Monroe, A Life on Film*, compiled and edited by John Kobal, introduction by David Robinson—oversize pictorial on Marilyn as seen through her films and film publicity. Color and black-and-white photos from the remarkable Kobal Collection. London: Hamlyn Publishing, 1974.

  *American reprint, New York: Exeter Books, 1984.

- *Monroe: Her Life in Pictures*, by James Spada with George Zeno—a chronological account of her life and career in more

than 230 photos, many unfamiliar. Mainly black-and-white, some excellent color. 8"x11". New York: Doubleday, 1982.
  *Published as a hardcover (in a small quantity), and as a quality paperback.

• *Marilyn Monroe*, by Tom Hutchinson—an eighty-page pictorial in the Screen Greats series, concentrating mainly on her film career. Decorated board covers, with dust jacket. London: Optimum Books, 1982.

• *Marilyn Monroe*—an illustrated biography by Janice Anderson. *The Unabridged Marilyn*: "Despite some good color and black-and-white photographs . . . just another stock MM bio." Sixty-one color photos, one hundred thirty black-and-white. London: Hamlyn, 1983.

• *Marilyn Monroe*, by Roger St. Pierre—12"x12" magazine, twenty-eight pages of familiar color photos. Originally sold in record stores, probably as a promotional giveaway. London: Anabas Look Book Series, 1985.

• *Marilyn Monroe, A Never-Ending Dream*, compiled and edited by Guus Luijters—more than 450 black-and-white photos. Text is by Marilyn, commentary matched to the photos. First published in Amsterdam in 1983. English edition, New York: St. Martin's Press, 1987.

• *Marilyn at Twentieth Century–Fox*, by Lawrence Crown— oversize, a complete illustrated history of Marilyn from starlet to troubled star, in two hundred photographs. Plus interviews and stories by coworkers. London: Comet Books, 1987.

• *Masters of Starlight: Photographers in Hollywood*, by David Fahey and Linda Rich. The catalogue to accompany a 1987 Los Angeles exhibit: the work of the Hollywood still photographer, from 1910 to 1970. Forty-three major photographers represented by over three hundred photos: 9"x11", 287

pages. Los Angeles, CA: Los Angeles County Museum of
Art, 1987.

  *Of the forty-three photographers here, at least ten pho-
  tographed Marilyn.

• *Marilyn Monroe and the Camera*, conception by Lothar
  Schirmer—the most lavish Marilyn book, a collection of the
  best, sexiest, most famous photos, from the earliest advertising and pinup sessions, to the starlet photos, to the classics
  by Avedon, Stern, Halsman, Beaton, and the paparazzi.
  9"x13" size, with 48 color plates and 104 black-and-white.
  Foreword by Jane Russell, plus a revealing interview from
  the October 1960 issue of *Marie-Claire*, published in English
  for the first time. Boston: Little, Brown and Co., 1989.

• *Marilyn*, by Neil Sinyard—oversize pictorial with over 130
  black-and-white and color photos. New York: Gallery Books,
  1989.

A pinup from
1952, the year
Marilyn became
world-famous for
another pinup
photo—as the
"Golden Dreams"
calendar nude.
[Photo courtesy
of Archive
Photos.]

- *Marilyn, A Hollywood Life,* by Ann Lloyd—oversize, over one hundred color and black-and-white photos. Includes Marilyn's horoscope. New York: Mallard Press, 1989.

- *Marilyn, Her Life and Legend,* contributing writer Susan Doll—oversize 14"x10" tribute, the many moods and guises of Marilyn in 450 photos, 190 in color: cheesecake, studio publicity shots, scene stills, candids. New York: Beekman House, 1990.

- *Marilyn Monroe,* by Roger Baker—her public and private life as seen in two hundred black-and-white photos from the files of the United Press. 10"x11". New York: Portland House, 1990.

- *Forever Marilyn,* by Marie Cahill—oversize pictorial, ninety-seven photos, color and black-and-white. The photos on pages 10 and 11 are of "promotional work for McDonald-Douglas in 1946," and have been reproduced in no other book, as far as I know. You will recognize the blonde on page 42—"Marilyn mugging for the camera"—as Jayne Mansfield. London: Bison Books, 1991.

- *The Marilyn Album,* by Nicki Giles—9"x12" pictorial with over six hundred photos, mainly black-and-white, tracing Marilyn's life and career. A good selection of photos, despite problems with chronology and identification (The photo of Marilyn as Richard Avedon's Lillian Russell is said to be from *A Ticket to Tomahawk,* a *Bus Stop* scene is grouped with *Clash by Night,* etc. New York: Gallery Books, 1991.

- *Marilyn: The Ultimate Look at the Legend*—by James Haspiel. Regarded as a leading archivist of Marilyn, Haspiel shares his friendship with her during the last eight years of her life. Whenever Marilyn was in New York, Haspiel waited around to take photos of her. Many were just fuzzy snapshots, others turned out to be very special. Over 150 color and black-and-white photos, many published here for the first time. New York: Henry Holt, 1991.

• *The Marilyn Monroe Auction*—118-page catalogue for auction held August 15, 1992, at the G. Ray Hawkins photography gallery in Santa Monica, California. 5½" x 8½" catalogue—black and white—most photo reproductions 4" x 5". An intriguing collection, many classics, many unfamiliar: John Bryson, Bruce Davidson, George Zimbel, much Milton Greene, Jasgur, Bernard, et al.

• *3-D Hollywood, Photos by Harold Lloyd*—edited by Suzanne Lloyd Hayes. Semiretired from the screen in the 1930s, the silent-film comedian avidly pursued his photography hobby. This is a selection of sixty-seven 3-D color photos, from the three hundred thousand Lloyd took. With the exception of the thirteen with Marilyn, they are of little interest. Most intriguing are the photos Lloyd took of Philippe Halsman photographing Marilyn for her first *Life* magazine cover. New York: Simon and Schuster, 1992.
   *Packaged with a pair of plastic 3-D glasses.

• *Those Lips, Those Eyes*—a celebration of classic Hollywood sensuality, by Edward Z. Epstein and Lou Valentino. Introduction by Judith Crist. 9"x12" pictorial, seventy-seven photos, mostly black-and-white, many oversize. Five of Marilyn, much of Lana Turner, Ava Gardner, Rita Hayworth, but also Jean Harlow, Clark Gable, Marlon Brando, Dolores Del Rio, more John Wayne than you'd expect. New York: Carol Publishing, 1992.

• *Marilyn*, by Kathy Rooks-Denes—pictorial (11½" x 11½") with lengthy biographical text. About 150 photos, mainly black-and-white, an unexciting selection. New York: BDD Illustrated Books, 1993.

- *Marilyn Monroe, Photographs 1945–1962*. Schirmer's Visual Library—5½" x 7½" paperback with forty-eight classic photos, color and duotone. With Truman Capote's "A Beautiful Child" story from *Music for Chameleons*. London/Munich: Schirmer/Mosel, 1994.

- *Young Marilyn: Becoming the Legend*, by James Haspiel— one hundred fifty rare photographs, fifty in color, documenting the transformation of Norma Jeane Dougherty into Marilyn Monroe: unpublished stills, costume tests, candid shots by fans, etc. New York: Hyperion, 1994.

- *Marilyn Monroe unCovers*, compiled by Clark Kidder, edited by Madison Daniels—9"x12" pictorial, photos of 279 Marilyn magazine covers from all over the world, in color. Many full-page. Photographers identified for many photos. Alberta, Canada: Quon Editions, 1994.

- *Magnum Cinema, Photographs from Fifty Years of Moviemaking*—text and introduction by Alain Bergala. Magnum, the world's most prestigious picture agency, has worked with filmmakers since its inception fifty years ago. This 360-page collection represents filmmaking from all over the world, in photos by fifty-nine photographers. London: Phaidon Press, 1995.

  *Magnum had exclusive rights to cover the filming of *The Misfits* (1961). The agreement called for two different photographers every two weeks, with Eve Arnold on hand for the entire two months because of her friendship with Marilyn. No other movie, maybe no other event, has been covered by so many of the world's most acclaimed photographers: Eve Arnold, Henri Cartier-Bresson, Bruce Davidson, Elliott Erwitt, Ernest Haas, Philippe Halsman, Erich Hartmann, Bob Henriques, Inge Morath, and Dennis Stock.

Magnum Cinema features twenty-six pages of photos from *The Misfits* by all of these photographers.

- *Marilyn by Moonlight*, a remembrance in rare photos, edited by Jack Allen, with reminiscences by Marilyn Monroe, introduction by Greg Schreiner—called the first "digitally designed" Marilyn book, this is a collection of over 120 color and black-and-white photos, mainly unfamiliar or unseen, and enhanced through computer wizardry. New York: Barclay House, 1996.

  *At this point, issued only in a numbered edition of five hundred copies, slipcased.

- *American Photo* magazine, May-June 1997—Collector's Issue devoted to Marilyn and her photographers. Rare and never-seen photos by Sam Shaw, John Florea, Milton Greene, Bob Henriques, Earl Moran, Douglas Kirkland, Alfred Eisenstaedt, Tom Kelley (a "Golden Dreams" outtake), Andre de Dienes, Philippe Halsman, Glenn Embree, Jock Carroll, Bruno Bernard, Bert Stern, Earl Leaf, Eve Arnold, Richard C. Miller, Ed Feingersh, George Barrish.

- *Marilyn*, by Jay Harrison—oversize 11"x12" pictorial with 173 black-and-white photos, 77 in color. Many are full-page. Originally published in Europe in 1992. American publication, NJ: BHB International (distributor), 1997.

A number of Marilyn photographers aren't yet represented with their own book, or in photo collections. (See Part 3, Chapter 15, Marilyn's "Escorts to Immortality," to identify and locate photos by the others.)

Chapter 20

Marilyn in Costume and Fashion

- *Hollywood Costume Design*, by David Chierichetti—photos of Marilyn in costumes by Orry-Kelly, Rene Hubert, and Travilla. New York: Harmony Books, 1976.

- *Fashion in Film*, edited by Regine and Peter W. Engelmeier, English translation by Eileen Martin. Munich: Prestel-Verlag, 1990.

- *In a Glamorous Fashion*, by W. Robert LaVine—includes a Cecil Beaton photo of Marilyn (arm across face) New York: Scribner's, 1980.

- *Costume Design in the Movies*, by Elizabeth Leese—brief biographies of designers, with complete filmographies. England: BCW Publishing, 1976.

- *Marilyn Monroe Paper Dolls*, by Tom Tierney, noted fashion illustrator—color illustrations of thirty-one costumes from twenty-four of her films. New York: Dover Books, 1979.

- *Star Style—Hollywood Legends as Fashion Icons*, by Patty Fox—the real-life wardrobes of ten actresses who defined, or defied, the fashions of her times, who created a personal style: Audrey Hepburn, Marilyn Monroe, Doris Day, Lucille Ball, Katharine Hepburn, Joan Crawford, Greta Garbo, Marlene Dietrich, Dolores Del Rio, Gloria Swanson. 130 black-and-white photos. Los Angeles: Angel City Press, 1995.

Chapter 21

Marilyn in Art

- *Homage to Marilyn Monroe*—exhibition catalogue, text by Sidney Janis. 26-page pamphlet of an exhibition of artwork by leading artists in homage to Marilyn Monroe, held December 6 to 30, 1967, at the Sidney Janis Gallery in New York City.

- *Marilyn in Art*, compiled by Roger G. Taylor—a collection representing the remarkable range of artwork inspired by Marilyn. 9"x9". Illustrations and paintings by Olivia, Warhol, Pepe Gonzales, de Kooning, Jon Whitcomb, and others of varying quality and originality. Salem, NH: Salem House, 1984.

- *Elvis + Marilyn: 2 x Immortal*, edited by Geri DePaoli— deluxe 9"x12" catalogue for a touring art exhibit. 170 pages, reproducing the 120 works of art—including images by Andy Warhol, Keith Haring, Robert Rauschenberg, Claes Oldenburg, and Christo—that document the transformation of Marilyn and Elvis into immortal symbols of gender, heroism, and even spirituality. Includes a series of thought-provoking essays. New York: Rizzoli International, 1994.

Chapter 22

Marilyn Biographies

◆

Books

- *The Marilyn Monroe Story* by Joe Franklin and Laurie Palmer—fan-magazine fluff. Issued in hardcover and as paperback. New York: Rudolph Field Company, 1953.

  *This is one of the highest-priced items on the collector's market, usually selling for around a thousand dollars. The pricing reflects the rarity and the fact that it is the first book on Marilyn. It does not reflect quality.

- *Will Acting Spoil Marilyn Monroe?*—a brief biography by Pete Martin. Marilyn in 1955, in transition from Hollywood to intellectual New York. Taken from a three-part series of interviews in the *Saturday Evening Post*. Photos. New York: Doubleday, 1956.

  *There's speculation about the photo on page 108—Marilyn riding an elephant, with her right breast spilling out of her costume. Was this photo deleted or replaced in subsequent editions? Close inspection of all copies of the book seen, including the paperback, have the photo intact.

- *Marilyn Monroe*—a biography by Maurice Zolotow. The first significant biography of Marilyn, written from direct interviews with the subject. Zolotow also knew most of the main

players, including DiMaggio and Arthur Miller. The interviews took place in New York in 1955. New York: Harcourt,
Brace and Co., 1960.

> *"Revised Edition" with new introduction and new epi-
> logue. Trade paperback. New York: Harper and Row,
> 1990.

> *Zolotow also wrote *Marilyn's Final Hours*, a six-part
> series for the New York *Daily News*, in September 1973.

• *Marilyn Monroe: "Her Own Story"*—a biography by George
Carpozi, Jr., with material that came from Marilyn herself,
beginning with a 1955 interview. Forty-five photos. New
York: Belmont Books paperback, 1961.

"It has autobiographical value for the very large number of
Marilyn's own words which are quoted in it."

—*Edward Wagenknecht, As Far As Yesterday*

> *Published in England as *The Agony of Marilyn Monroe*,
> 1962, World Distributors.

• *The Fifty Year Decline and Fall of Hollywood*, by Ezra
Goodman, a *Time* magazine film critic, and Hollywood
correspondent—an informative and lively report of
Hollywood in decline: The last days of D. W. Griffith;
Louella Parsons, Hedda Hopper, and the kept press; the
publicity-proud, talent-shy directors and stars. New York:
Simon and Schuster, 1961.

> *Goodman did two months of intensive research for a
> *Time* cover story, interviewing more than a hundred
> people including Andre de Dienes, Natasha Lytess,
> Billy Wilder, and publicists Harry Brand and Roy Craft.
> His research was not used for the cover story.

> Goodman writes, "Monroe has a neat habit of latch-
> ing onto people, of having them mother and father her,
> and then dumping them unceremoniously by the way-

side when she has done with them. She acquires—and gets rid of them—in shifts. She likes to change people like other women change hats."

- *Marilyn: The Tragic Venus*—a biography by Edwin P. Hoyt. Photos. New York: Chilton Books, 1965.

"[A] hatchet job. [Hoyt] relied heavily upon Nunnally Johnson...who despised Marilyn until shortly before the end of her life, when he did a kind of right-about-face without, apparently, ever achieving a consistent all-over view. Even the pictures have obviously been chosen to show Marilyn in her least attractive poses."

—*Edward Wagenknecht, As Far As Yesterday*

*"Not another biography!" said *Time* magazine in 1965. Little did they suspect.

- *Skouras, King of Fox Studios*, by Carlo Curti—a strange one. The first of three sections is about mogul Skouras. Part two is about Marilyn, part three about Elizabeth Taylor as Cleopatra. Los Angeles: Holloway House, 1967. Paperback original.

"The portion on Monroe is scandal-mongering in the old *Confidential* magazine style. It is a distasteful, ill-advised, non-documented collection of stories."

—*George Rehrauer, Cinema Booklist, 1972*

- *Norma Jean: The Life of Marilyn Monroe*, by Fred Lawrence Guiles—probably the best Marilyn biography. Norman Mailer credited it as his main source, and *The Unabridged Marilyn* calls it "the consummate cradle-to-career-to-tomb biography." It is a very calm, civilized, and contemplative book, filled with obvious affection and respect. (Which is quite a stunt when you're dealing with such an explosive subject as Marilyn.) Fully illustrated, with rare photos and snapshots. New York: McGraw-Hill, 1969.

*See also *Legend*, this section, a 1984 revision of this book.

- *Marilyn*, by Joe Hembus—a brief, lively biography of interest because it quotes from European sources. Photos. Originally published in West Germany in 1973 as *Marilyn Monroe, Die Frau Des Jahrbunderts*. English translation, London: Tandem Books, 1973. Paperback.

"With her seductive walk, the blonde is Eve, the snake and the apple all in one."

—*Jean Desternes in* Cahier du Cinema

- *Marilyn*, edited by Lawrence Schiller, with a biography by Norman Mailer—109 photos by twenty-four top photographers. 9"x10". New York: Grosset and Dunlap, 1973.

(See this chapter, "Marilyn and Norman Mailer," for further details and outrage.)

- *Marilyn Monroe*, by Joan Mellen—a comprehensive overview with photos, filmography. From the series *The Pyramid Illustrated History of the Movies*. New York: Pyramid, 1973. Paperback original.

*Reversing the usual procedure, the reprint is a hardcover book.

- *Legend: The Life and Death of Marilyn Monroe*—by Fred Lawrence Guiles. A revision/updating of his seminal 1969 biography *Norma Jean*. Contains additional interviews with Jim Dougherty, Lee Strasberg, Arthur Miller. New York: Stein and Day, 1984.

*The *New York Times* reviewer felt the impetus for this revision was to discuss openly the Marilyn–Bobby

Kennedy relationship, which had been hidden behind pseudonyms in the first book.

- *Goddess: The Secret Lives of Marilyn Monroe*, by Anthony Summers—a biography by an investigative journalist, with a motherlode of new details and speculations. New York: Macmillan, 1985.

  "When he gets around to examining the theory that Monroe was murdered, he seems to have it both ways, first enticing us with its possible truth and then concluding that he doesn't believe it."
  —*The New York Times, September 19, 1985*

- *Requiem for Marilyn*, by Bernard of Hollywood (Bruno Bernard)—a biography/appreciation/investigation by one of Marilyn's first photographers. He tells of meeting her on the street, and how his photos helped her get into Twentieth Century–Fox. He writes a common-sense analysis of her death/suicide. Many photos, his own and others. London: Kensal Press, 1986.

  "Marilyn's greatest creation...was the creation of Marilyn Monroe herself."
  —*Bruno Bernard*

- *Marilyn*, by Gloria Steinem, with photos by George Barris— a feminist viewpoint. Steinem says Marilyn was rewarded for remaining childlike and dependent. New York: Henry Holt, 1986.
  *See also Part 4, Chapter 18, "Marilyn by Her Photographers," George Barris.

- *The Marilyn Scandal—Her True Life Revealed by Those Who Knew Her*, by Sandra Shevey—hard to read: Shevey seems to be trying to cram all the existing theories into one big theory. Photos. New York: William Morrow, 1987.

*The paperback edition has *additional* material and speculation!

- *The Unabridged Marilyn, Her Life from A to Z*, by Randall Riese and Neal Hitchens, 578 pages—a biographical breakdown of Marilyn's life, categorized into people, places, and things, with more than 1,500 entries. 150 rare photos. Essential. New York: Congdon and Weed, 1987.

- *Marilyn on Location*, by Bart Mills—a biography, despite the inapt title, and a routine one at that. Photos. London: Sidgwick and Jackson, 1989.

- *Marilyn: The Last Take*, by Peter Brown and Patte Barham—a detailed look at the last fourteen weeks of Marilyn's life. Photos. New York: Dutton, 1992.

"The authors' main evidence against a conclusion of suicide is odd: that in recently discovered footage of her last and unfinished film, *Something's Got to Give*, she looks terrific and performs marvelously.

"After its promise to reveal explosive truths [it] ends with conjecture: 'Here's the story as we see it ...' What follows is the not-unfamiliar theory about murder resulting from her affairs with the Kennedys.

"In fact, the book that set out to tell 'the true and full story... a story which has never been told,' ends up admitting that Marilyn Monroe and her death remain 'an enduring riddle which may never be solved.'"

—*John Rechy, Los Angeles Times Book Review, October 18, 1992*

*The paperback edition has a ninety-page afterword with new speculations.

- *Marilyn's Men: The Private Life of Marilyn Monroe*, by Jane Ellen Wayne. Photos. New York: St. Martin's Press, 1992.
  *On the third page of the preface, we read of a "gold lamé see-through gown" (not likely); we read that Marilyn

"very rarely, if ever, achieved the ultimate orgasm" (huh?); and that she "preferred the freedom of nudity irrelevant to sex" (huh?, again).

Then we get Marilyn's quote about the girlie photographers she posed for, that "they wanted to sample the merchandise. If you didn't go along, there were twenty-five girls who would." But now the quote is used to refer to Hollywood moviemakers.

Somehow you don't feel like reading any further.

• *Marilyn Monroe: The Biography*, by Donald Spoto—possibly the definitive biography, certainly the most important for its wealth of new information from original research and interviews, and from previously unavailable material. Spoto had exclusive access to more than 35,000 pages of unseen material, including the papers of Dr. Ralph Greenson. Also, through canceled checks, Spoto shows that Marilyn was shopping in Beverly Hills on the day Robert Slatzer says they were being married in Tijuana, Mexico. A major, 698-page work. Photos. New York: Harper-Collins, 1993.

    *Spoto outlines the step-by-step development of "the Great Conspiracy" behind Marilyn's death—making a convincing case for attention-grabbing greed, jealousy, nonsense, hypocrisy. Disregard it at your own risk.

• *Marilyn Monroe, "Quote Unquote,"* by Janice Anderson—a brief biography/appreciation with photos and memorable sayings. Eighty pages, forty-four familiar black-and-white and color photos. New York: Crescent Books, 1995.

• *Marilyn: The Story of a Woman*, by Kathryn Hyatt—a "fictionalized biography" in the form of a graphic novel—that is, a comic book for adults. 180 pages, black-and-white drawings, not as professional as you might like. New York: Seven Stories Press, 1996.

◆

Magazine Biographies

(the "cover-to-cover" special issues)

• *Marilyn*, by Sidney Skolsky—a full-length magazine biography by a friend and advocate. New York: Dell Publishing, 1954.

> "Disappointingly sophomoric and superficial."
>
> —*The Unabridged Marilyn*

• *Marilyn: Her Tragic Life*—fully illustrated magazine, text by George Miller. New York: Escape Magazines, 1962.

• *Marilyn Monroe: The Complete Story of Her Life, Her Loves and Her Death*—by John Pascal. New York: Popular Library, 1962.

• *Marilyn Monroe: Her Last Untold Secrets*—contains "The Mother No One Knew About" (Natasha Lytess); "Marilyn's Children Tell What They Thought of Her" (actually, the children of Arthur Miller and Joe DiMaggio); "The Man Who Might Have Saved Her" (Jose Bolanos, who says he *didn't* call the night she died). No publishing information given.

• *Marilyn's Life Story*—edited by Agnes Birnbaum. Dell Publishing, 1962.

• *Marilyn*, edited by Milburn Smith—a magazine devoted to Marilyn, fully illustrated. Published as *Barven Screen Greats No. 4*, 1971.
  > *Recycled in 1980 as *Marilyn, Screen Greats Vol. II*, by Starlog Press.
  > *Recycled in the 1990s as *Screen Greats presents Marilyn*, Starlog Signet Special, with eight giant fold-out pinups.

- *Marilyn Monroe: "Her Own Story,"* by George Carpozi, Jr.— a 1980smagazine edition of the paperback biography first published in 1961.

- *The Marilyn Chronicles,* edited by Milburn Smith—the text is a chronology of Marilyn's life. Over one hundred color photos, even more black-and-white. Color cover is a half-successful attempt at a 3-D effect. New York: Starlog, 1994.

◆

Marilyn in Biography Collections

- *Pete Martin Calls On...* forty interviews from the *Saturday Evening Post.* Contains "Did Acting Spoil Marilyn Monroe?" plus interviews with Marlon Brando, Clark Gable, Hedy Lamarr, Grace Kelly, Yul Brynner, Gary Cooper, et al. New York: Simon and Schuster, 1962.

- *Seven Daughters of the Theater,* by Edward Wagenknecht. Studies of three stage actresses: Sarah Bernhardt, Ellen Terry, Julia Marlow; two opera singers: Mary Garden, Jenny Lind; a dancer, Isadora Duncan; and a film star, Marilyn Monroe—a dazzling array of feminine genius and beauty in the performing arts. Photos. Norman, OK: University of Oklahoma Press, 1964.

  "His estimation of Monroe's potential as a serious actress is a thoughtful tribute."
  —*George Rehrauer, Cinema Booklist*

- *The Fox Girls,* by James Robert Parish—biography, filmography and photos of the studio's top female stars: Theda Bara, Janet Gaynor, Shirley Temple, Alice Faye, Loretta Young, Betty Grable, June Haver, Jeanne Crain, Marilyn Monroe, Sheree North, Raquel Welch. Unassailable research and conclusions. New York: Arlington House, 1971.

- *The Decline and Fall of the Love Goddesses*, by Patrick Agan. Ten stars on their way up, at the peak, on the way down: Rita Hayworth, Jayne Mansfield, Betty Hutton, Linda Darnell, Veronica Lake, Betty Grable, Susan Hayward, Dorothy Dandridge, Frances Farmer, Marilyn Monroe. Standard stuff. A few photos. Los Angeles: Pinnacle Books, 1979.

- *A Star is Torn*, by Robyn Archer and Diana Simmonds. What thirteen singer-superstars had in common—tragic lives, alcohol and drug addictions, untimely deaths, and a great deal of talent. Marie Lloyd, Bessie Smith, Helen Morgan, Jane Froman, Carmen Miranda, Billie Holiday, Edith Piaf, Judy Holliday, Judy Garland, Dinah Washington, Marilyn Monroe, Patsy Cline, Janis Joplin. New York: Dutton, 1986.

- *Fallen Angels*, by Kirk Crivello. The lives and untimely deaths of fourteen Hollywood beauties: Marilyn Monroe, Sharon Tate, Gail Russell, Inger Stevens, Barbara Payton, Carole Landis, Barbara Bates, Natalie Wood, Suzan Ball, Jean Seberg, Susan Peters, Marie McDonald, Gia Scala, Jayne Mansfield. Photos. Secaucus, NJ: Citadel, 1988.

- *Va Va Voom!—Bombshells, Pinups, Sexpots and Glamour Girls*, by Steve Sullivan. The sexy superstars of the Fabulous Fifties: Marilyn Monroe, Jayne Mansfield, Mamie Van Doren, Brigitte Bardot, Betty Page, Tempest Storm, and cult favorites June Wilkinson, Candy Barr, Meg Myles, et al. Capsule biographies of many more. Over two hundred photos, a few in color. 9"x12" quality paperback. Los Angeles: General Publishing Group, 1995.

◆

Biographies for Young Readers

- *Marilyn Monroe*, by Frances Lefkowitz. A 128-page biography for teenagers, with photos. Introduction by Leeza

Gibbons: "Hopefully, by studying the lives and achievements of these pop culture legends, we will learn more about ourselves." New York: Chelsea House, 1995.

- *Marilyn Monroe*, by Adam Woog. A title in the Mysterious Deaths series that includes Abraham Lincoln, John F. Kennedy, Wolfgang Amadeus Mozart, Amelia Earhart. Photos. San Diego, CA: Lucent Books, 1997.

- *Marilyn Monroe: Norma Jeane's Dream*, by Katherine E. Krohn. Black-and-white and color photos. Minneapolis: Lerner Publications, 1997.

◆

Marilyn and Berniece Baker

- *My Sister Marilyn*, by Berniece Baker Miracle. Norma Jeane was twelve and Berniece was nineteen when they learned that they were half-sisters—with the same mother but different fathers. Their relationship was separated by distance, but lasted until Marilyn's death; Berniece picked out the dress Marilyn was buried in. Photos and letters, most published for the first time. Chapel Hill, NC: Algonquin Books, 1994.

◆

Marilyn and Jim Dougherty

- *The Secret Happiness of Marilyn Monroe*, by Jim Dougherty. Marilyn's first husband gives his account of their marriage, written thirty years later. Photos. Chicago: Playboy Press, 1976, paperback original.

◆

Marilyn and Joe DiMaggio

- *Marilyn and Joe DiMaggio*, by Robin Moore and Gene Schoor. A fan magazine–type account of a romance that made history. New York: Manor Books, 1977, paperback original.

• *Joe and Marilyn*, a memory of love, by Roger Kahn. The story as seen by a writer of classic baseball books (*The Boys of Summer*), but who did not personally know either of them—and Joe refused to be interviewed. The *New York Times* called it "a worthy compilation of anecdotes." *Newsweek* criticized the lack of details on their lives after divorce: Kahn doesn't even mention the weekly roses. New York: William Morrow, 1986.

In 1952, this was the Villa Nova Restaurant on Sunset Boulevard, where a friend arranged for Marilyn and Joe DiMaggio to meet. (She was two hours late.) It's now the Rainbow Bar and Grill. [Photo courtesy of Patrick V. Miller.]

◆

Marilyn and Arthur Miller

"But you're Arthur Miller—how can you be so boring?"
—from the musical **Marilyn: An American Fable**

• "My Wife Marilyn," essay by Arthur Miller, *Life* magazine, December 22, 1958—accompanying Richard Avedon's "Fabled Enchantresses" color photo essay.

• *The Misfits*—the screenplay by Arthur Miller. A dreadful betrayal: Arthur Miller admitting to the world that he was defeated by Marilyn. He gave Marilyn's character dialogue that came from her own life. And there was worse to come, with *After the Fall*. New York: Viking Press, 1961.

　　*Reprinted in *Film Scripts Three*, which also contains *Charade* (screenplay by Peter Stone) and *The Apartment* (screenplay by Billy Wilder and I. A. L. Diamond). New York: Appleton-Century-Crofts, 1972. In spiral binder.

　　*Reprint, New York: Irvington Publishers, 1989, quality paperback.

• *The Misfits*—"a synthesis of screenplay and novel" by Arthur Miller. With photos from the film, and the original short story from *Esquire* (October 1957). Written "to create a fiction which might have the peculiar immediacy of image and the reflective possibilities of the written word" (Miller). New York: The Viking Press, 1961.

　　*Also published in *Arthur Miller's Collected Plays*, Volume II. New York: The Viking Press, 1981. This book also contains *After the Fall*, three other plays, and the script for the TV movie *Playing for Time* (1980).

"He could have written me anything, and he comes up with this. If that's what he thinks of me, well, then, I'm not for him and he's not for me."
—Marilyn on **The Misfits**

Publicity photo for *The Misfits*, before the filming became an ordeal. [Photo courtesy of Photofest.]

• *The Story of The Misfits*—by James Goode. An objective day-by-day account of the filming, interspersed with interviews. "Reveals the key figures more honestly and dramatically than a sensational approach." (*The New York Times*) Sixteen pages of photos. Indianapolis: Bobbs-Merrill, 1963.

  *Reprint, as *The Making of The Misfits*. New York: Limelight, 1986, quality paperback.

• *After the Fall*, the play by Arthur Miller. New York: The Viking Press, 1964. Arthur Miller's odyssey of self-discovery, "a drama of revealment," wrote Tom Prideaux in *Life* magazine, February 7, 1964: "He tears from himself a confession that when Maggie, with whom married life had become unbearable, was on the brink of death from an overdose of sleeping pills he felt a wave of gratitude that his ordeal with her was ending."

Robert Brustein, in *The New Republic*, February 8, 1964, was even rougher:

"... A shameless piece of tabloid gossip, an act of exhibition-ism which makes us all voyeurs.

"It is astonishing that a playwright, whose major business is perception, could live with this unfortunate woman for over four years, and yet be capable of no greater insight than those of ... a professional theater columnist."

After the Fall was the first presentation of the Repertory Theater of Lincoln Center, in New York City, opening on January 23, 1964. Jason Robards, Jr., starred as Quentin/Arthur Miller, and Barbara Loden was Maggie/Marilyn. It was directed by Elia Kazan, who is himself a character in the play. The other women in Quentin's life were played by Virginia Kaye, Mariclare Costello, Salome Jens, and Zohra Lampert. Also in the large cast were David Wayne, Hal Holbrook, Ralph Meeker, John Phillip Law, and Faye Dunaway as a nurse.

   *Also issued in limited edition of 500 signed copies, slipcased.

   *"Revised final stage version," April 1964.

- *Timebends: A Life*—the autobiography of Arthur Miller. 614 pages, thirty-two pages of photos. New York: Grove Press, 1987.

"He presents [Marilyn] as a victim of what he calls 'the American illness' that will not allow sexuality and seriousness to coexist in the same woman. Monroe prized her beauty and needed admiration, yet she despaired at the universal assumption that she lacked brains and talent. In what may be the most carefully crafted passage in the book, Miller writes: 'The secret of her wit's attractiveness was that she could see around it, around those who were laughing with her, or at her.

Like almost all good comics, she was ruefully commenting on herself and her own pretensions to being more than a dumb sex kitten; like most comics, she despaired of her dignity, and her remarks and her wryness itself were self-generated oxygen that allowed her to breathe at all.'

"Drawn to her, Miller recognized that he could lose himself in sensuality. He thought perhaps he could rescue her, but disabled by barbiturates and the paranoia that became particularly accented when she was on a movie set, Monroe included him among those she imagined had betrayed her. Beneath all her insouciance and wit, death was her companion everywhere and at all times, and it may be that its unacknowledged presence was what lent her poignancy, dancing at the edge of oblivion as she was."

—*Time* magazine, November 16, 1987

*Also issued in a signed first edition privately printed by the Franklin Mint.

- *Everybody Wins*—an original screenplay by Arthur Miller, with a preface by him. Fifteen photos from the film. New York: Grove Weidenfeld, 1990, paperback original.

Everybody Wins was filmed in 1989, starring Debra Winger and Nick Nolte, and directed by Karel Reisz. The story is of criminal attorney Nolte hired by shady lady Winger to save a young man wrongfully convicted of murder. Gradually Nolte learns that the Winger character had an affair with the district attorney, that she's regarded as little more than a hooker, that she's been mentally unstable if not schizophrenic, and that the whole town is rotten.

Dismissed by the critics as a pretentious flop, David Denby of *New York* magazine (February 5, 1990) found a point of interest: "Am I crazy or is Arthur Miller still wrestling with the ghost of Marilyn Monroe? Winger plays an unfathomable woman, a beauty abused yet noble, a liar and near-psychopath who overpowers men and then slips away, unreachable, tormented, tormenting.... It is the Marilyn of Miller's autobiography."

◆

Marilyn and the Kennedys

- *The Mysterious Death of Marilyn Monroe*, by James A. Hudson. One of the first books to suggest murder, and to implicate the Kennedys. New York: Volitant Books, 1968, paperback original.

- *Legend: The Life and Death of Marilyn Monroe*, by Fred Lawrence Guiles. A revision/updating of his 1969 biography *Norma Jean* to discuss openly the Marilyn–Bobby Kennedy relationship. New York: Stein and Day, 1985.

- *Capitol Hill in Black and White*, by Robert Parker. A memoir by a Washington insider—former chauffeur and bodyguard for LBJ; headwaiter of the Senate dining room; and the waiter who says he saw JFK and MM together in the Mayflower Hotel. New York: Dodd, Mead, 1986
    *Paperback editions, New York: Jove Books, 1989 and 1992.

- *A Woman Named Jackie*, an unauthorized biography by C. David Heymann. New York: Lyle Stuart, 1989.
    *Contains many details on Marilyn Monroe's supposed mad love for JFK and then for Bobby. It has the story of Marilyn calling Jackie at the White House, with Jackie offering to divorce JFK and step aside—if Marilyn is prepared to live openly in the White House. (The story is credited to Peter Lawford.) Lawford on at least one occasion took photographs of Marilyn performing fellatio on Kennedy while JFK lounged in a large marble

bathtub. Kennedy also could not resist Jayne Mansfield, who had "a more realistic view of men than her more celebrated rival."

- *Peter Lawford: The Man Who Kept the Secrets*, an investigative biography by James Spada. The story of a personable and popular actor (1923–1984) who will probably be seen by history as a procurer. 504 pages. Photos. New York: Bantam Books, 1991.

"He reveals Peter's role in leading John F. Kennedy on his 'hunting expeditions' for girls in Los Angeles, and in introducing the President to Marilyn Monroe. He discusses the connection between Kennedy, Sinatra, and the leading Mafia dons. And he offers the most plausible scenario to date of events leading to Marilyn's death as well as Peter's part in the ensuing cover-up."
—from the dust jacket

- *The Kennedys in Hollywood*, by Lawrence Quirk. Photos. Dallas: Taylor Publishing, 1996. A history that goes from Joseph Kennedy's business interests and torrid affair with Gloria Swanson...through Jack's numerous liaisons with Gene Tierney, Angie Dickinson, Marilyn Monroe...to Maria Shriver's marriage to Arnold Schwarzenegger, and John Jr.'s relationship with Daryl Hannah.
  *Says Quirk: Marilyn and JFK met at a party in 1954, and began their "back street" affair that lasted until her death—eight years. Which would mean Marilyn had been trysting with JFK in various hotels, private homes, and yachts, while she was married to Joe DiMaggio and to Arthur Miller—"to the annoyance of both husbands."
  *Also: "Marilyn felt her marriage to Joe really broke up because he didn't like to be fellated, and rebelled against her insistence along those lines."

◆

Marilyn and Norman Mailer

"I needed money very badly."
—*Norman Mailer, 60 Minutes (CBS, July 13, 1973)*

- *Marilyn*, a biography by Norman Mailer, produced by Lawrence Schiller. Hired to write an introduction to a collection of photographs, Mailer caught the Marilyn bug and wound up with a book-length biography/appreciation/meditation/whatever. He borrowed freely from Fred Lawrence Guiles's biography, and subsequent editions of this book carried a statement acknowledging Guiles's spadework. Mailer was the first to print the name Robert Kennedy—irresponsibly—and to *speculate* about Kennedy involvement. There were no complaints about the excellent collection of photos. New York: Grosset and Dunlap, 1973.
  - *Also issued in a deluxe edition in slipcase, signed by Mailer and Schiller.
  - *1975 mass-market paperback has a new chapter in which Mailer raises new questions about Marilyn's death.

- *Of Women and Their Elegance*, a book of photos by Milton Greene—for which Mailer was again hired to do an introduction, and again got carried away. He came up with "an imaginary memoir of Marilyn . . . a set of interviews that never took place." Thirty-six photos of Marilyn, but also Marlene Dietrich, Ava Gardner, Grace Kelly, Sophia Loren, Catherine Deneuve, Audrey Hepburn, and a number of high-fashion models. New York: Simon and Schuster, 1980.
  - *A 1991 French edition of this book reprinted just the Mailer text, under the title *Mémoires Imaginaires de Marilyn*. Editions Robert Laffont, 1982.

- "Marilyn Monroe's Sexiest Tapes and Discs"—in *Video Review* magazine for February 1982. Mailer evaluates her movies on videotape and laser disc.

"It's less about Marilyn than about Mailer's quest for Marilyn"
—*Vanity Fair, April, 1986*

- *Strawhead*, a play inspired by Marilyn, excerpted in *Vanity Fair* magazine, April 1986. It was performed at the Actors Studio in New York for two weeks, with Mailer's own daughter Kate portraying Marilyn. Kate posed as Marilyn for photos by Bert Stern.

◆

They Knew Marilyn—Or Say They Did

(directors and coworkers, friends, lovers, leeches, onlookers)

Lauren Bacall

- *By Myself*—an autobiography of a full life, that ends with the death of her actor husband Humphrey Bogart. (A recent second volume continued her story.) She briefly discusses working with Marilyn on *How to Marry a Millionaire* (1953); she was irritated by some of Marilyn's quirks but there was no real animosity. Photos. New York: Knopf, 1979.

James Bacon

- *Hollywood Is a Four-Letter Town*—by the Los Angeles journalist James Bacon. The drinking, gambling, loving habits of the stars. Includes a twenty-five-page chapter on Bacon's (questioned) affair/friendship with Marilyn at the time she was living in producer Joseph M. Schenck's guest house. Photos. Chicago: Henry Regnery, 1976.

Truman Capote

- *Music For Chameleons*—new writing, including an account, called "A Beautiful Child," of an afternoon spent with Marilyn after the funeral of Constance Collier (1878–1955), the actress-coach with whom Marilyn had briefly studied. This account sounds misremembered or manufactured. New York: Random House, 1980.

    *Capote's Marilyn piece is reprinted as the introduction to *Marilyn Monroe, Photographs 1945–1962*, Schirmer/Mosel paperback, 1994.

Jack Cardiff

- *Magic Hour*—the autobiography of the British cinematographer, with a twenty-page chapter on *The Prince and the Showgirl* (1957). Cardiff and Marilyn became good friends. Photos. London/Boston: Faber and Faber, 1996.

Jack Cole

- *Unsung Genius*—a biography by Glenn Loney. A legendary figure in the history of dance, Jack Cole (1914–1974) worked with Marilyn on five films. Photos. New York: Franklin Watts, 1984.

    "Few are aware of the enormous contribution he made to the creation of the legend that was Marilyn."
    —from the dust jacket

g. Peter Collins

- *I Remember... Marilyn*—an account of a seven-month romance that began when they met at the Stage Deli in New York in 1959. Collins's only photo memory (and proof) is a snapshot taken on *The Misfits* location in 1960, of Marilyn talking to a man with his back to the camera. It could be Collins, but how remarkable that he's wearing a shirt identical to the one worn in the film by Montgomery Clift. This 1995 book seems to have been sold mainly through the mail: The Vestal Press, 320 N. Jensen Road, Vestal, New York, 13851.

*Writing sample:

> "For however we felt, and for as much endless devotion we now all pledge individually and together, on that August night, so very long ago, she undertook her longest journey alone."

George Cukor

"I think she was quite mad."

—*George Cukor*

• *On Cukor*—by Gavin Lambert. A biography of the director in the form of a series of interviews, with more than one hundred photos. Four pages on working with Marilyn on *Let's Make Love* (1960): "She never could do the same thing twice, but, as with all the true movie queens, there was an excitement about her." New York: Putnam, 1972.

Tony Curtis

"There's been a lot of bullshit written about that Hitler remark of mine. It was just a throwaway line."

—*Tony Curtis*

• *Tony Curtis, the Autobiography*—with Barry Paris. How Bernie Schwartz from the Bronx became a top movie star. Tony tells his story, and Barry Paris follows behind to drop

in the relevant details and background. Photos, 83-title filmography. New York: William Morrow, 1993.

> *Tony remembers Marilyn from 1949 when she wore see-
> through blouses to attract attention. Tony and Marilyn
> borrowed Howard Duff's Malibu house to spend a night
> together at the beach.

Tay Garnett

• *Light Your Torches and Pull Up Your Tights*—the autobiography of Tay Garnett, director and screenwriter. 130 small
photos. New York: Arlington House, 1973.

> *Four pages on making *The Fireball* (1950), cowritten
> with novelist Horace McCoy. Seeking a backer for the
> project, Garnett went to see Joseph M. Schenck who
> agreed to finance the film and to release it. When more
> money was needed, Schenck again agreed.
>
> Garnett makes no reference to Marilyn, but in cross-
> checking dates, you find that Marilyn and Joe Schenck
> were very good friends at this period.

Sydney Guilaroff

"'You know, Sydney, I know a lot of secrets about what has
gone on in Washington...Dangerous ones!'"

—*Crowning Glory*, Sydney Guilaroff

• *Crowning Glory—Reflections of Hollywood's Favorite Confidant*, by Sydney Guilaroff—as told to Cathy Griffin;
introduction by Angela Lansbury. MGM's hair stylist to the
stars, the first to receive a screen credit; a veteran of more
than 2,000 films. Photos. CA: General Publishing Group,
1996.

*Stories of romances with Garbo and Ava Gardner; creating Louise Brooks's bangs; running into Lana Turner buying a butcher knife the day Johnny Stampanato was stabbed; telling Joan Crawford where to adopt children; and other stories that *really* make you wonder.

Most seriously, he tells of how Marilyn called him in tears on August 4, 1962, saying that she had threatened to arrange a tell-all press conference to expose Bobby Kennedy... and that he had threatened to keep her quiet.

Radie Harris

"The tragedy of the Strasbergs' influence—they motivated her into a lot of pretentious rot!"

—*Radie Harris*

• *Radie's World*—the memoirs of the veteran columnist for the *Hollywood Reporter*. Photos. New York: Putnam, 1975.

*Features a thirteen-page chapter on Marilyn: at a 1950 dinner dance for Laurence Olivier and Vivien Leigh, which Marilyn attended with agent/protector Johnny Hyde—she never said a word; at a 1957 party for Marilyn given by the Oliviers; on the set of *The Prince and the Showgirl*; at Madison Square Garden, May 19, 1962. Radie seems a bit more perceptive than some of her sisters-in-print.

Howard Hawks

"Marilyn Monroe was the most frightened little girl who had no confidence in her ability. Very strange girl. And yet she had this strange effect when she was photographed."

—*Howard Hawks*

• *Hawks on Hawks*, interviewed by Joseph McBride. Hawks directed Marilyn in *Monkey Business* (1952) and *Gentlemen Prefer Blondes* (1953). He speaks only briefly of Marilyn in this book. Photos. Berkeley: University of California Press, 1982.

John Huston

• *An Open Book*—the autobiography of the veteran director. Huston directed Marilyn in her first important film, *The Asphalt Jungle* (1950)—"Marilyn didn't get the part because of Johnny Hyde. She got it because she was damned good."—and in her last completed film, *The Misfits*, ten years later. New York: Knopf, 1980.

    *John Huston narrated the 1966 documentary *The Legend of Marilyn Monroe*.

Nunnally Johnson

• *Screenwriter, the Life and Times of Nunnally Johnson*—a biography by Tom Stempel. Johnson wrote many classic screenplays, including *Jesse James* (1939), and *The Grapes of Wrath* (1940), from the John Steinbeck novel. Photos. Filmography. Cranbury, NJ: A. S. Barnes, 1980.

    *Seven-page chapter on Marilyn. Johnson wrote the screenplays for *We're Not Married* and *How to Marry a Millionaire*. He rewrote the screenplay of *My Favorite Wife* (RKO, 1939), retitling it *Something's Got to Give*, and convinced Marilyn to do it. The minute Johnson left town, Cukor ordered rewrites, which Marilyn took as a slap for having had an opinion about the screenplay.

Ted Jordan

- *Norma Jean: My Secret Life With Marilyn Monroe*—Ted Jordan's account of a passionate affair that began at the Ambassador Hotel in Los Angeles, where he was a lifeguard. Photos, including two nude studies that Jordan says he took of Marilyn but which have since been identified as being of Arline Hunter. New York: William Morrow, 1989.

    *The 1996 HBO movie *Norma Jean and Marilyn*, featuring Ashley Judd and Mira Sorvino, was loosely based on this book.

    *Jordan claimed to possess Marilyn's "little red book," given him by the actress, but on examination it proved not to be the one with all the top-secret information the Kennedy brothers supposedly had told to Marilyn.

Elia Kazan

- *A Life*—the autobiography of the stage and film director. A massive, 848-page memoir full of famous names. Photos. New York: Knopf, 1988.

    *Kazan says he was sexually involved with Marilyn while she was married to Joe DiMaggio, and also later, while she was married to Arthur Miller (a longtime Kazan friend and associate). Kazan was himself married at the time.

Fritz Lang

- *The Films of Fritz Lang*—by Frederick W. Ott. The typical Citadel book treatment: Every film by the director, with casts, credits, synopses, reviews, production notes, more than five hundred photos. Secaucus, NJ: Citadel Press, 1979.

Clash by Night (1952) was from an Odets play, starring a miscast Barbara Stanwyck and a very forceful Marilyn. Lang, quoted on Marilyn: "She was a very peculiar mixture of shyness and uncertainty—I wouldn't say 'star allure'—but . . . she knew exactly her impact on men."

Hans Jorgen Lembourn

• *Diary of a Lover of Marilyn Monroe*—a Danish journalist (Lembourn) writes of a forty-day love affair that supposedly happened in the late 1950s while she was still married to Arthur Miller, when he was writing *The Misfits* for her. Originally published in Denmark in 1979. New York: Arbor House, 1979.

" [S]he never for a moment appears to have taken part in real life . . . She enacts only movie clichés, utters only dialogue that Hollywood keeps in the files."

—*Quentin Crisp, New York magazine, March 19, 1979*

Joshua Logan

• *Movie Stars, Real People, and Me*—autobiography of the Broadway-Hollywood director who worked with Marlon Brando, Bette Davis, Henry Fonda, Ezio Pinza, Vanessa Redgrave, Maurice Chevalier, et al. Sixty-five photos. Complete list of his Broadway shows and Hollywood movies. New York: Delacorte, 1978.

*Twenty-six pages, six photos, on directing Marilyn in *Bus Stop*. He had refused at first, protesting that she couldn't act, until Lee Strasberg told him that of the hundreds of actors he'd worked with, two stood out: Brando and Marilyn.

Joseph L. Mankiewicz

"Imagine Marilyn alive today—very fat, boozing it up. I think she'd have been a pitiful, dreadful mess, and nobody would be able to remember what they do remember."

—"More About All About Eve," interview with Gary Carey

- *All About Eve*—the complete screenplay. New York: Random House, 1951

- *More About All About Eve*—the complete screenplay plus a lengthy interview with Gary Carey. New York: Random House, 1972

- *Pictures Will Talk: The Life and Films of Joseph L. Mankiewicz*—by Kenneth L. Geist. New York: Scribner's, 1978.

    *Two passing references to Marilyn: that she "required an extraordinary number of takes," the scene with George Sanders in the theater lobby requiring twenty-five takes; and how she lost out on *Guys and Dolls* (MGM, 1955).

Yves Montand

- *You See, I Haven't Forgotten*—an autobiography, written with Herve Hamon and Patrick Rotman. Translated from the French by Jeremy Leggatt. The son of Italian peasants who became a legendary music-hall performer, film star, and political activist. Much on his affair with Marilyn while filming *Let's Make Love*. Photos. New York: Knopf, 1992.

Eunice Murray

- *Marilyn: The Last Months*—by Eunice Murray, with sister-in-law Rose Shade. Marilyn's housekeeper-companion-nurse tells her version of the final story...and seemed to change it every time she told it. Photos. Paperback original. New York: Pyramid Books, 1975.

Jean Negulesco

• *Things I Did...and Things I Think I Did*—memoirs of the Rumanian-born director who came to Hollywood in the 1940s. He guided Marilyn through *How to Marry a Millionaire*, and was to replace Cukor as director of *Something's Got to Give* in 1962. He felt he could have cheered her up but wasn't allowed to approach her because of the litigious snit everyone was in. There is a thirteen-page chapter on Marilyn: "Marilyn Monroe, A Vulnerable Phenomenon," with photos, drawings. New York: Simon and Schuster, 1984.

Sir Laurence Olivier

"I refused to treat Marilyn as a special case—I had too much pride in my trade and would at all times treat her as a grown-up artist of merit, which in a sense she was."

—*Sir Laurence Olivier*

• *Confessions of an Actor*—an autobiography. Nine-page chapter on directing and starring with Marilyn in *The Prince and the Showgirl*. Photos, one with Marilyn. New York: Simon and Schuster, 1982.

"A very short way into the filming, my humiliation at Marilyn's rudeness had reached depths I would not have believed possible."

• *The Prince, the Showgirl and Me*—by Colin Clark. Six months on the set with Marilyn and Olivier, as seen by a young gofer who kept a dairy of perceptive, touching, and hilarious observations. Photos. First published in Great Britain by HarperCollins, 1995. American publication, New York: St. Martin's Press, 1996.

*An excerpt from Clark's diary:

"FRIDAY, 2 OCTOBER: There is no denying that MM has problems. She is herself one gigantic problem. But she is also the solution! As long as she can get to the studio and walk onto the set, it is worth everything to film her. This plump, blonde (?) young lady with the big eyes is certainly very hard to control. Right now, she is almost too much for a young, smart producer (Milton), a top playwright and intel-lectual (AM), America's foremost dramatic coaching couple (the Strasbergs) and England's best actor/director (SLO). MM is just a force of nature. This is sort of wonderful for us, to watch and be associated with, but it must be very uncom-fortable for her. I wonder if Garbo was like this, or Chaplin."

Gloria Pall

• *The Marilyn Monroe Party*—an account of Ray Anthony's party for Marilyn and Ray, by blonde showgirl-actress Gloria Pall, who was promoted as a rival to Marilyn. According to Gloria, and to the press clippings she reprints, the reporters were looking for something new—and Gloria was it. A self-published, spiral-bound, xeroxed limited edition. Los Angeles, 1992.

Louella O. Parsons

• *Tell It to Louella*—an affectionate and revealing review of the past two decades in Hollywood, with profiles of Clark Gable, Marlon Brando, Judy Garland. Features "Doubting

Cinderella," a twenty-eight-page chapter on Marilyn—her story up to *The Misfits*. New York: Putnam, 1961.

Lena Pepitone

"She told me that [JFK] was always putting his hand on her thigh."

—Lena Pepitone

- *Marilyn Monroe Confidential*—by Lena Pepitone, with William Stadiem. An account by Marilyn's New York maid and (supposed) friend and confidante, with details on Marilyn's personal hygiene that many find offensive. Also described as "tabloid trashy... exploitative and vulgar" by *The Unabridged Marilyn*. Sixteen pages of photos. New York: Simon and Schuster, 1979.

Otto Preminger

"Directing her was like directing Lassie. You need fourteen takes to get the bark right."

—Otto Preminger

- *Preminger*—an autobiography. The Vienna-born director, apprentice to Max Reinhardt, made his name with *Laura* (1944), and never made another decent movie—*River of No Return* included. Contains a short chapter on making the film, mainly on his problem with "fake" drama coach Natasha Lytess. He denies making the above "Lassie" quote. One photo with Marilyn. New York: Doubleday, 1977.

"Her Psychiatrist Friend"

- *Violations of the Child Marilyn Monroe*—by "her psychiatrist friend." One of the first to jump on the Marilyn money-wagon, this anonymous but still-modest author claims to have made the last phone call. New York: Bridgehead Books, 1962.

Mickey Rooney

- *Life Is Too Short*—the autobiography of Mickey Rooney, indefatigable entertainer. There are several brief references to Marilyn: He says he got her the part in *The Fireball*; and that Marilyn went the naughty route, that she made naughtiness a personal trademark. And he says he saw her at the White House, in a crowd listening to President Kennedy. New York: Villard Books, 1991.

Norman Rosten

- *Marilyn: An Untold Story*—Rosten and his wife Hedda were Marilyn's closest friends and confidants for the final seven years of her life. Paperback original. New York: Signet Books, 1973.

  "A memoir, an insider's account, written with a poet's sensibility and gentle wit."
  —Carolyn Gaiser, *The Village Voice*, November 8, 1973

- *Marilyn Among Friends*—by Sam Shaw and Norman Rosten. A collection of two hundred Shaw photographs, with text by Rosten: an account of Shaw's relationship with Marilyn, and then an extended account of his and his wife's close friendship with her. New York: Henry Holt, 1987.

Jane Russell

- *That Girl*—a 5"x4" pocket magazine. Sixty-eight pages, about fifty photos. New York: Affiliated Magazines, 1953.

- *My Path and My Detour*—an autobiography of Jane Russell. Several pages on filming *Gentlemen Prefer Blondes*, and how director Howard Hawks also had trouble with Natasha Lytess. Photos, one with Marilyn. New York: Franklin Watts, 1985.

Sidney Skolsky

"'I'm going to marry Arthur Miller,' Marilyn said. I looked at her as though she were crazy. 'Arthur Miller! You just got home from a honeymoon!'"

—*Sidney Skolsky*

• *Don't Get Me Wrong—I Love Hollywood*—the anecdotal auto-biography of "Hollywood's favorite columnist." He covered the movie scene from Schwab's drugstore, and was an early, enthusiastic promoter and close friend of Monroe's. With a twenty-six-page chapter on Marilyn, plus eight photos. New York: G. P. Putnam, 1975.

June 26, 1953: Marilyn and Jane Russell leave their hand- and footprints at Grauman's Chinese Theater. Marilyn had suggested it might be more appropriate if she left the imprint of her buttocks, and Jane the imprint of her bust. [Photo courtesy of Photofest.]

The Strasbergs

• *Bittersweet*—Susan Strasberg's first autobiography. The daughter of acting coach Lee Strasberg, she was a Broadway success and an emotional failure, but she survived. She openly recounts her feelings of rivalry with surrogate sister Marilyn. Photos, two with Marilyn. New York: Putnam, 1980.

• *A Method to Their Madness*—the history of the Actors Studio, by Foster Hirsch, the workshop that produced Marlon Brando, James Dean, Geraldine Page, Robert DeNiro, Al Pacino, and where Marilyn escaped to private classes with the Strasbergs. Brief discussion of how the Strasbergs influenced Marilyn's subsequent movies. Photos. New York: Norton, 1984.

• *Marilyn and Me: Sisters, Rivals, Friends*—Susan's firsthand account of Marilyn's becoming part of the Strasberg family in 1954. Lee and Paula became Marilyn's teachers, therapists, parents, with no time for their own unhappy children. Photos. New York: Warner Books, 1992.

Simone Signoret

• *Nostalgia Isn't What It Used to Be*—the autobiography of the blonde French cinema legend. She accompanied husband Yves Montand to Hollywood while he was starring opposite Marilyn in *Let's Make Love*, then returned to Paris to wait out the much-publicized Monroe-Montand affair. New York: Harper and Row, 1978. (First published in France in 1976.)

Billy Wilder

"Marilyn's whole success is she can't act. If she takes it seriously, it is the end of Monroe."

—*Billy Wilder in Hollywood*, Maurice Zolotow

- *Billy Wilder in Hollywood*—a biography by Maurice Zolotow. Wilder worked with Marilyn twice: on *The Seven Year Itch* and *Some Like It Hot*. The first film was trouble but the second was a nightmare that he blamed on the New York sophisticates. He said, "I have never met anyone as utterly mean as Marilyn Monroe. Nor as utterly fabulous on the screen, and that includes Garbo." 364 pages. Photos. New York: Putnam, 1977.

Shelley Winters

- *Shelley II: The Middle of My Century*—a biography by Shelley Winters. New York: Simon and Schuster, 1989.
  *Shelley repeats her usual story of Marilyn washing lettuce with a Brillo pad. She also says that when she heard of Marilyn's death, she was so angry she was able to stand up on water skis the first time she tried.

"In civilized parts of the globe, cannibals eat the flesh of their adversaries in the hope that the virtues of a worthy opponent will pass into their own blood streams. It is in a less noble spirit that the bodies of women like Miss Monroe and Miss Garland are forever being savaged. Their lives are thought to point the smug moral that however rich you may become, however much admiration you may inspire, you can still come to nothing in the end. Their corpses have occasioned a satanic miracle of loaves and fishes. However often their addictions, their neuroses, their drunkenness are paraded like entrails before us, there always seems to be more on which the press, their husbands, and their lovers can feed."

—*Quentin Crisp, New York magazine, March 19, 1979*

(Also see Part 3, Chapter 14, for further information about these people.)

◆

Marilyn in Comic Books

- *Crossfire* comic, numbers 12 and 13—featuring a two-part story on "The 24th Annual Death of Marilyn Monroe," solved by the masked superhero Crossfire. Cover illustration on number 12 is by Dave Stevens. Guerneville, CA: Eclipse Comics, 1985.

- *Madonna vs. Marilyn*—Kirk Lindo, editor–art director. Not strictly a comic book, but with full-page color illustrations of the subjects. Northport, New York: Celebrity Comics, 1991.

- *Marilyn Monroe*—written by Steven Spire III, drawn by Bill O'Neill and Bob Dignan. Massapequa, New York: Personality Classics, 1991.

- *The Marilyn Monroe Conspiracy*—edited by Todd Loren. San Diego, CA: Conspiracy Comics, 1991.

- *Marilyn Monroe: Suicide or Murder?*—edited by Todd Loren. San Diego, CA: Revolutionary Comics, 1991.

- *Monroe and DiMaggio*—editor and publisher Alfonso Alfonso. Miami, FL: Conquest Comics, 1992.

- *Marilyn Monroe: Suicide or Murder?*—edited by Jay Sanford. San Diego, CA: Revolutionary Comics, 1993.

- *Tragic Goddess: Marilyn Monroe*—edited by Adam Post. Westport, CT: POP Comics, division of Whitney Publishing, 1995.

Marilyn's Addresses

- *Marilyn Monroe in Hollywood*—by Marsha Bellavance-Johnson. Forty-two-page pamphlet, a guide book to the main homes, theaters, and restaurants in Marilyn's life. Ketchum, ID: The Computer Lab, 1992.

- *Marilyn's Addresses*—by Michelle Finn. A fan's guide to the places she knew. Two hundred locations associated with her life, with thirty photos. London: Smith Gryphon Publishers, 1995.

Chapter 23

How Did Marilyn Die?

◆

A Compendium of Conspiracies

(conspiracies listed in order of publication)

Murder by Bobby Kennedy and the "Communist Conspiracy"

• *The Strange Death of Marilyn Monroe*—by Frank A. Capell, an ultra-right-wing, red-baiting journalist. Capell says that all of them—Bobby Kennedy, the housekeeper Mrs. Murray, psychiatrist Dr. Ralph Greenson, the lawyer Mickey Rudin, publicist Pat Newcomb—*all* of them were either Communists or thinking about it. Capell says Bobby Kennedy used his "personal Gestapo" to cover up Marilyn's murder. A 7"x 9" pamphlet with stiff covers. Eighty pages, with photos, documents. Zarephath, NJ: The Herald of Freedom, 1964.

> *This went through various printings, with addenda added in 1967 and 1969.

Spontaneous Suicide or Suicide as Revenge

• *Sudden Endings*—by M. J. Meaker. Thirteen in-depth profiles and analyses of famous suicides: Ernest Hemingway,

Diana Barrymore, Virginia Woolf, Hart Crane, Joseph Goebbels, et al. A quote from Marilyn: "I feel a queer satisfaction in punishing the people who are wanting me now. But it's not them I'm really punishing. It's the long-ago people who didn't want Norma Jeane." New York: Doubleday, 1964.

Premeditated Suicide

• *Norma Jean: The Life of Marilyn Monroe*—by Fred Lawrence Guiles, New York: McGraw-Hill, 1969.

• *Legend: The Life and Death of Marilyn Monroe*, by Fred Lawrence Guiles, New York: Stein and Day, 1984.
    *Together, these two books comprise the best biography of Marilyn, written with compassion but also with a certain objective, levelheaded distance from the subject.
    *An excerpt from *Legend*:

    "Marilyn was a compulsive potential suicide. If [Arthur] Miller saved her three times after she actually had crossed the line of tolerance in her pill intake, consider what drove her to that point. Nothing visible, of course, only a sense of worthlessness that no amount of love and reassurance could overcome. And that last weekend she was in the grip of some final compulsion—a compulsion that had become determination."

Blackmail/Accidental Suicide

• *The Beauties and the Beasts*—by Hank Messick. The Mob in show business: Frank Sinatra, George Raft, the murder of Paul Bern, and Marilyn's accidental suicide in a failed attempt to blackmail Bobby Kennedy. New York: McKay, 1973.

Murder by Bobby Kennedy
or Dr. Greenson

• *The Life and Curious Death of Marilyn Monroe*—by Robert
  F. Slatzer, "an old friend and confidant." Photos, copies of
  autopsy reports and other important documents. New York:
  Pinnacle House, 1974.

  *It was Slatzer who first revealed to the world that
  Marilyn was going to hold a press conference to
  denounce both John F. Kennedy and brother Robert
  Kennedy—each had promised to marry her—and it is
  this improbable event that becomes the basis for most of
  the murder theories: She had to die because she was
  going to denounce and ruin the Kennedys.

  Yet on page 272 here, Slatzer himself says, "I knew
  Marilyn, and when [a man] began to grate on her nerves or
  bore her, she simply tossed him over. Is it really possible
  that Marilyn could have wanted to take her life ... simply
  because Bobby Kennedy—or Jack Kennedy—for that
  matter, any lover—had spurned her?"

  Also, on page 250, Slatzer makes reference to an
  unknown statement reportedly made by Bobby Kennedy
  to the Los Angeles police, implicating JFK and Marilyn.
  Slatzer wonders if Bobby is "trying to shift the blame to
  his brother?" Bobby is also said to have told the police
  of Dr. Greenson giving Marilyn an injection in her
  armpit.

• *The Marilyn Files*—by Robert Slatzer. Eighteen years later,
  Slatzer has no more doubts—Robert Kennedy killed Marilyn
  Monroe with specialists from the Secret Service and the CIA,
  a team of doctors and publicists, and a team of legal and cor-
  porate types. (One question: What is "the sound of something being lowered onto a bed?" What exactly does that

sound like?) Photos. Reproductions of the usual documents. New York: Shapolsky Books, 1992, paperback original.

> *This book was the basis for the 1992 KTLA-TV special of the same name.

> *And this just in!—Slatzer and Milo Speriglio announced in 1996 that Marilyn had been killed because she knew the truth about the government cover-up of "the Roswell incident"—when an alien spacecraft crashed in the desert outside Roswell, New Mexico, in 1947.

"Very Probable Suicide" —Coroner, Thomas J. Noguchi

• "Conversation with Dr. Thomas Noguchi"—interview by Donald Carroll, *Oui* magazine, February 1976.

> *Dr. Thomas Noguchi, the Los Angeles County medical examiner, believes it was suicide. Scientific data indicated she had taken thirty or forty Nembutals in a short period of time. There was no trace of these in her stomach, because her body was used to the drug and processed it much faster than would someone who had never taken it before.

> The physical examination was coupled with a psychological autopsy: "Her whole lifestyle pointed toward suicide."

• *Coroner*—a "career highlights" tome by Thomas T. Noguchi, the medical examiner who performed the autopsy on Marilyn and lived to regret it. Other important deaths discussed: Robert F. Kennedy, Sharon Tate, Janis Joplin, William Holden, Natalie Wood, John Belushi. New York: Simon and Schuster, 1983.

Revenge Murder by Fidel Castro... or by Right-Wing CIA Operatives

- *Who Killed Marilyn?*—by Tony Sciacca (aka Anthony Scaduto). This expands the article "Who Killed Marilyn Monroe?" which first appeared in the October 1975 *Oui* magazine. The CIA guys were bitter about JFK bungling the Bay of Pigs... or Castro was angered by assassination attempts on his life. Photos. Paperback original. New York: Manor Books, 1976.

Accidental Suicide... or Murder by Bobby

- *Goddess: The Secret Lives of Marilyn Monroe*—by Anthony Summer. Dumped by Bobby Kennedy, Marilyn accidentally overdosed, and Bobby, Peter Lawford, and the FBI cleaned up, cleared out, covered up. New York: Macmillan, 1985.
    - *However, in the 1986 paperback edition of *Goddess*, Summers has a new chapter in which he discusses the deadly injection by Dr. Ralph Greenson (page 435); and then he writes of "the Marilyn tapes," which have the sounds of Bobby Kennedy and Peter Lawford killing Marilyn (page 442).
    - *But wait—there's more!* Summers also discusses Marilyn as a security risk because she'd been told classified information about nuclear testing and about the attempt to kill Castro (page 439).

Dr. Ralph Greenson and His Big Needle

- "Marilyn Was Murdered: An Eyewitness Account"—by James E. Hall, article in *Hustler* magazine, May 1986. Hall was an ambulance driver for Schaefer Ambulance. He says he and his partner found Marilyn dying; they began CPR and her color started to come back. Dr. Greenson appeared, and pulled out a hypodermic with a huge needle. He pushed Marilyn's breast aside and stuck the needle into her chest. She died immediately.

Murder by the CIA to Save the Kennedys from Scandal

- *The World's Greatest Secrets*—by Allan Hall. Jack the Ripper, Adolph Eichmann, Mata Hari, the Duke of Windsor and Mrs. Wally Simpson, The Manhattan Project, Fatty Arbuckle, The President and Marilyn Monroe, etc. London: Hamlyn, 1989.
    *Quote: "[JFK] had many illicit affairs during his marriage...both before he stepped into the White House and after."
    *Quote: "Several noted journalists...believe that Mafia bosses—sick of the war waged on them by the Kennedys—may have decided to fake Marilyn's suicide in order to lure Bobby Kennedy into a trap."
    *The author quotes Robert Slatzer, and then quotes Milo Speriglio on Marilyn's press conference: Not only was she going to spill the beans about her love affairs with the brothers, but would reveal the secrets of JFK's attempts to kill Castro. So the CIA killed Marilyn to prevent scandal from engulfing the White House.

Mercy Killing by Bodyguard

- Larry Buchanan, director of the film *Goodbye, Norma Jean* (1976), and the recycled version called *Goodnight, Sweet Marilyn* (1989), was quoted in the *Los Angeles Times* on March 30, 1990: "We got an awful lot of lies from the powers that be in Los Angeles, down in City Hall and from the coroner's office. We got a lot of garbage from all of them so we came forward with a very simple truth."

The truth, according to Buchanan, is that Monroe's death was the result of a mercy killing. Buchanan claims a bodyguard named "Mesquite" entered into a pact with the actress that would prevent her from being institutionalized for mental problems. Although there never has been any evidence made public to support his claim, Buchanan contends that Mesquite administered a lethal dose of drugs to help Marilyn "to the other side."

Buchanan repeats this story in *Filmfax* magazine (April-May 1993), but in this version "Mesquite" is a bit player.

Personally Smothered with a Pillow by Robert Kennedy

- *Marilyn: The Ultimate Look at the Legend*—by James Haspiel. Photos. New York: Henry Holt, 1991.

    *Haspiel presents *Rasho-Monroe*, his version of the classic film *Rashomon* (although he gets the plot wrong). Bobby and Peter Lawford tell Marilyn she must stop seeing the President, she's endangering his career. She won't listen. One of them knocks her to the floor (hence the bruises). They put her on the bed, Bobby grabs a pillow and holds it over her face. Bobby leaves, ordering Lawford to make it look like a suicide.

    Suddenly, Lawford realizes Marilyn is not dead, and calls an ambulance. She dies in the ambulance, so they turn around and take her back. Lawford proceeds with the "suicide" details.

    Haspiel says this story "in its entire pathetic and convincing detail had been revealed to me halfway through the 1980s ... Welcome to reality, people."

Revenge Murder by the Mob

- *Double Cross*—the inside story of Sam Giancana, the mobster who controlled America, by his godson and his brother, Sam and Chuck Giancana. Photos. New York: Warner Books, 1992.

  *See if you can follow this: The Mob made John F. Kennedy the President, in return for favors. The Mob also made Marilyn a star, through Mob-connected Joseph M. Schenck, cofounder of Twentieth Century–Fox, and Harry Cohn, head of Columbia Pictures. JFK used Marilyn and actress Angie Dickinson as couriers to deliver confidential FBI memos to Sam Giancana. The CIA used Marilyn as bait to compromise world leaders, including President Sukarno of Indonesia.

  Then, know-it-all J. Edgar Hoover, head of the FBI, confronted the Kennedys, forcing them to begin severing Mob ties. Giancana, outraged, ordered Marilyn killed to compromise Bobby...who somehow weaseled out of it. And you can probably guess Giancana's next two assassinations.

Murder by Bobby Kennedy

- *Marilyn: The Last Take*—by Peter Harry Brown and Patte B. Barham. Photos. New York: Dutton Books, 1992.

  "Compelling evidence that Marilyn was the victim of two conspiracies that, together, brought about her professional and personal downfall—shattering, totally authenticated revelations!"

  *Including Marilyn saying, "I'm going to blow the lid off this thing!"...to Robert Slatzer.

Murder by Bobby Kennedy and J. Edgar Hoover—for the Good of the Country

- *The Murder of Marilyn Monroe*—an "autobiography" of Marilyn, speaking through a group of psychics: Leonore Canevari, Jeanette van Whye, Christian Dimas, Rachel Dimas. Foreword and afterword by Brad Steiger. Photos. New York: Carroll and Graf, 1992, quality paperback.

    *Marilyn says she was murdered because of the press conference she was going to hold. She was going to discuss her relationship with Bobby Kennedy, the Bay of Pigs fiasco, the Kennedys' use of the Mob for political reasons, and her concern over U.S. air strength being so weak.

    Marilyn: "I told Peter [Lawford] that I missed my period and wasn't sure which one, Bobby or John, was the father. But, I told him that I would think about who I would blame depending on which one called first."

    *One suspects Robert Slatzer's heavy hand in all this: When the apparition of Marilyn appears, the first question the psychics ask her is, "It was rumored that you married Bob Slatzer. Did you actually marry him?" And Marilyn answers, "Yes."

    Marilyn's spirit appeared to Bob on August 4, 1973. His report:

    "She had on white slacks with a little black-and-white, splash-pattern top, little white loafers, and I could see a shock of blond hair.

    "The ghostly figure moved down the street and walked through a couple of small drainage ditches before she vanished into thin air. Slatzer noticed that while his shoes left imprints on the concrete from the water in the ditches, the spirit of Marilyn Monroe had left none."

    You can't put nothing over on this guy!

Murder Ordered by John F. Kennedy— Committed by Dr. Ralph Greenson

• A book yet to be published: *Confidentially Marilyn*—by George Carpozi, Jr., who published a credible biography of Marilyn in 1961. In the newsletter of the All About Marilyn Fan Club, October 1992, Carpozi is interviewed about his relationship with Marilyn. After the 1961 book, Marilyn said, "You don't have my real story. Someday...perhaps soon...I may let you write the real story...." Eighteen months later she was dead!

Carpozi researched her life and death for three decades. In his new book, *Confidentially Marilyn*, he will reveal "How Marilyn Was Murdered:"

  • Frank Sinatra negotiated it;
  • Milton "Mickey" Rudin, his lawyer, arranged it;
  • President John F. Kennedy ordered it;
  • Attorney General Robert F. Kennedy supervised it;
  • Dr. Ralph Greenson, her psychiatrist, committed it; and
  • Peter Lawford covered it up.

Shapolsky Publishers featured *Confidentially Marilyn* in its Fall 1992 catalogue. It promised additional stunning revelations:

  • that Marilyn had a secret life as a Hollywood call girl;
  • that Marilyn participated in sexual "orgies" with JFK, RFK, and stars like Frank Sinatra and Dean Martin;
  • plus new evidence that Marilyn was pregnant with Robert F. Kennedy's child when she was murdered.

(Shapolsky Publishers declared themselves bankrupt before this book could be published.)

Accidental Death or Murder by Dr. Greenson and Mrs. Murray

• *Marilyn Monroe*, the biography by Donald Spoto. New York: HarperCollins, 1993.

> *Dr. Greenson was trying to reduce Marilyn's dependence on Nembutal. Dr. Engelberg wrote a prescription for it without Greenson's knowledge. Housekeeper Eunice Murray gave Marilyn a chloral hydrate enema, at Dr. Greenson's direction . . . and the interaction of the two drugs was fatal.

Three conspiracies offered by detective Milo Speriglio:

1. Murder by Hoffa-Giancana Group to Destroy Bobby Kennedy

• *Marilyn Monroe: Murder Cover-Up*—by Milo Speriglio. Paperback original. New York: Seville Publishers, 1982.

• *The Marilyn Conspiracy*—by Milo Speriglio. An updating of the above book. Paperback original. New York: Pocket Books, 1986.

"My investigation has shown that Bobby Kennedy had dangerous adversaries who shrank at nothing to destroy him. In the final weeks of July 1962, RFK's most deadly enemies, the Jimmy Hoffa–Sam Giancana group, found in an abandoned sex star grasping at delusions the opportunity to expose Bobby in a bizarre Hollywood love affair that would ruin his political career." (page 169)

2. Mob Hit Ordered by Joseph Kennedy to Protect John F. Kennedy

• *Crypt 33: The Saga of Marilyn Monroe—The Final Word—* by Adela Gregory and Milo Speriglio. Marilyn had to die because she was pregnant with Bobby Kennedy's child, and people would have thought it was JFK's. Joseph Kennedy ordered the hit, by Sam Giancana, who was seeking to blackmail/control the Kennedys. The hit men were Phil "Milwaukee" Alderisio, Johnny "the Angel of Death" Roselli, Anthony "the Ant" Spilotro, Chuckie Nicoletti, Frank Schweihs, and Frank Cullotta—who collectively were involved in over three hundred murders. Photos. New York: Carol Publishing, 1993.

3. Marilyn Knew of Government Cover-up of Flying-Saucer Crash

*In 1996, Milo Speriglio and Robert Slatzer announced that Marilyn had been killed because she knew the truth about the government cover-up of the Roswell incident—in which an alien spacecraft crashed in the desert outside Roswell, New Mexico, in 1947, and the government denied it ever happened.

Murder by CIA Renegades to Destroy the Kennedys

• *The Men Who Murdered Marilyn*—by Matthew Smith, investigative journalist. Introduction by Robert Mitchum. London: Bloomsbury Publishing, 1996.

*Smith modestly says he thought that his theory of "a right-wing group of malcontents in the CIA providing the 'mechanics' to murder Marilyn" was originated by him—but that others had reached the same conclusion: novelist Norman Mailer and columnist Dorothy Kilgallen!

Then Smith also modestly reminds readers that he earlier had uncovered evidence of CIA renegades being involved in the conspiracy to assassinate President Kennedy and Robert Kennedy.

Chapter 24

Marilyn in Poem and Prose

(alphabetical by author)

• George Axelrod, *Will Success Spoil Rock Hunter?*—a play. A comedy of a Marilyn-type actress. Jayne Mansfield created the part on Broadway in 1955 and then starred in the 1957 movie version. New York: Random House, 1956.

• Jon Barraclough and Neil Norman, *Insignificance: The Book.* A lengthy essay on "the making of myth," and the screenplay by Terry Johnson for the 1985 Nicolas Roeg film. Quality paperback. London: Sidgwick and Jackson, 1985.

  *A black comedy of a hot New York night in 1954, when Marilyn, Joe DiMaggio, Senator Joe McCarthy, and scientist Albert Einstein get together to discuss life, death, sex, and the universe. First produced at London's Royal Court Theatre in 1982 with Australian Judy Davis as the Actress. The 1985 film version starred Roeg's wife Theresa Russell, Tony Curtis, Gary Busey, Michael Emil, and Will Sampson. In the play, the fifth character is "a tall, dark mobster type, probably CIA." In the film, he's an Indian.

  Leonard Maltin's *Movie and Video Guide* (1998) understands it better than I do: "Striking, gloriously cinematic examination of the meaning of fame in America and the perils of atomic warfare." Whatever you say, Leonard.

- George Bernau, *Candle in the Wind*—a novel of sex symbol Marilyn Lane, who survives an overdose, then undergoes "a drama more dangerous, more tempestuous than any she'd played on the screen." New York: Warner Books, 1990.

- Alvah Bessie, *The Symbol*—a novel. Marilyn's life, told as the story of Wanda Oliver who wants to be loved for herself, not her body. "Trash," said *Time* magazine. "A pig's-eye view of Marilyn's life," said Edward Wagenknecht. New York: Random House, 1966.
    *This was the basis for the 1974 ABC-TV film *The Sex Symbol*, starring Connie Stevens. Alvah Bessie also wrote the teleplay.

- John W. Blanpied, editor; *Movieworks*—stories and poems about movies. An anthology of ninety-three poems and stories by fifty-seven writers, including "To Marilyn" by Elizabeth Patton. Rochester, New York: The Little Theater Press, 1990.

- Marilyn Bowering, *Anyone Can See I Love You*—a cycle of Marilyn poems, written in the first person. Several of the poems use words attributed to Marilyn. Ontario: The Porcupine's Quill, 1987.

- Phyllis Burke, *Atomic Candy*—a novel. "A frontal assault on the cultural icons of the last half of the twentieth century"— from the dust jacket. New York: Atlantic Monthly Press, 1989.
    *Marilyn, JFK, Richard M. Nixon, and the atomic bomb are shown on the dust jacket.

- Ernesto Cardenal, *Marilyn Monroe and Other Poems*. "The world's foremost poet writing in Spanish"—from the dust jacket. London: Search Press, 1975.

- Jock Carroll, *The Shy Photographer*—a novel by the Canadian author and photographer whose photographs of Marilyn for *Niagara* were not published in book form until 1996, as *Falling for Marilyn: The Lost Niagara Collection.* New York: Stein and Day, 1964. "A comic novel, a black comedy about movie queen Gloria Heaven who came to a tragic end because of the pressures of her life."

- Paddy Chayefsky, *The Goddess* (a screenplay). New York: Simon and Schuster, 1957.

Rita: "How nice do I have to be?
Casting Director: "If you're not Bette Davis, you gotta be very nice."

    *New York, summer 1955: Lee Strasberg wanted Marilyn to meet the best writers in town, and so introduced her to Paddy Chayefsky. Chayefsky gave her an advance copy of *Middle of the Night*, due to open on Broadway in February 1956.

    Marilyn read the play overnight and called the writer the next day, saying she was in love with the part of the secretary, the beautiful young woman with the soul of a child. After the play opened, Marilyn made Chayefsky promise he would not give the screen rights to anyone other than Marilyn Monroe Productions.

    Putting everything else on hold, Chayefsky spent considerable time and energy revising the play for Marilyn. When the first draft was completed, he had trouble reaching Marilyn or Milton Greene. He was told she had a new literary adviser: Arthur Miller.

    While Marilyn and Arthur were honeymooning in England, word was sent to Chayefsky that she was no longer interested in doing the movie. He was asked if he was interested in writing a screenplay about Jean Harlow.

Paddy Chayefsky got angry. He spent the next two years writing and producing *The Goddess*.

"This original script would ultimately depict the rise and fall of Rita Shawn, a major Hollywood movie star whose unquenchable ambition and shattered life were eerily similar to Marilyn Monroe's. What would later surprise many about *The Goddess* was not that he had used Marilyn Monroe as his prototype, but that he captured her inner longing and despair so accurately."

—*Shaun Considine, Mad as Hell: The Paddy Chayefsky Story*

Chayefsky forwarded the first copy of *The Goddess* to Marilyn—a bold move, but why not? It was a good script. Marilyn read it and said she wanted to play the part. But Arthur was jealous and hated the script, and changed his wife's mind.

A scene from *The Goddess* (1958), with Kim Stanley as a despairing blonde sex symbol, and Lloyd Bridges as her husband the sports hero. Paddy Chayefsky wrote the original screenplay, apparently to get even with Marilyn. [Photo courtesy of Photofest.]

Kim Stanley was a highly regarded Broadway star, and a member of the Actors Studio. She created the role of Cherie in the original production of *Bus Stop*. Because Marilyn got to do the movie, it was seen as fitting that Kim Stanley should do the part of Marilyn in *The Goddess*.

Betty Lou Holland, who played the mother, was the same age as Kim Stanley. Five-year-old Patty Duke was "the goddess" as a girl. Joan Copeland was the aunt—a very interesting choice in that the actress was Arthur Miller's sister, and thus Marilyn's sister-in-law. Elizabeth Wilson played Natasha Lytess–Paula Strasberg. Lloyd Bridges and Steven Hill were the two husbands.

At the time the film was set to open, Harry Cohn, president of Columbia Pictures, died of a heart attack—leaving behind no one who knew how to market an offbeat little film like *The Goddess*. It premiered without fanfare in a small New York art house on Fifty-fifth Street and was left to wither away. The film received rave reviews all over the world, and was given the jury's Special Prize at the 1957 Brussels Film Festival, but Columbia apparently did not hear about it.

Viewers who see the film now are usually not prepared for the film's strong emotional impact.

• Kenn Davis and John Stanley, *Bogart '48*. Who's plotting to blow up the 1948 Academy Awards show? Humphrey Bogart and friends race against the clock. New York: Dell Publishing, 1980, paperback.

• Henry Denker, *The Director*—a novel. The filming of *Mustang!*—starring Preston Carr, king of the superstars, and Daisy Donnell, a sex symbol terrified of her career and filled with "a constant sense of doom." The *New York Times Book*

Review called it "a generally entertaining charade." New York: Richard W. Baron Publishing, 1970.

- Henry Denker, *Venus at Large*—a Hollywood comedy. It opened on Broadway in April 1962, to negative reviews. David Wayne starred in *Venus at Large*, as a Hollywood agent haunted by the fact that he's not Jewish. (He thinks of becoming a Wandering Presbyterian.) William Prince was an Arthur Miller type, Boris Tumarin a Lee Strasberg type, Jack Bittner a Paddy Chayefsky type, and Leon Janney was Jack Carr, a Jack Paar type. Joyce Jameson was praised in the Marilyn role.

"The girl sex symbol . . . is not only amusing but, thanks to the spectacular Miss Jameson's skillful portrayal, is also genuinely touching in her childlike earnestness."

—*Richard Watts, Jr.,* **The New York Post,** *April 13, 1962*

"Possibly Mr. Denker is inhibited by the laws of libel or by a realization that the saga of a Marilyn Monroe among the dedicated Methodists has an honest, touching side. Or it may be that satire is not his métier."

—*Howard Taubman,* **The New York Times,** *April 13, 1962*

- Carole Nelson Douglas, editor; *Shades of Blonde*—a 352-page collection of "what if?" short stories about Marilyn Monroe. Most of the entries are by mystery and horror writers. New York: Forge, 1997.

- Lucinda Ebersole and Richard Peabody, editors; *Mondo Marilyn: An Anthology of Fiction and Poetry.* Excerpts from novels by Doris Grumbach, Sam Toperoff, John Rechy; poems by Charles Bukowski, Lyn Lifshin, Taylor Mead, and much more. New York: St. Martin's Press, 1995, quality paperback original.

- Jonathan Fast, *The Inner Circle*—a show-business murder mystery. A mysterious cult worships a Mexican panther god which must be appeased every ten years with a human sacrifice. Victims are from the film industry and have included (characters based upon) Jean Harlow, Marilyn Monroe, James Dean, Freddie Prinze. New York: Delacorte Press, 1979.

- Donald Freed, *American Iliad*—a play featuring Richard M. Nixon, JFK, and Marilyn Monroe. It was given a reading at Loyola University in Los Angeles in August of 1996.

- Philip French and Ken Wlaschin, editors; *The Faber Book of Movie Verse*—an anthology of 340 poems by 227 English-language poets. London/Boston: Faber and Faber, 1993.
     *Four Marilyn poems: "Marilyn" by Lee L. Berkson; "Marilyn and You" by Alan Jenkins; "The Earth: To Marilyn" by Judith E. Johnson; and "Marilyn" by Lawrence P. Spingarn.

   "Marilyn has probably been the subject of more poems... than any other star or filmmaker in the history of cinema."
   —*The Faber Book of Movie Verse*

- William Goldman, *Tinsel*—a novel by the successful screenwriter. New York: Delacorte Press, 1979.

   "It's about the financing and casting of a film about the last hours of Marilyn Monroe. When Raquel Welch refuses to appear nude in the part, the field is opened to three sex symbols in varying degrees of professional eclipse. *Tinsel* is nasty, hard-edged entertainment."
   —*Newsweek, August 13, 1979*

- E. J. Gorman, *The Marilyn Tapes*. New York: Tom Doherty Associates, 1995.

   "[A] novel of the days just after Marilyn's death... and how J. Edgar Hoover, Louella Parsons, the Mafia, and the Kennedy brothers battle each other for possession of the provocative tape-recordings secretly made in Marilyn's own bedroom—tapes that could topple the Kennedy administration and make J. Edgar Hoover the most powerful man in America."

—from the dust jacket

"A dum-dum between the eyes...[it] will blow the back of your skull off."

—Popular novelist Joe Gores

• Corinne Griffith, *Hollywood Tales*. "Based somewhat on fact...each tale is dedicated to one of Hollywood's 'greats,' and challenges the reader to imagine [the star] in its central role"—*The Hollywood Novel*, Anthony Slide. The stories are for Marilyn, Frank Sinatra, David Niven, Corinne Griffith, Gary Cooper, Eddie Anderson, Bob Hope. Los Angeles: Frederick Fell, 1962.

> *The authoress is more interesting than any of her stories. Corinne Griffith (1894–1979) was a major star of the silents who later claimed that she was not the actress Corinne Griffith but her stand-in, who took over when the real actress died. (Details from Anthony Slide, *The Hollywood Novel*)

• Doris Grumbach, *The Missing Person*—a novel. New York: Putnam, 1981.

"A portrait of extraordinary public glamour and private misery. The nation's number one pinup: Franny Fuller...sexy, voluptuous actress whose whispery voice and glorious blond mane have aroused the fascination of every moviegoer in the country."

—from the dust jacket

• Brett Halliday, *Kill All the Young Girls*—a murder mystery. Characters apparently based on Marilyn and Darryl F. Zanuck and other ruthless types out to kill each other. New York: Dell Publishing, 1973, paperback.

• Ben Hecht, *The Sensualists*—a novel. The story of a woman who falls in love with her husband's mistress...who turns out to be a character obviously patterned on Marilyn. New York: Julian Messner, 1959.

> She held her head like an animal strutting and sniffing. "She acts is if she's a champion of something or other, probably sex."
>
> *—from The Sensualists*

• William Hegner, *The Idolators*—a novel. New York: Trident Press, 1973.

> "Loosely based on the life of Marilyn Monroe. The central character is raped as a teenager, becomes a successful screen star, marries a baseball player and a prize-winning playwright, but kills herself because she cannot become pregnant or fully return a man's love."
>
> *—Anthony Slide, The Hollywood Novel*

• Terry Johnson, *Insignificance*—a play. A black comedy of a hot New York night in 1954 when Marilyn, Joe DiMaggio, Senator Joe McCarthy, and scientist Albert Einstein get together to discuss life, death, sex, and the universe. First produced at London's Royal Court Theater in 1982 with Australian Judy Davis as "Actress." London: Methuen paperback, 1982.

• Garson Kanin, *Come On Strong*—a play based in part on Marilyn. The story of blonde actress Virginia Karger (vocal coach Fred Karger was one of Marilyn's important loves) who marries an aging millionaire who drops dead on their honeymoon. The play was on Broadway briefly in 1962, with Carroll Baker and Van Johnson. Acting version published by Dramatists Play Service.

- Garson Kanin, *Moviola*. New York: Simon and Schuster, 1979.

  "An overwrought, eulogistic novel about the film business...a greenhorn-to-mogul saga with cameo performances by great stars of the distant and recent past...Much space is devoted to a novelization of the rise and fall of Marilyn Monroe. [The fictional mogul's] conclusion: 'It was just a case of bad luck, mismanagement. She met the wrong people, she got bad advice.'"

  —*Time magazine, December 31, 1979*

- Michael Korda, *The Immortals*—a novel of Marilyn's affairs with the Kennedy brothers. The supporting cast features a full complement of conspirators: J. Edgar Hoover, Jimmy Hoffa, the Mafia. Korda lists his published source material, a fairly disreputable lineup. He excerpts the "red diary," as quoted in Ted Jordan's book. New York: Poseidon Press, 1992.

  "Someone was bound to write something this staggeringly vulgar, and now it is out of the way."

  —*John Rechy, The Los Angeles Times Book Review*

  "It's a pretty tacky novel."

  —*Booklist*

- Lyn Lifshin, *Marilyn Monroe*—poems. Portland, OR: Quiet Lion Press, 1994.

  "[Her poems] are nightmarish snapshots, sharp visual details turned in a flash into emotional significance."

  —*Ms. Magazine*

- Nellie McClung, *"My Sex Is Ice Cream"—The Marilyn Monroe Poems*. Using Marilyn's own poetry as inspiration, Nellie

McClung re-creates Marilyn's sexuality, her vulnerability, her intelligence. Includes a selection of Marilyn's own poetry, transcribed from her notebooks by Norman Rosten. Victoria, B.C., Canada: Ekstasis Editions, 1996, paperback.

• Vardis Margener, *Double Take*—a novel based on a screenplay by Alfred Sole and Colin Pahlow. A millionaire Marilyn collector meets a woman who could have been Marilyn's twin; she makes the guy's fantasies come true. But then he sees a photo of her daughter.... New York: Playboy Press, 1982, paperback original.

• Roger Newman, *The Hardest Part of It* (aka *Public Property*)—a 1979 play about Marilyn Monroe that was staged in London under the first title, then in New York under the second.

• Ann Pinchot, *52 West*—a novel of success in our time. The title refers to a New York boarding house catering to artists, musicians, actors. New York: Farrar, Straus and Cudahy, 1962.

"A group of 1930s boarders gather together in 1961 to help the owner out of her current financial problems, and among their number is an actress who became a starlet after posing in the nude; she contemplates suicide and has some of the same characteristics as Marilyn Monroe."

—*Anthony Slide, The Hollywood Novel*

• John Rechy, *Marilyn's Daughter*. A 531-page novel by the controversial author of *City of Night*. An eighteen-year-old girl discovers a letter asserting that she is the daughter of Marilyn Monroe, and goes on a search for the truth. New York: Carroll and Graf, 1988.

*Maurice Zolotow, Marilyn's first biographer, reviewed this book for the *Los Angeles Times Book Review*: "I knew most of the significant individuals in her personal life and in her career...and so, yes, I feel that Rechy's book neither reflects reality nor distorts it interestingly."

- Ron Renaud, *Fade to Black*. A novelization of Vernon Zimmerman's 1980 film, with Linda Kerridge as a Marilyn look-alike, being stalked by a murderous movie nut played by Dennis Christopher. New York: Pinnacle Books, 1980, paperback.

- Martin Ryerson, *The Golden Venus*—a novel of Robyn Bonney, and her rise from orphan to sex symbol. New York: Award Books, 1968, paperback original.

- Ben Staggs, *MMII: The Return of Marilyn Monroe*—a "what if?" novel. What if Marilyn didn't die but escaped to New York where, disguised as a redhead, she pursued a serious acting career...while working at a Doubleday bookstore? New York: Donald Fine, 1991.

- Roseanne Daryl Thomas, *The Angel Carver*—a novel. A retelling of the Pygmalion myth. Two artists take different approaches to re-creating Marilyn. Jack is a wood carver who meets Lucille, who dreams of getting rich from her resemblance to Marilyn. Jack carves a wooden, bejeweled statue of her. Buddy meets Lucille and with the help of plastic surgeons turns her into Marilyn Monroe "in all her nodding, blue-eyed, comatose glory." New York: Random House, 1993.

- Sam Toperoff, *Queen of Desire*—a novel based on Marilyn's life, blending truth and invention, real people and fictional characters. New York: HarperCollins, 1992.

"A defect that sabotages Mr. Toperoff's work throughout: his real-life characters tend to be pallid facsimiles of the vibrant originals."
—*The New York Times Book Review*, May 3, 1992

Chapter 25

Marilyn's Films

(books covering all her films)

- *The Films of Marilyn Monroe*—by Michael Conway and Mark Ricci. Fully illustrated filmography, an early title in the Citadel Press's "Films of" series. New York: The Citadel Press, 1964.

- *The Films of Marilyn Monroe*—by Richard Buskin. 9"x11" pictorial. Less text than Citadel's, but with slick quality paper and one hundred color photos. Lincolnwood, IL: Publications International, 1992.

**(books on individual films—
chronological by film release date)**

All About Eve (1950)

- *All About Eve*—the complete screenplay. New York: Random House, 1951.
- *More About All About Eve*—the screenplay plus lengthy discussion with director Joseph L. Mankiewicz and editor Gary Carey. New York: Random House, 1972.

The Fireball (1950)

- *Light Your Torches and Pull Up Your Tights*—the autobiography of director Tay Garnett. Garnett devotes four pages to the problems in filming *Fireball*. He makes no reference to Marilyn...but does say that Marilyn's friend mogul Joseph M. Schenck financed the film. New York: Arlington House, 1973.

The Asphalt Jungle (1950)

• *The Asphalt Jungle*—a screenplay by Ben Maddow and John Huston, from the novel by W. R. Burnett. Afterword by W. R. Burnett. A few photos, one with Marilyn. Southern Illinois University Press, 1980.

Niagara (1953)

• *Falling for Marilyn: The Lost Niagara Collection*—photos by Jock Carroll. (See Part 4, Chapter 18, "Jock Carroll.")

The Seven Year Itch (1955)

• *The Seven Year Itch*—the play by George Axelrod. Photos from the film. New York: Bantam Books, 1955, paperback.
• *Marilyn Monroe as The Girl*, by Stanley Kauffmann. (See Part 4, Chapter 18, "Sam Shaw.")
• *The Great Movies—Live!*—a pop-up book featuring classic scenes from *King Kong, High Noon, Casablanca, Gone With the Wind*, and Marilyn's skirt-blowing scene from *The Seven Year Itch*. New York: Fireside–Simon and Schuster, 1987.

Bus Stop (1956)

• *Bus Stop*—the original play by William Inge. New York: Random House, 1955.

- *Bus Stop—A Story Based on the 20th Century–Fox CinemaScope Film Starring Marilyn Monroe.* A 5"x7" British paperback—a novelization of the film, with fifty-four black-and-white photos, plus other stories on the film and on Marilyn, with sixteen photos. London: Charles Buchan's, 1956.

The Prince and the Showgirl (1957)

- *The Prince and the Showgirl*—the screenplay by Terence Rattigan, from his play. Photos from the film. New York: Signet, 1957, paperback original.
- *The Prince, the Showgirl and Me*—six months on the set with Marilyn and Laurence Olivier—by Colin Clark. (Discussed at length in Part 4, Chapter 22, "They Knew Marilyn ... "— Laurence Olivier.)

Some Like It Hot (1959)

- *Some Like It Hot*—the screenplay by Billy Wilder and I. A. L. Diamond. Nine photos from the film. New York: Signet, 1959, paperback original.
- "The Day Marilyn Needed 47 Takes to Remember to Say, 'Where's the Bourbon?'" by I. A. L. Diamond, in *Roots* magazine, December 1985.
- *Tony Curtis: The Autobiography* has much to say on the irritations of making this film. (See Part 4, Chapter 22, "They Knew Marilyn ... "—Tony Curtis.)
- *Some Like It Hot*—original movie script. Large format paperback, one of a series published by *Premiere—The Movie Magazine*. Monterey Park, CA—O.S.P. Publishing, Inc., 1994.

Let's Make Love (1960)

- *Let's Make Love*, by Matthew Andrews—a novelization of the screenplay by Norman Krasna. New York: Bantam Books, 1960, paperback original.

The Misfits (1961)

(See listings under Part 4, Chapter 22, "Marilyn and Arthur Miller.")

- *Marilyn Monroe: An Appreciation*, by Eve Arnold, has much to say about filming *The Misfits*. (See Part 4, Chapter 18, "Eve Arnold.")

Chapter 26

Marilyn, the Apotheosis

◆

Marilyn as Pop-Culture Icon, Legend, Symbol, Living Goddess

- *Demon*, by John Varley. A sci-fi novel of the goddess Gaea who is able to manifest herself in whatever form she wishes. In the excellent cover illustration by Steve Ferris, she takes the form of a nearly nude Marilyn Monroe. New York: Berkley Books, 1984, hardcover book club edition (the only hardcover edition).

- *How to Impersonate Famous People*—by Christopher Fowler. Illustrations by Stuart Buckley. Step-by-step instructions for impersonating Marilyn, Groucho Marx, Bette Davis, the Elephant Man, Carmen Miranda, Elvis Presley, et al. New York: Crown Books, Prince Paperbacks, 1984.

- *Son of Celluloid*—a graphic novel by Clive Barker, illustrated by Les Edwards. A dying hoodlum crawls into a fleabag movie theater to hide. His cancer assumes a monstrous life of its own, killing wantonly. The spirits of the Movies—personified by John Wayne and Marilyn Monroe—come to the rescue. Forestville, CA: Eclipse Books, 1991.
    *A true horror comic, not for the faint of heart. The cover illustration has Marilyn licking blood.

- *Dying to Be Marilyn*, by Yvette Paris—"the Queen of Burlesque," a successful Marilyn look-alike. How Marilyn's fame and personality can become embodied in those who imitate her, and how these imitators can become captured and enslaved by "the Marilyn Vortex." Also describes many of the famous and successful Marilyn look-alikes and impersonators. Cheyenne, WY: Lagumo Corp., 1996.

Chapter 27

What's Marilyn All About?

• *The Celluloid Sacrifice: Aspects of Sex in the Movies*—by Alexander Walker. An examination of sex appeal and censorship, with a chapter comparing Jean Harlow and Marilyn. Illustrated, one Marilyn photo. New York: Hawthorne Books, 1967.

• *The Hollywood Cage*—by Charles Hamblett. A London journalist gives a sensationalized portrait of the Hollywood that killed Marilyn. Includes an account of *The Misfits* production that is obviously not firsthand. Of value is Henry Hathaway's remarks on how Marilyn was mistreated and her talent wasted (pages 145–47). 150 photos. New York: Hart Publishing, 1969.

 *Originally published in England as *Who Killed Marilyn Monroe?—or, Cage to Catch Our Dreams*. London: Leslie Frewin, 1966.

• *Marilyn Monroe: A Composite View*—edited by Edward Wagenknecht. A valuable collection of pieces not otherwise readily available. New York: Chilton Books, 1969.

 *Interviews by Richard Meryman (*Life*) and Alan Levy (*Redbook*).

 *Memories by film critic Hollis Alpert, Arthur Miller's father, poet Edith Sitwell, six top photographers, *Photoplay* editor Adele Whitely Fletcher, and poet Norman Rosten.

*Reflections by photographer Cecil Beaton, acting-guru Lee Strasberg (the funeral eulogy); analyses by art/social critics Lincoln Kirstein, Diana Trilling, David Robinson, Alexander Walker, and Wagenknecht himself.

• *From Reverence to Rape: The Treatment of Women in the Movies*—by Molly Haskell. A study of sex and sexism, showing how the situation has deteriorated over the years. With an important analysis of Marilyn. Photos. New York: Holt, Rinehart and Winston, 1974.

   *Second edition, updated—The University of Chicago Press, 1987.

"The one thing in Marilyn that we can never forget, and perhaps never forgive, is the painful, naked and embarrassing need for love."

— *Molly Haskell*

• *Marilyn Lives!*—by Joel Oppenheimer. Oversize, quality paperback, fully illustrated. Mostly about Marilyn's fans and how they were affected by her. New York: Delilah Books, 1981.

• *Film Comment* magazine for September-October 1982— with two important cover stories: David Thomson on Marilyn as a pinup photo supreme, and David Stenn on the Marilyn industry.

• *Heavenly Bodies: Film Stars and Society*—by Richard Dyer. How the image of three stars is reflected in the attitudes and experiences of a particular social group: Judy Garland in gay cultural iconography; Paul Robeson as related to black issues; and Marilyn Monroe in the context of feminist debates about images of women. About forty pages on Marilyn, with photos. New York: St. Martin's Press, 1986.

- *Marilyn Monroe, A Life of the Actress*—by Carl E. Rollyson, Jr. The first serious evaluation of her talent as an actress ... evaluating her movies as crucial events in the shaping of her identity. Ann Arbor, MI: UMI Research Press, 1986.

    * Dust jacket features color production of Audrey Flack's beautiful painting of a young Marilyn.

- *Marilyn Monroe*—by Graham McCann. A reexamination of her life and representation, drawing on critical theory, feminism, and film studies. NJ: Rutgers University Press, 1988.

    "The definitive study of a movie star as icon, as odalisque, and as slave."
    —*Quentin Crisp*

- *Lovesick: The Marilyn Syndrome*—by Susan Israelson and Elizabeth Macavoy. Exploring the notion that some people are so emotionally deprived as children that they are handicapped in adult relationships. New York: S. P. I. Books, 1992.

    *The paperback edition is called *The Marilyn Syndrome*.

- *Why Norma Jean Killed Marilyn Monroe*—by Lucy Freeman. The author of *Fight Against Fears* explores why Marilyn was driven to suicide. Chicago: Global Rights, Ltd., 1992.

- *American Monroe: The Making of a Body Politic*—by S. Paige Baty. Berkeley: University of California Press, 1995.

    "By using the latest tools of deconstruction and gender studies, [Baty] has done her best to turn a human being into a bloodless text, an object, a toy for pompous academics. Pretentious, solipsistic and utterly devoid of humor and common sense."
    —*Michiko Kakutani, The New York Times, August 1, 1995*

• *Marilyn Monroe: The Life, The Myth*—edited by Giovan Battista Brambilla, Gianni Mercurio, Stefano Petricca. Published on the occasion of the Italian exhibit *Marilyn, Il Mito*. A major 320-page collection of international memorabilia tracing Marilyn's life and career from orphan to goddess. 9" x 12". New York: Rizzoli, 1996.

*Includes reproductions of 142 magazine covers plus numerous reprints of fan magazine stories; Earl Moran color illustrations; features on the photos of Milton Greene, Douglas Kirkland, George Barris. Plus, essays on Marilyn and Andy Warhol, Marilyn as a pop icon, reminiscences by photographers Sam Shaw and Eve Arnold, Marilyn and star-style fashion, Marilyn memorabilia, etc. "Marilyn nude" photos identify Candy Barr as the star of *The Apple, Knockers, and the Coke Bottle*, and say that the nude in Ted Jordan's book is "perhaps" really Marilyn—but both ladies have long been identified as Arline Hunter.

Chapter 28

A Marilyn Bibliography

- *Marilyn Monroe, A Bibliography*—by Frederic Cabanas. Preface by Fred Lawrence Guiles. A 122-page quality paperback: a worldwide bibliography of Marilyn. Small reproductions of book covers. Barcelona: Ixia Libres, 1992. Multilingual.

Chapter 29

The Essential
Marilyn Library

- Guiles, Fred Lawrence, *Norma Jean and Legend*—together, the best biographies, levelheaded and loving. (See pages 273–4.)
- Spoto, Donald, *Marilyn Monroe, The Biography*—the most important book on Marilyn because of the massive amount of new research and the author's willingness to take on bad guys and phonies. (See page 277.)
- Hitchens, Neal, and Randall Riese, *The Unabridged Marilyn*—near definitive, alphabetical reference. (See page 276.)
- Buskin, Richard, *The Films of Marilyn Monroe*—the best filmography. (See page 335.)
- Wagenknecht, Edward, *Marilyn: A Composite View*—a valuable collection of hard-to-find interviews, essays, reviews. (See page 341.)
- Doll, Susan, *Marilyn: Her Life and Legend*—the most photos for the money. (See page 262.)
- Belmont, George, editor; *Marilyn and the Camera*—the best collection of the classic photos, with superior reproduction. (See page 261.)

- de Dienes, Andre, *Marilyn, Mon Amour*, and Milton Green, *Milton's Marilyn*—the best Marilyn photos. (See pages 249–50.)
- Rosten, Norman, *Marilyn, An Untold Story*—a friend as seen through the eyes of a poet. (See page 302.)
- Clark, Colin, *The Prince, the Showgirl and Me*—the best behind-the-scenes book ever, with a revealing firsthand account of Marilyn. (See page 299.)

Chapter 30

Marilyn on the Internet

(and how to find her)

What is it about Marilyn and the Web?

It's anyone's guess whether it would be more accurate to say that the Internet and the World Wide Web were invented just for people like Marilyn fans, or if the superhighway had not fallen into place when it did, Marilyn followers would have had to invent it. Either way, no matter how much you know about Marilyn, or how big your Marilyn collection is—you ain't seen nothin' yet!

Once you've logged on and connected with your browser (Netscape Navigator, Microsoft Explorer, whatever) you can get an idea of your Marilyn options in cyberspace by searching for "Marilyn Monroe" through any of a number of search engines and web guides. Here's what a few quick searches done the week of the thirty-fifth anniversary of Marilyn's death turned up:

- Yahoo! (a popular web guide) came up with fifty-two sites divided into two main categories, "Entertainment: Actors and Actresses," and "Business and Economy: Companies: Entertainment: Movies and Film: Memorabilia: Monroe, Marilyn."

- Lycos, another commonly-used Web guide, turned up 11,694 matches on a search of "Marilyn Monroe." The Alta Vista search engine identified a total of 176,250 documents relating to Marilyn available on the World Wide Web.

But what is all this stuff? And where does one begin? And how do you keep from going broke?

A great place to begin your Marilyn Monroe cyberspace odyssey is what many net-surfing Marilyn fans and collectors refer to as "Peggy Wilkins' page," or just "Peggy's page." You get there by keying in this address: http://mozart.lib.uchicago.edu/Marilyn/

In a few moments, you discover the wonderful service Ms. Wilkins provides. Very easy-to-follow web pages give you well-organized and clearly described one-click access to many of the best, most interesting and useful Marilyn Monroe locations on the Internet. You can see unfamiliar photos, read bios and film reviews. You learn about Marilyn Merlot wines, look at original Marilyn artwork, and see digitally enhanced MM images. Another opportunity at this one location is to sign on with a "list-serve" subscriber list where any subscriber can post a message or query to be read by all and responded to as one sees fit.

Once you've spent a little time at this "Marilyn Monroe" address, you can try doing your own MM searches. Chances are, you'll click from Peggy's page to someone else's who offers yet another link to something you want to investigate. (On the Internet user/news groups, a good starting place is: alt.movies.marilyn-monroe.) And on it goes.

If you're looking for recent books about Marilyn, the web offers stay-at-home book buying services—one is Amazon Books, based in Portland, Oregon. Their web address is: http://www.amazon.com

The bigger bookstore chains will be giving Amazon a run for your money. The Barnes and Noble web site, for instance, offers discounts on all titles ordered through them (not their stores). Here's where they live in cyberspace: http://www.barnesandnoble.com

So now you're off and running. And if your personal computer and online service access provider can keep up, you're entering a brave new world of Marilyn Monroe wonders. So surf, download, scan, and enjoy. But, remember copyright laws—a lot of what you may be tempted to grab is owned. And, share your knowledge, ideas, and opinions with the same respect you want from others.

In fact, you could look at the Internet as being one big Marilyn Monroe fan club, with members communicating to others from all over the world. Some existing fan clubs can already be reached on-line. Others still rely on the postal service.

Chapter 31

The Marilyn Fan Clubs

(currently active)

- The Legend Club for Marilyn Monroe
  c/o Dale Notinelli
  2401 Artesia Boulevard
  Redondo Beach, CA 90278
  *Offers Marilyn scrapbooks.

- The Marilyn Lives Society: Marilyn Monroe Fan Club
  c/o Michelle Finn
  14 Clifton Square
  Corby, Northants, NN172DB
  United Kingdom
  *Issues a monthly newsletter.

- Marilyn Monroe Australian Fan Club
  P.O. Box 60
  Richmond, Victoria 3121
  Australia

- The Marilyn Monroe International Fan Club
  c/o Ernie Garcia
  842 Linden Avenue
  Long Beach, CA 90813
  *Mails occasional listings of Marilyn material for sale.
  Specify areas of interest.

- Marilyn Remembered
  c/o Greg Schreiner
  1237 Carmona Street
  Los Angeles, CA 90019
  (213) 931-3337
  > *The only club known to have regularly scheduled meetings. If you plan to be in the Los Angeles area, call ahead for the next meeting.

- Marilyn Reporter
  c/o Debbie Jasgur
  1648 S. Crystal Lake Drive, Suite 40
  Orlando, FL 32806
  (407) 898-6387

- Marilyn Then and Now
  c/o Ray Zweidinger
  97-07 63rd Road, Suite 15H
  Rego Park, NY 11374
  > *A new fan club formed in 1997, with plans to hold regularly scheduled meetings for members in the New York City area. Sample newsletter is $3; one-year subscription is $20.

- Some Like It Hot
  (Marilyn Monroe Fan Club)
  c/o Tina Muller
  Linkstr. 2,
  31134 Hildscheim,
  Germany
  > *Issues an English-language newsletter.

ANSWERS TO QUIZZES

Answers to "The Men Who Made Merry"

1. (h) James Dougherty, Marilyn's first husband.
2. (e) David Conover, Army photographer.
3. (f) Andre de Dienes, photographer.
4. (r) Joseph M. Schenck, Twentieth Century–Fox mogul.
5. (r) Joseph M. Schenck, who married Norma of the Talmadge sisters.
6. (k) Fred Karger, Columbia Pictures musical director.
7. (f) Andre de Dienes, photographer.
8. A—(k) musical director Fred Karger; B—(j) agent Johnny Hyde.
9. (g) Joe DiMaggio, baseball legend, Marilyn's second husband.
10. (q) Hal Schaefer, Twentieth Century–Fox music director.
11. (c) Marlon Brando, actor.
12. A—(o) playwright Arthur Miller, Marilyn's third husband; B—(p) Yves Montand, Marilyn costar and lover.
13. (s) Frank Sinatra, singer, actor, friend, maybe lover.
14. (n) Douglas Kirkland, photographer.
15. (l) Elia Kazan, director.
16. (i) Milton Greene, photographer.
17. (g) Joe DiMaggio was married to Dorothy Olsen from 1939 to 1945. Joe DiMaggio, Jr., was born in 1941.
18. (d) Charlie Chaplin, Jr., actor.

19. (a) Milton Berle, comedian.
20. (p) Yves Montand, singer and actor.
21. (m) John F. Kennedy, President of the United States.
22. (g) Joe DiMaggio again.
23. (t) President Sukarno of Indonesia.
24. (r) Joseph M. Schenck again.
25. (u) Robert Slatzer, journalist-filmmaker, claims he and Marilyn were married in Tijuana, Mexico, on October 4, 1952.

Answers—Trivia Challenge Part One

1. *Don't Bother to Knock* (1952).
2. She suggested this for her own tombstone:
   ### HERE LIES MARILYN MONROE
   ### 37–22–35
3. She sang for him, to prove that it was her own voice he heard in *Gentlemen Prefer Blondes* (1953).
4. a. Michael Redgrave and Barbara Bel Geddes.
   b. Francis Lederer and Shirley MacLaine.
5. Marilyn's contemptuous name for Sir Laurence Olivier, while filming *The Prince and the Showgirl*.
6. Cary Grant.
7. Her hands.
8. Hedda Hopper, July 29, 1946.
9. *Hometown Story* (1951), an industrial film financed by General Motors, and not intended for commercial release.
10. Montgomery Clift.
11. The third statement is incorrect. Marilyn was born in 1926. Harlean Carpenter did not change her screen name to Jean Harlow until 1928.

12. Marilyn's mother, Gladys Baker, who infrequently visited when Marilyn was living with the Bolenders, a foster family.

13. John Steinbeck narrated *O. Henry's Full House* (1952).

14. Russia. Johnny Hyde, Michael Chekhov, and Lee Strasberg were born in Russia. Natasha Lytess claimed to be Russian but was German.

15. Lois Maxwell, who played Miss Moneypenny in the James Bond movie series.

16. John Florea.

17. Marion Davies (1897–1961).

18. False. She was called "Sweetheart of the Month."

19. Frank Powolny.

20. Her drama coach Natasha Lytess, to whom she looked for approval after each take.

Answers to "Pretenders to the Throne"

1. (h) Arline Hunter.
2. (n) Marion Michaels.
3. (a) Lola Albright.
4. (e) Diana Dors.
5. (g) Joy Harmon.
6. (l) Jayne Mansfield.
7. (p) Barbara Nichols.
8. (q) Sheree North.
9. (t) Stella Stevens.
10. (x) Yvette Vickers.
11. (b) Carroll Baker.
12. (e) Diana Dors.
13. (c) Brigitte Bardot.

14. (f) Dixie Lee Evans.
15. (i) Adele Jergens, in *Ladies of the Chorus*.
16. (j) Hope Lange, in *Bus Stop*.
17. (l) Jayne Mansfield.
18. (w) Mamie Van Doren, in *The Private Lives of Adam and Eve* (Universal, 1960).
19. (s) Roxanne Rosedale.
20. (k) Joi Lansing.
21. (m) Beverly Michaels.
22. (o) Cleo Moore.
23. (r) Kim Novak, in *Vertigo* (Paramount, 1958).
24. (u) Greta Thyssen.
25. (v) Barbara Valentin.
26. (k) Joi Lansing.
27. (o) Cleo Moore.
28. (p) Barbara Nichols, in *Sweet Smell of Success* (United Artists, 1957).
29. (b) Carroll Baker, (c) Brigitte Bardot, (e) Diana Dors, (h) Arline Hunter, (l) Jayne Mansfield, (r) Kim Novak, (t) Stella Stevens, and (w) Mamie Van Doren all appeared in *Playboy*.

Answers—Trivia Challenge Part Two

21. Uncle Lon.
22. Syndicated columnist Sidney Skolsky.
23. Don Murray starred in *Bus Stop*, and then as RFK in the 1974 TV film *The Sex Symbol*.
24. *The Creature from the Black Lagoon* (Universal, 1954).
25. Singing "Happy Birthday, Mister President" to JFK on May 19, 1962.

26. Ella Fitzgerald.

27. She received it as payment for appearing on the Jack Benny show.

28. Your guess is as good as mine—Marilyn and Joe DiMaggio spent their wedding night there.

29. She plays "The Girl" in *The Seven Year Itch*.

30. The alias under which Marilyn flew to New York, just before Christmas 1954, to begin a new life.

31. She was seen out with Arthur Miller, who was on record as showing sympathy for the Communist cause.

32. Blonde.

33. She played the ghost of Gladys, in *Goodnight, Sweet Marilyn* (Studio Entertainment, 1989).

34. Zsa Zsa Gabor.

35. (1) Tom Ewell: *Seven Year Itch* (Twentieth Century–Fox, 1955) with Marilyn; *Will Success Spoil Rock Hunter?* (Twentieth Century–Fox, 1957) and *The Girl Can't Help It* (Twentieth Century–Fox, 1956), with Jayne.

    (2) Tommy Noonan: *Gentlemen Prefer Blondes* (1953), with Marilyn; *Promises, Promises* (NTD Inc., 1963), with Jayne.

    (3) Groucho Marx: *Love Happy* (United Artists, 1949), with Marilyn; *Will Success Spoil Rock Hunter?* (Twentieth Century–Fox, 1957) with Jayne.

    (4) Tony Randall: *Let's Make Love* (1960), with Marilyn; *Will Success Spoil Rock Hunter?* (Twentieth Century–Fox, 1957), with Jayne.

36. (1) March 31, 1955: riding a pink elephant in Mike Todd's benefit circus for the Arthritis and Rheumatism Foundation.

    (2) May 19, 1962: singing "Happy Birthday" to President John F. Kennedy.

37. Dr. Ralph Greenson, Marilyn's Los Angeles psychiatrist.

38. On a gold money-clip from Tiffany's.

39. One of her favorite fashion designers. Marilyn was buried in a pale sea-green dress designed by Pucci.

40. When the film was released in America in 1956, the title was changed to *The Pursuit of the Graf Spee*. It stars John Gregson and Peter Finch.

Answers—Trivia Challenge Part Three

41. Tay Garnett directed Jean Harlow in *China Seas* (MGM, 1935), Lana Turner in *The Postman Always Rings Twice* (MGM, 1946), and Marilyn in *Fireball* (Twentieth Century–Fox, 1950).

42. A rhinestone.

43. Marilyn wears the same outfit in all of them—a tightly woven sweater dress from her own wardrobe.

44. June Haver is the first actress and Natalie Wood, the second.

45. Montgomery Clift's former secretary, she worked briefly for Marilyn in New York. But mainly her name was used as a decoy, when Marilyn lived on Doheny Drive in 1961. It was Marjorie's name on the doorbell.

46. Richard Meryman, writer for *Life* magazine, as he finished what would be her last interview.

47. Entertaining American troops in Korea in February 1954.

48. Marilyn's character in *We're Not Married* is a mother.

49. Ronald Reagan was the superior officer of David Conover, of the First Motion Picture Unit. Reagan dispatched Conover to the Radioplane factory to photograph women for military magazines. Conover spotted Marilyn and asked her to pose for him, which led to many memorable things.

50. Bob Hope.

51. In college, a friend suggested that "Isadore Diamond" sounded too Jewish. So the writer used the initials I. A. L., which stood for Interscholastic Algebra League, of which he had been champion.

52. Jean Peters and Howard Hughes.

53. Agoraphobia is an abnormal fear of crossing through or being in open or public places.

54. Jeanette MacDonald (as told to photographer Jock Carroll).

55. *Monkey Business* (Twentieth Century–Fox, 1952).

56. A scene in the film has a rancher serenading the photo of his dead wife—and they used a photo of Marilyn!

57. Marilyn was the model for the fairy Tinker Bell in the Disney cartoon feature *Peter Pan* (1953).

58. The church refused to recognize DiMaggio's divorce from his first wife Dorothy Arnold.

59. Carl Sandburg.

60. "She was the best waitress in Duluth. I guess it was the way she put the beer on the table," says George.

BIBLIOGRAPHY

Agan, Patrick. *The Decline and Fall of the Love Goddesses*. Los Angeles: Pinnacle, 1979.

Alfonso, Alfonso, editor. *Monroe & DiMaggio*. Miami: Conquest Comics, 1992.

Allen, Jack, editor. *Marilyn by Moonlight*. New York: Barclay, 1996.

Anderson, Janice. *Marilyn Monroe*. London: Hamlyn, 1983.

_____. Marilyn Monroe, *"Quote Unquote."* New York: Crescent, 1995.

Andrews, Matthew. *Let's Make Love*, novelization. New York: Bantam Doubleday Dell, 1960.

Arnold, Eve. *The Unretouched Woman*. New York: Alfred A Knopf, 1976.

_____. *Marilyn Monroe: An Appreciation*. New York: Alfred A Knopf, 1987.

Archer, Robyn and Diana Simmonds. *A Star Is Torn*. New York: Dutton/Signet, 1986.

Avedon, Richard. "Color Essay of the Year." *1960 Photography Annual*.

_____. "Fabled Enchantresses" photo feature. *Life*, December
22, 1958.

_____. "The Persistence of Marilyn." *American Photographer*, July 1984.

_____. "Photos by Richard Avedon." *The New Yorker*, March 21, 1994.

Axelrod, George. *Will Success Spoil Rock Hunter?* New York: Random House, 1956.

Bacall, Lauren. *By Myself*. New York: Alfred A Knopf, 1979.

Bacon, James. *Hollywood Is a Four-Letter Town*. Chicago: Regnery Publishing, 1976.

Baker, Roger. *Marilyn Monroe*. New York: Portland, 1990.

Barker, Clive. *Son of Celluloid*, graphic novel. Forestville, CA: Eclipse, 1991.

Barris, George. *Marilyn*, with a biography by Gloria Steinem. New York: Henry Holt & Co., 1986.

_____. *Marilyn, Her Life in Her Own Words*. New York: Henry Holt & Co., 1995.

Baty, S. Paige. *American Monroe, The Making of a Body Politic*. Berkeley: University of California Press, 1995.

Beaton, Cecil. *Cecil Beaton, Photographs* 1920-1970. New York: Stewart, Tabori & Chang, Publishers, 1995.

Beauchamp, Antony. *Focus on Fame*. London: Odhams, 1958.

Bellavance-Johnson, Marsha. *Marilyn Monroe in Hollywood*. Ketchum, Idaho: Computer Lab, 1992.

Bergala, Alain, text. *Magnum Cinema, photographs from 50 years of movie-making*. London: Phaidon, 1995.

Bernard, Susan, editor. *Bernard of Hollywood's Marilyn*. New York: St. Martin's Press, 1993.

Bernau, George. *Candle in the Wind*. New York: Warner Books, 1990.

Bessie, Alvah. *The Symbol*. New York: Random House, 1966.

Birnbaum, Agnes, editor. *Marilyn's Life Story*. New York: Bantam Doubleday Dell, 1962.

Blanpied, John W., editor. *Movieworks*. Rochester, NY: Little Theatre Press, 1990.

Bowering, Marilyn. *Anyone Can See I Love You*. Ontario: Porcupine's Quill, 1987.

Boyd, Herb, editor. *Marilyn Monroe: Seductive Sayings*. Stamford, CT: Longmeadow, 1994.

Brambilla, Giovan Battista and Gianni Mercurio, Stefano Petricca. *Marilyn Monroe: the Life, the Myth*. New York: Rizzoli International Publications, 1996.

Brandon, Henry. *As We Are*. New York: Bantam Doubleday Dell, 1961.

Brown, Peter and Patte B. Barham. *Marilyn: The Last Take*. New York: Dutton/Signet, 1992.

Bruno of Hollywood (Bruno Bernard). *Requiem for Marilyn*. London: Kensal, 1986.

Burke, Phyllis. *Atomic Candy*. New York: Atlantic, 1989.

Buskin, Richard. *The Films of Marilyn Monroe*. Lincolnwood, IL: Publications International, 1992.

Cahill, Marie. *Forever Marilyn*. London: Bison, 1991.

Canevari, Leonore and Jeanette van Whye, Christian Dimas, Rachel Dimas. *The Murder of Marilyn Monroe*. New York: Carroll & Graf Publishers, 1992.

Capell, Frank A. *The Strange Death of Marilyn Monroe*. Staten Island, NY: Herald of Freedom, 1964.

Capote, Truman. *Music for Chameleons*. New York: Random House, 1980.

Cardiff, Jack. *Magic Hour*. London/Boston: Faber & Faber, 1996.

Carpozi, George Jr. *Marilyn Monroe: "Her Own Story."* New York: Belmont, 1961. (Published in England as *The Agony of Marilyn Monroe*.)

Carroll, Donald, interviewer. "Conversation with Dr. Thomas Noguchi." *Oui*, February 1976.

Carroll, Jock. *Falling for Marilyn: The Lost Niagara Collection*. New York: Michael Friedman Publishing Group, 1996.

_____. *The Shy Photographer*. New York: Stein, 1964.

Chayefsky, Paddy. *The Goddess, a screenplay*. New York: Simon & Schuster, 1957.

Chierichetti, David. *Hollywood Costume Design*. New York: Harmony Books, 1976.

Clark, Colin. *The Prince, the Showgirl and Me*. New York: St. Martin's Press, 1996.

Collins, g. Peter. *I Remember... Marilyn*. Vestal, NY: Vestal, 1995.

Conover, David. *The Discovery Photos, Summer 1945*. Ontario: Norma Jeane Enterprises, 1990

_____. *Finding Marilyn*. New York: Grosset & Dunlap Publishers, 1981.

Conway, Michael and Mark Ricci. *The Films of Marilyn Monroe*. New York: Citadel Press,1964.

Crivello, Kirk. *Fallen Angels*. Secaucus, NJ: Citadel Press, 1988.

Crown, Lawrence. *Marilyn at Twentieth Century–Fox*. London: Comet, 1987.

Curti, Carlo. *Skouras, King of Fox Studios*. Los Angeles: Holloway House Publishing Co., 1967.

Curtis, Tony. *Tony Curtis, the Autobiography*. New York: William Morrow & Co., 1993.

Davis, Kenn and John Stanley. *Bogart '48*. New York: Bantam Doubleday Dell, 1980.

de Dienes, André. *Marilyn, Mon Amour*. New York: St. Martin's Press, 1985.

Denker, Henry. *The Director*. New York: Baron, 1970.

DePaoli, Geri, editor. *Elvis + Marilyn: 2 x Immortal*. New York: Rizzoli International Publications, 1994.

Diamond, I. A. L. "The Day Marilyn Needed 47 Takes to Remember to Say, 'Where's the Bourbon?'." *Roots*, December 1985.

Dillinger, Nat. *Unforgettable Hollywood*. New York: William Morrow & Co., 1982.

Doll, Susan, editor. *Marilyn: Her Life and Legend*. New York: Beekman Publishers, 1990.

Dougherty, James E. *The Secret Happiness of Marilyn Monroe*. Chicago: Playboy, 1976.

Douglas, Carole Nelson, editor. *Marilyn: Shades of Blonde*. New York: Forge, 1997.

Dyer, Richard. *Heavenly Bodies: Film Stars and Society*. New York: St. Martin's Press, 1986.

Eisenstaedt, Alfred. *Eisenstaedt's Album*. New York: Viking, 1976.

Engelmeier, Regine and Peter W. *Fashion in Film*. Munich: Prestel, 1990.

Epstein, Edward Z. and Lou Valentino. *Those Lips, Those Eyes*. New York: Carol Publishing Group, 1992.

Evanier, Mark and Dan Spiegle. "The 24th Annual Death of Marilyn Monroe." *Crossfire* numbers 12 and 13. Guerneville, CA: Eclipse Comics, 1985.

Fahey, David and Linda Rich. *Masters of Starlight: Photographers in Hollywood*. Los Angeles: County Museum of Art, 1987.

Fast, Jonathan. *The Inner Circle*. New York: Delacorte Press, 1979.

Feingersh, Ed. *Marilyn: March 1955*. New York: Delta Books, 1990.

Finn, Michelle. *Marilyn's Addresses*. London: Smith Gryphon, 1995.

Fowler, Christopher. *How to Impersonate Famous People*. New York:Crown, 1984.

Fox, Patty. *Star Style: Hollywood legends as fashion icons*. Los Angeles: Angel City,1995.

Franklin, Joe and Laurie Palmer. *The Marilyn Monroe Story*. New York: Field, 1953.

Freeman, Lucy. *Why Norma Jean Killed Marilyn Monroe*. Chicago: Global Rights, 1992.

French, Philip and Ken Wlaschin, editors. *The Faber Book of Movie Verse*. London/Boston: Faber & Faber, 1993.

Garnett, Tay. *Light Your Torches and Pull Up Your Tights*. New Rochelle, NY: Arlington,1973.

Geist, Kenneth L. *Pictures Will Talk: The Life and Films of Joseph L. Mankiewicz*. New York: Scribners, 1978.

Giancana, Sam and Chuck. *Double Cross*. New York: Warner Books, 1992.

Giles, Nicki. *The Marilyn Album*. New York: Gallery, 1991.

Goldman, William. *Tinsel*. New York: Delacorte Press, 1979.

Goode, James. *The Story of* The Misfits. Indianapolis: Bobbs, 1961.

Goodman, Ezra. *The Fifty Year Decline and Fall of Hollywood*. New York: Simon & Schuster, 1961.

Gorman, E. J. *The Marilyn Tapes*. New York: Doherty, 1995.

Grant, Neil. *Marilyn In Her Own Words*. New York: Crescent, 1991.

Greene, Milton. *Milton's Marilyn*. Munich: Schirmer, 1994.

_____. *Of Women and Their Elegance*. New York: Simon & Schuster, 1980.

Griffith, Corinne. *Hollywood Tales*. Los Angeles: Fell, 1962.

Grumbach, Doris. *The Missing Person*. New York: The Putnam Berkley Group, 1981.

Guilaroff, Sydney. *Crowning Glory*. Los Angeles: General, 1996.

Guiles, Fred Lawrence. *Legend: The Life and Death of Marilyn Monroe*. New York: Stein, 1984.

_____. Norma Jean: *The Life of Marilyn Monroe*. New York: McGraw-Hill, 1969.

Hall, Allan. *The World's Greatest Secrets*. London: Hamlyn, 1989.

Hall, James E. "Marilyn Was Murdered: An Eyewitness Account." *Hustler*, May 1986.

Halliday, Brett. *Kill All the Young Girls*. New York: Bantam Doubleday Dell, 1973.

Halsman, Philippe. *Philippe Halsman's Jump Book*. New York: Simon & Schuster, 1959.

_____. "Three Encounters with a Love Goddess." *Hollywood Dreamgirl*, No. 1, 1955

Hamblett, Charles. *The Hollywood Cage*. New York: Hart, 1959. (Originally published in England as *Who Killed Marilyn Monroe? Or, Cage to Catch Our Dreams*).

Harris, Radie. *Radie's World*. New York: The Putnam Berkley Group, 1975.

Harrison, Jay. *Marilyn*. Surrey, England: Colour Library, 1992.

Haskell, Molly. *From Reverence to Rape*. New York: Henry Holt & Co., 1974.

Haspiel, James. *Marilyn: The Ultimate Look at the Legend*. New York: Henry Holt & Co., 1991.

_____. *The Young Marilyn: Becoming the Legend*. New York: Hyperion, 1994.

Hawkins, G. Ray. *The Marilyn Monroe Auction*, a catalog. Los Angeles: G. Ray Hawkins Gallery, 1992.

Hayes, Suzanne Lloyd, editor. *3-D Hollywood, photos by Harold Lloyd*. New York: Simon & Schuster, 1992.

Hecht, Ben. *The Sensualists*. New York: Messner, 1959.

Hegner, William. *The Idolators*. New York: Trident, 1973.

Hembus, Joe. *Marilyn*. London: Tandem, 1973.

Heymann, C. David. *A Woman Named Jackie*. New York: Stuart, 1989.

Hirsch, Foster. *A Method to Their Madness*. New York: Norton, 1984.

Hoyt, Edwin P. *Marilyn: The Tragic Venus*. New York: Chilton, 1965.

Hudson, James A. *The Mysterious Death of Marilyn Monroe*. New York: Volitant, 1968.

Huston, John. *An Open Book*. New York: Alfred A Knopf, 1980.

Hutchinson, Tom. *Marilyn Monroe*. London: Optimum, 1982.

Hyatt, Kathryn. *Marilyn, The Story of a Woman*. New York: Seven Stories, 1996.

Inge, William. *Bus Stop*, novelization of the film. London: Buchan's, 1956.

_____. *Bus Stop*, the play. New York: Random House, 1955.

Jakubowski, Maxim and Ron Vander Meer. *The Great Movies—Live!* New York: Simon & Schuster, 1987.

Janis, Sidney, text. *Homage to Marilyn Monroe*, exhibition catalog. New York: Sidney Janis Gallery, December 6-30, 1967.

Jasgur, Joseph. *The Birth of Marilyn: the lost photographs of Norma Jean.* New York: St. Martin's Press, 1991.

Johnson, Terry. *Insignificance: the book*, with the screenplay. London: Sidgwick, 1985.

_____. *Insignificance*, the play. London: Methuen, 1982.

Jordan, Ted: *Norma Jean: My Secret Life With Marilyn Monroe.* New York: William Morrow & Co., 1989.

Kahn, Roger. *Joe & Marilyn: A Memory of Love.* New York: William Morrow & Co., 1986.

Kanin, Garson. *Come On Strong.* New York: Dramatists Play Service, 1962.

_____. *Moviola.* New York: Simon & Schuster, 1979.

Kazan, Elia. *A Life.* New York: Alfred A Knopf, 1988.

Kidder, Clark, compiler. *Marilyn Monroe unCovers.* Alberta, Canada: Quon, 1994.

Kirkland, Douglas. *Light Years.* New York: Thames, 1989.

_____. *Icons: Creativity with Camera and Computer.* San Francisco: HarperCollins Publishers, 1993.

Kobal, John, editor. *Marilyn Monroe: A Life on Film.* London: Hamlyn, 1974. (1984 American reprint by Exeter, New York.)

Korda, Michael. *The Immortals.* New York: Poseidon, 1992.

Krohn, Katherine E. *Marilyn Monroe: Norma Jeane's Dream.* Minneapolis: Lerner, 1997.

Lambert, Gavin. *On Cukor.* New York: The Putnam Berkley Group, 1972.

LaVine, W. Robert. *In a Glamorous Fashion.* New York: Scribner's, 1980.

Leese, Elizabeth. *Costume Design in the Movies.* England: BCW, 1976.

Lefkowitz, Frances. *Marilyn Monroe.* New York: Chelsea Publishing Co., 1995.

Lembourn, Hans Jorgen. *Diary of a Lover of Marilyn Monroe.* New York: Arbor, 1979.

Levy, Alan, interviewer. "A Good Long Look at Myself." *Redbook*, August 1962.

Lifshin, Lyn. *Marilyn Monroe*. Portland: Quiet Lion, 1994.

Lindo, Kirk, editor. *Madonna vs. Marilyn*. Northport, NY: Celebrity Comics, 1992.

Lloyd, Ann. *Marilyn: A Hollywood Life*. New York: Mallard, 1989.

Logan, Joshua. *Movie Stars, Real People and Me*. New York: Delacorte Press, 1978.

Loney, Glenn. *Unsung Genius* (Jack Cole). New York: Watts, 1984.

Loren, Todd, editor. *The Marilyn Monroe Conspiracy*. San Diego: Conspiracy Comics, 1991.

Luitjers, Guus, editor. *Marilyn Monroe: A Never-Ending Dream*. New York St. Martin's Press, 1987.

_____. *Marilyn Monroe in Her Own Words*. New York: Omnibus, 1991.

McBride, Joseph. *Hawks on Hawks*. Berkeley: University of California Press, 1982.

McCann, Graham. *Marilyn Monroe*. New Brunswick: Rutgers University Press, 1988.

Macavoy, Elizabeth and Susan Israelson. *Lovesick: The Marilyn Syndrome*. New York: Fine, 1991. (Paperback edition is called *The Marilyn Syndrome*.)

McClung, Nellie. "My Sex Is Ice Cream," *The Marilyn Monroe Poems*. Victoria, B. C., Canada: Ekstasis, 1996.

Mailer, Norman. *Marilyn*. New York: Grosset & Dunlap PublishersP, 1973.

_____. "Marilyn Monroe's Sexiest Tapes and Discs." *Video Review*, February 1982.

_____. *Of Women and Their Elegance*. With photos by Milton Greene. New York: Simon & Schuster, 1980.

_____. *Strawhead*, a play. Excerpted in Vanity Fair, April 1986.

Mankiewicz, Joseph L. *All About Eve*, the screenplay. New York: Random House, 1951.

_____. *More About All About Eve*. Screenplay, interview with Gary Carey. New York: Random House,1972.

Margener, Vardis. *Double Take*. Chicago: Playboy, 1982.

Martin, Pete. *Pete Martin Calls On....* New York: Simon & Schuster, 1962.

_____. *Will Acting Spoil Marilyn Monroe?* New York: Bantam Doubleday Dell, 1956.

Meaker, M.J. *Sudden Endings.* Garden City, NY: Bantam Doubleday Dell, 1964.

Mellen, Joan. *Marilyn Monroe.* New York: Pyramid, 1973.

Meryman, Richard, interviewer. "Fame may go by and—so long, I've had you." *Life*, August 3, 1962.

Messick, Hank. *The Beauties & the Beasts.* New York: McKay, 1973.

Miller, Arthur. *After the Fall.* New York: Viking, 1964.

_____. *Everybody Wins*, screenplay. New York: Grove, 1990.

_____. *The Misfits*, "synthesis of screenplay and novel." New York: Viking, 1961.

_____. *The Misfits*, the screenplay. New York: Viking, 1961.

_____. "My Wife Marilyn." *Life*, December 22, 1958.

_____. *Timebends*, autobiography. New York: Grove, 1987.

Miller, George. *Marilyn: Her Tragic Life.* New York: Escape Magazines, 1962.

Mills, Bart. *Marilyn on Location.* London: Sidgwick, 1989.

Miracle, Berniece Baker. *My Sister Marilyn.* Chapel Hill, NC: Algonquin Books of Chapel Hill, 1994.

Monroe, Marilyn. *My Story.* New York: Stein, 1974.

Montand, Yves. *You See, I Haven't Forgotten.* New York: Alfred A Knopf, 1992.

Moore, Robin and Gene Schoor. *Marilyn and Joe DiMaggio.* New York: Manor, 1977.

Murray, Eunice with Rose Shade. *Marilyn: The Last Months.* New York: Pyramid, 1975.

Negulesco, Jean. *Things I Did...and Things I Think I Did.* New York: Simon & Schuster, 1984.

Noguchi, Thomas T. *Coroner.* New York: Simon & Schuster, 1983.

Olivier, Laurence. *Confessions of an Actor.* New York: Simon & Schuster, 1982.

Oppenheimer

Oppenheimer, Joel. *Marilyn Lives!* New York: Delilah, 1981.

Ott, Frederick W. *The Films of Fritz Lang.* Secaucus, NJ: Citadel Press, 1979.

Pall, Gloria. *The Marilyn Monroe Party.* Los Angeles, self-published, 1992.

Paris, Yvette. *Dying To Be Marilyn.* Wyoming: Lagumo, 1996.

Parish, James Robert. *The Fox Girls.* New Rochelle, NY: Arlington, 1971.

Parker, Robert. *Capitol Hill in Black and White.* New York: Dodd, 1986.

Parsons, Louella O. *Tell It to Louella.* New York: The Putnam Berkley Group, 1961.

Pascal, John. *Marilyn Monroe: The Complete Story of Her Life, Her Loves and Her Death.* New York: Popular, 1962.

Peabody, Richard and Lucinda Ebersole, editors. *Mondo Marilyn: An Anthology of Fiction and Poetry.* New York: St. Martin's Press, 1995.

Pepitone, Lena with William Stadiem. *Marilyn Monroe Confidential.* New York: Simon & Schuster, 1979.

Pinchot, Ann. *52 West.* New York: Farrar, Straus & Giroux, 1962.

Post, Adam. *Tragic Goddess: Marilyn Monroe.* Westport, CT: POP Comics, 1995.

Preminger, Otto. *Preminger: an awtobiography* (sic). New York: Bantam Doubleday Dell, 1977.

"Psychiatrist friend." *Violations of the Child Marilyn Monroe.* New York: Bridgehead, 1962.

Quirk, Lawrence. *The Kennedys in Hollywood.* Dallas: Taylor, 1996.

Rattigan, Terence. *The Prince and the Showgirl*, the screenplay. New York: Signet, 1957.

Rechy, John. *Marilyn's Daughter.* New York: Carroll & Graf Publishers, 1988.

Renaud, Ron. *Fade to Black.* New York: Pinnacle, 1980.

Riese, Randall and Neal Hitchens. *The Unabridged Marilyn: Her Life from A to Z.* New York: Congdon, 1987.

Rollyson, Carl E., Jr. *Marilyn Monroe: A Life of the Actress.* Ann Arbor: UMIP, 1986.

Rooks-Denes, Kathy. *Marilyn.* New York: Bantam Doubleday Dell, 1993.

Rooney, Mickey. *Life Is Too Short.* New York: Villard, 1991.

Rosten, Norman. *Marilyn: An Untold Story*. New York: Signet, 1973.

_____. *Marilyn Among Friends*. Photos by Sam Shaw. New York: Henry Holt & Co., 1987.

Russell, Jane. *Jane Russell: My Path & My Detours*. New York: Watts, 1985.

_____. *That Girl*. Los Angeles: Affiliated Magazines, 1953.

St. Pierre, Roger. *Marilyn Monroe*. London: Anabas, 1985.

Sanford, Jay, editor. *Marilyn Monroe: Suicide or Murder?* San Diego: Revolutionary Comics, 1993.

Schiller, Lawrence, editor. *Marilyn*. With a biography by Norman Mailer. New York: Grosset & Dunlap Publishers, 1973.

Schirmer, Lothar, conception. *Marilyn Monroe and the Camera*. Boston: Little, 1989.

_____. *Marilyn Monroe, Photographs 1945-1962*. Munich: Schirmer, 1994.

Schonauer, David, editor. "Rare Marilyn: a portfolio of work." *American Photo*, May/June, 1997.

Sciacca, Tony (Anthony Scaduto). *Who Killed Marilyn?* New York: Manor, 1976.

Shaw, Sam. *The Joy of Marilyn*. New York: Exeter, 1979.

_____. *Marilyn Monroe as The Girl*. New York: Ballantine, 1955.

_____. and Norman Rosten. *Marilyn Among Friends*. New York: Henry Holt & Co., 1987.

Shevey, Sandra. *The Marilyn Scandal*. New York: William Morrow & Co., 1987.

Signoret, Simone. *Nostalgia Isn't What It Used to Be*. New York: HarperCollins Publishers, 1978.

Sinyard, Neil. *Marilyn*. New York: Gallery, 1989.

Skolsky, Sidney. *Marilyn*. New York: Bantam Doubleday Dell, 1954.

_____. *Don't Get Me Wrong—I Love Hollywood*. New York: The Putnam Berkley Group, 1975.

Slatzer, Robert. *The Life and Curious Death of Marilyn Monroe*. New York: Pinnacle, 1974.

_____. *The Marilyn Files*. New York: Shapolsky, 1992.

Smith, Mathew. *The Men Who Murdered Marilyn*. London: Bloomsbury, 1996.

Smith, Milburn, editor. *Marilyn.* New York: Barven, 1971.

_____. *The Marilyn Chronicles.* New York: Starlog, 1994.

Spada, James with George Zeno. *Monroe: Her Life in Pictures.* New York: Bantam Doubleday Dell, 1982.

Spada, James. *Peter Lawford: The Man Who Kept the Secrets.* New York: Bantam Doubleday Dell, 1991.

Speriglio, Milo. *The Marilyn Conspiracy.* New York: Pocket Books, 1986.

_____. Marilyn Monroe: *Murder Cover-Up.* New York: Seville, 1982.

_____ with Adela Gregory. *Crypt 33: The Saga of Marilyn Monroe—The Final Word.* New York: Carol Publishing Group, 1993.

Spire, Steven. "Marilyn Monroe." *Personality Classics #2.* NY: Massapequa, 1991.

Spoto, Donald. *Marilyn Monroe, the Biography.* New York: HarperCollins Publishers, 1993.

Staggs, Ben. *MMII, the Return of Marilyn Monroe.* New York: Fine,1991.

Steinem, Gloria. *Marilyn.* Photos by George Barris. New York: Henry Holt & Co., 1986.

Stempel, Tom. *Screenwriter, the life and times of Nunnally Johnson.* New York: Barnes & Noble Books, 1980.

Stern, Bert. "The Last Nude Photo of Marilyn." *Playboy,* January 1984.

_____. *The Last Sitting,* a selection. New York: William Morrow & Co., 1982.

_____. *The Last Sitting,* 101 selected photos. Munich: Schirmer, 1993.

_____. "The Last Sitting Photos." *Eros,* Autumn 1962.

_____. "The Marilyn Files." *American Photo,* November/December 1992.

_____. *Marilyn Monroe: The Complete Last Sitting.* Munich: Schirmer,1992.

_____. "The Marilyn Monroe Trip: a portfolio of serigraphic prints." *Avant-Garde,* March 1968.

Strasberg, Susan. *Bittersweet.* New York: The Putnam Berkley Group, 1980.

_____. *Marilyn and Me: Sisters, Rivals, Friends.* New York: Warner Books, 1992.

Sullivan, Steve. *Va Va Voom! Bombshells, Pin-Ups, Sexpots and Glamour Girls.* Los Angeles: General,1995.

Summers, Anthony. *Goddess: The Secret Lives of Marilyn Monroe*. New York: Macmillan, 1985.

Taylor, Roger G. *Marilyn in Art*. Salem, NH: Salem, 1984.

_____. *Marilyn Monroe: In Her Own Words*. London: Kwintner, 1983.

Thomas, Roseanne Daryl. *The Angel Carver*. New York: Random House, 1993.

Thomson, David. "Baby Go Boom!" *Film Comment*, September-October 1982

Tierney, Tom. *Marilyn Monroe Paper Dolls*. New York: Dover, 1979.

Toperoff, Sam. *Queen of Desire*. New York: HarperCollins Publishers, 1992.

Varley, John. *Demon*. (Cover art of Marilyn.) New York: Berkley, 1984.

Wagenknecht, Edward. *Marilyn Monroe: A Composite View*. Philadelphia: Chilton, 1969.

_____. *Seven Daughters of the Theater*. Norman: Oklahoma University Press, 1964.

Walker, Alexander. *The Celluloid Sacrifice*. New York: Hawthorne, 1967.

Wayne, Jane Ellen. *Marilyn's Men: The Private Life of Marilyn Monroe*. New York: St. Martin's Press, 1992.

Weatherby, W. J. *Conversations with Marilyn*. New York: Mason, 1976.

Weiner, Leigh. *Marilyn: A Hollywood Farewell*. Los Angeles: self-published, 1990.

Wilder, Billy and I. A. L. Diamond. *Some Like It Hot*, the screenplay. New York: Signet, 1959.

Willoughby, Bob. *The Hollywood Special*. New York: Takarajima, 1993.

Winters, Shelley. *Shelley II, the Middle of My Century*. New York: Simon & Schuster, 1989.

Woog, Adam. *Mysterious Deaths: Marilyn Monroe*. San Diego: Lucent, 1997.

Zerbe, Jerome. *Happy Times*. New York: Harcourt, 1973.

Zolotow, Maurice. *Billy Wilder in Hollywood*. New York: The Putnam Berkley Group, 1977.

_____. *Marilyn Monroe*. New York: Harcourt Brace & Co., 1960.

_____. Revised Edition with new introduction and new epilogue. NY: HarperCollins Publishers, 1990

INDEX

ABOUT THE AUTHOR

Ernest Wayne Cunningham and his sisters were given movie names at birth: Shirley (Temple), Margaret (O'Brien), (John) Wayne, Linda (Darnell), and Mildred (Pierce). Only Ernest took it seriously, and began going to the movies as often as possible.

He went to New York and wrote headlines for movie ads at Diener-Hauser-Bates, the world's first movie advertising agency. He went to Los Angeles to write screenplays, but instead wrote advertising headlines for network television sitcoms and movies of the week.

He now sells movie memorabilia; writes freelance headlines; and does freelance editing, proofreading, and research. This is his first book.

Ernest Cunningham considers himself a student of the Marilyn phenomenon, rather than a fan. He senses that it is just beginning.